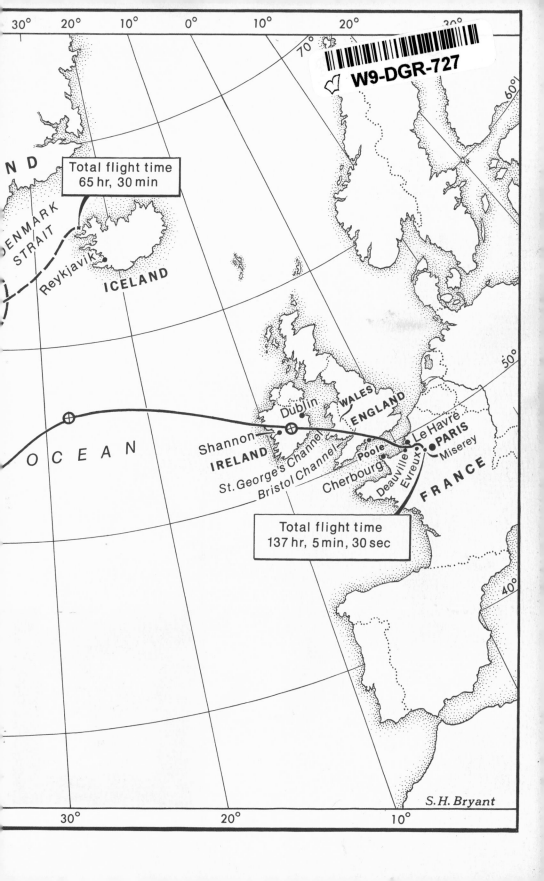

Total flight time
65 hr, 30 min

DENMARK
STRAIT

Reykjavik

ICELAND

N D

O C E A N

Dublin

Shannon

WALES

ENGLAND

Le Havre **PARIS**

IRELAND

Poole

St. George's Channel

Bristol Channel

Cherbourg

Deauville Evreux Miserey

FRANCE

Total flight time
137 hr, 5 min, 30 sec

S. H. Bryant

DOUBLE EAGLE

Ben Abruzzo
Maxie Anderson
Larry Newman

DOUBLE EAGLE

by Charles McCarry

Little, Brown and Company — Boston — Toronto

LIBRARY OF CONGRESS CATALOGUE CARD NUMBER 79–17732

FIRST EDITION

Picture Credits

1: Lt. John J. Walters. 2–10: Dick Kent. 11–15, 17: Double Eagle II. 16, 19, 21: Gamma/Liaison. 18: Pierre Vauthey, Sygma. 20: Lepeuve, Gamma/Liaison. 22: Mark Bulka, Sipa Press/Black Star.

BP

Designed by Susan Windheim

*Published simultaneously in Canada
by Little, Brown & Company (Canada) Limited*

PRINTED IN THE UNITED STATES OF AMERICA

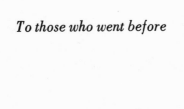

To those who went before

When men cease to take up the challenges that are before them, when they cease to cross new frontiers, then as a society we are no longer moving forward.

— Ben Abruzzo

The first flight was a great adventure; the second flight was a great expedition.

— Maxie Anderson

Dad! We did it, Dad!

— Larry Newman

Foreword

At 7:49 P.M. European daylight time (1549 Greenwich mean time) on August 17, 1978, the helium balloon *Double Eagle II* landed in a barley field near the village of Miserey, France, on the outskirts of Paris. It had lifted off from a clover field near Presque Isle, Maine, five days, seventeen hours, five minutes, and fifty seconds earlier, and its landing marked the completion of the first crossing of the Atlantic Ocean by a free manned balloon.

The crew, three businessmen from Albuquerque, were Ben L. Abruzzo, Maxie L. Anderson, and Larry Newman. At least seventeen other balloons had attempted the Atlantic Crossing since 1873. Five pilots had died in the attempt.

Max Anderson and Ben Abruzzo had themselves nearly joined the list of victims the previous September, when they were forced into the sea off Iceland in an earlier attempt to make this voyage in a balloon called *Double Eagle*. Abruzzo and Anderson are the only men in the history of ballooning to challenge the Atlantic twice, and to win the second time.

They named both their craft in honor of Charles A. Lindbergh, the Lone Eagle, whose solo flight to Paris took place in 1927, fifty years before the first attempt by Abruzzo and Anderson.

The arrival of *Double Eagle II* in France ignited a celebration by the French people that recalled the welcome given to Lindbergh himself, and the *Double Eagle* pilots were subsequently decorated and honored by France and the United States, and by other governments and organizations.

The successful crossing of the Atlantic by a balloon was rightly compared to Speke's discovery of the source of the Nile, to Peary's dash to the North Pole, to Lindbergh's flight, to the conquest of

Everest by Hillary and Norkay. Like all of these feats, the flights of *Double Eagle*, both the failure in 1977 and the triumph in 1978, were monumental tests of human skill and courage, and they thrilled the world with the glad news that the age of human adventure was not yet over.

This book is the story of the adventures of Ben Abruzzo and Maxie Anderson, and of Larry Newman, as remembered by them and their families and their ground staff. Nothing is invented or fictionalized; the story requires no transfusion of imagination.

The words quoted in these pages are those spoken in life, as transcribed from hundreds of hours of recorded interviews and the transcription of radio broadcasts between the balloons and ground stations. The balloonists' thoughts are the thoughts they recall having, and they are invariably expressed in the balloonists' own words.

During the flight of the first *Double Eagle*, a tape recorder was inadvertently left running in the gondola, and all quotations are taken verbatim from the recordings. The words exchanged aboard *Double Eagle II* have been reconstructed from the balloonists' memory of events, and from tape recordings of their radio transmissions.

The reader will find that the memories of the balloonists do not always agree on specific details. Each man experienced the ordeal and triumph of these flights in his own way, and each has his own mental picture of what happened to him, a brave man under great stress, in the skies above the Atlantic. Because Maxie Anderson and Ben Abruzzo and Larry Newman are honest men as well as courageous ones, all of the pictures, flattering and unflattering, are displayed in this book, which is the gallery of their great feat.

DOUBLE EAGLE

 In the winter of 1977, Maxie L. Anderson of Albuquerque, New Mexico, was melancholy in a peculiarly American way. Nothing on the glittering surface of his life explained his discontent. Max Anderson was a gifted engineer. He was a millionaire with interests in uranium, copper, gold, and silver. He had been married for twenty-five years to a blond and beautiful woman and they had four bright children. He controlled his own mining company. He owned a handsome house, a stable of Arabian horses, a ski condominium at Taos, cars, airplanes, a sailboat moored in the Gulf of California — even a balloon.

Still, he felt the seed of unrest within him. He was forty-two years old that winter, a handsome man with a boyish lick of dark blond hair falling on his forehead and the clean-cut impassive features of his Scandinavian ancestors. For a time he had let himself go a little fat, for he enjoys his table, but now he was back to 168 pounds, his college wrestling weight. He had the broken nose of a man who stands his ground, and one mysterious blinded eye. Despite this handicap, he rarely lost at the fast man-on-man games he liked best.

What Max Anderson felt that winter, what he had been feeling for some time, is a thing that many successful men feel as they pass forty. He had done everything he was supposed to do, but he was not certain that he had done what he wanted in his heart to do. Looking at himself at forty-two, he saw a man he could admire; he did not always see the man he had hoped to see.

"All of a sudden," says Max, "what I guess you'd call my impossible dream came back to haunt me. This feeling came over me. I couldn't analyze it, but I kept on thinking that there was some test I hadn't passed."

In business, Max had more than once put everything on the line. He had walked right up to men who held guns in their hands on disputed mining claims, for even today mining in the West can be a business that is done with fists and firearms — but he did that for gain. He had flown airplanes and balloons and hang-gliders and taken every kind of risk in sport. Max had survived all these risks. He had never taken a risk he did not believe he would survive. Max is an analytical man, he measures everything and weighs it twice before he pays for it. But Max, with his life half over, had never done the impossible.

Max is a voracious reader. He devours popular magazines and scientific journals, biographies and novels; he has worked his way through the long shelf of the Durants' *Story of Civilization.* Just as unselfconsciously, he consumes a dozen comic books a week: it relaxes his mind to see good triumph over evil, to follow the adventures of Spider-Man, Superman, the Incredible Hulk.

Sleepless one February night, he was rummaging through the unread magazines in his study. He came upon the February issue of *National Geographic,* and it caught his eye at once. On the cover was a color photograph of a helium balloon in flight: a sphere on a cone, silver at the top and jet black below, with the American flag hanging limp from the balloon's equator — and below it, limitless and blue, the Atlantic Ocean. The balloon was *Silver Fox,* and its builder and pilot, visible as a tiny figure in the gondola suspended below the balloon, was Ed Yost of Sioux Falls, South Dakota.

Max knew Yost slightly — they had met when Yost came to Albuquerque to act as balloonmeister for the World Hot-Air Balloon Championships. Yost was considered by many to be the preeminent balloonist in the world. Inside the magazine was an account, as terse as Yost is taciturn in life, of his attempt to fly across the Atlantic alone in a helium balloon. Like the other nine balloons that had attempted the Atlantic since 1958, Yost's *Silver Fox* had failed, splashing into the Atlantic seven hundred miles short of the coast of Portugal and the European mainland. Yost had been aloft for 107 hours and thirty-seven minutes, breaking the previous record for manned flight of eighty-seven hours; he had flown a great-circle route distance of 2,745.03 miles, 578.18 miles beyond the old record.

It was a noble failure, but it was a failure. Max read the *Geographic* article again, examined the pictures. In one double-page spread, Yost's balloon hung in an azure void like a period at the end of a sentence, with the sun's rays bursting from its disk; it was a sun out of a religious painting. As he read the account of Yost's flight, Max had a feeling, too deep for words or even thought, that the seed of his unrest had been germinated. Here was an act to complete. Nobody, not even the supremely skilled and self-confident Ed Yost, had ever made it across the Atlantic in a balloon. This voyage was the last thing that men, naked to the elements, using their hands and their courage as the tools of tools, had not yet done. How many had tried? How many had died trying? Max did some quick research.

Counting aborted launches and publicity stunts, there had been a total of fourteen vain attempts since 1873, when Donaldson, Ford, and Hunt in *Daily Graphic* lifted off from Brooklyn in what is regarded as the first serious attempt to conquer the Atlantic. Five balloonists had died. Malcolm Brighton and Rodney and Pamela Anderson were lost in *Free Life*, a helium balloon, in 1970, after a flight of about fourteen hundred miles. Tom Gatch disappeared beyond Bermuda in *Light Heart* in 1974, and Bob Berger in *Spirit of Man* plunged to his death twelve miles off the New Jersey coast in the same year.

It was possible to die. But if you did, you would first have lived through the worst things a man can face: storms at great altitudes, wind, rain, snow, ice, lightning — uncontrollable and unimaginable forces. You would go in one side of the unknown in an open gondola, suspended beneath a bag filled with gas so slippery, so thin, that it could pour through a mere pinhole in the fabric, hemorrhaging helium as a pierced heart spurts blood. If you had the skill and the nerve, and the Spartan discipline, to come out the other side alive, you would be a man unlike any other. That was intensely appealing to Max Anderson.

Max Anderson values proofs of courage, in himself and in others. His greatest hero since boyhood had been Charles A. Lindbergh. He had read about Lindbergh, thought about Lindbergh, off and on for most of his life. Lindbergh had seemed to Max — who of course had not been born when Lindbergh won his fame and paid for it — to be a truly free man. He had done something nobody had ever done before. And, having done it, had entered history. The flight of

The Spirit of St. Louis had been an absolutely pure act — done for its own sake, done in solitude and almost in stealth; and, having been done, could never be done again.

Max, learning to fly as a fourteen-year-old on vacation from military school, had loved flying for the freedom it gave him: no one was there with you in the sky to tell you what to do, and no one to save you. He had thought of Lindbergh then — a hero, a man who had gone beyond the ordinary limits of manhood.

Max was an experienced pilot of hot-air balloons. Alone and with his friend, a self-made millionaire named Ben Abruzzo, he had logged hundreds of hours aloft in the five years they had owned balloons in partnership. But neither Max Anderson nor Ben Abruzzo had ever flown, even as a passenger, in a helium balloon, and only a helium balloon had a hope of making it across the Atlantic.

A hot-air balloon gets its lift, as its name suggests, from heated air: propane burners are mounted at the mouth of the balloon and fill the envelope from the bottom with heat. If you want the balloon to go up, you burn gas; if you want it to go down, you let it cool. Even the largest hot-air balloon can carry only enough propane, in heavy metal tanks, for a few hours' flight. The hot-air balloon ordinarily uses no ballast.

The gas balloon is a different and altogether more subtle device. It is carried aloft by a bag filled with helium. When heated by the sun, the helium expands and lifts the balloon. If the helium expands beyond the capacity of the envelope, the excess gas vents automatically through a duct. As the bag cools at sunset, the helium contracts, and the balloon with its gondola descends. Ballast — sand or lead pellets or anything that has weight — is then thrown overboard to halt the descent. In certain circumstances, a spongeful of water, squeezed over the side of the gondola, can cause a helium balloon to rise twenty feet. The skilled pilot can keep a balloon of sufficient size aloft for a week or more (though nobody in February 1977 had yet done so over the Atlantic).

Max Anderson had a rudimentary grasp of these principles. He is an aviator and an engineer. But it would be many months before he fully understood the problems involved, before he and Ben Abruzzo tried to solve the complicated equation of a transatlantic flight. For the moment, Max knew one central fact: nobody had ever landed a transatlantic balloon on dry land.

Max Anderson and Ben Abruzzo had had one of the first hot-air balloons ever flown in Albuquerque, a city that came to be known, in the language of its Chamber of Commerce, as "the hot-air balloon capital of the world." They were the first to fly over the Sandia Mountains. Together, they had won a lot of trophies. Alone, each had won many ballooning events, including Ben's triumph in the first Pikes Peak balloon race, and Maxie's in a solo race in 1973 over salt water from Cat Cays in the Bahamas to Fort Lauderdale, Florida.

The victories of Anderson and Abruzzo were not always popular with their fellow balloonists. Ballooning was just one of their enthusiasms, and though they were interested in the sport, they weren't mesmerized by it. They seldom went to meetings of their balloon club. They would just show up at the meet and win. To be rich *and* good is not an easily forgivable combination. Often they would miss out on a victory because, in their devil-may-care hurry, they would omit some silly detail. Once, the competing balloonists were supposed to throw little sandbags with pennants attached to them at a target on the ground. Ben and Max flew closer to the target than anyone, but then they discovered they had forgotten to put sand in the sandbags. The empty bags, pennants fluttering, flew away like moths.

They would go up in any weather. "We'd launch that sucker in a fifteen-knot wind when the balloon was completely laid over on the ground and it took ten strong men to hold it down," says Max. "Ben would crawl in and I'd crawl in and we'd go for a flight. Indirectly, it made you fearless because you didn't know any better." Max, with an FAA inspector aboard to examine him for his license, almost hit a water tower and landed in a garbage dump on a Pueblo Indian reservation. Max got the license — perhaps, Ben observes, because the inspector did not want to fly with Max again.

Ben, when flying in the World Championship qualifying round, saw his balloon "streamer" above him. It had collapsed inward and was falling out of the sky. He tore at the mouth of the envelope, trying to open the balloon at the bottom so that more hot air could enter with the burners wide open. The variometer, which registers rate of ascent and descent, had pegged out at fifteen hundred feet per minute, the maximum measured by the instrument, so the balloon, "a totally deformed monster," was falling even faster than that. Ben saw power lines below. "I climbed out," says Ben, "climbed all the way out of the gondola to jump. I was standing on the rails, coming straight

7

down on this 144,000-volt line. I had the blast going. Decided to jump. Patty Anderson, who was driving the chase car, was on the ground, screaming. Couldn't hear her, of course, because those pylons are about seventy-five feet high, so I must have been at a hundred feet. Just as I was getting to the power line I got enough wind shift so that the balloon passed over the line. I climbed back in, kept burning, and hit a house right on the apex of the roof. Knocked a bunch of shingles off. Bounced across the street, landed in a great big willow tree, bounced into another tree, and all this time I'm burning, just burning the hell out of the bottom of the balloon, and finally got enough heat so I was able to fly it out of there. Well, I went back, and the balloonmeister was Ed Yost and I reported it to him as an unusual incident, and Ed says, 'Not possible. That doesn't happen.' He gave me the theory. I said, 'I don't care about the theory. It happened.' "

Ben and Max had also been through some memorable crashes together. Once, coming into the beach as sure winners of a Bahamas-to-Florida race, Max (says Ben) hit the burners on their balloon just before touchdown. The balloon rose, flew over some houses, and was flung by a strong ground wind into the only dead oak tree for twenty miles around. The branches poked dozens of holes in the envelope. Max, laughing, claims that his quick thinking saved them from a landing in the water, which would have been a worse disaster; Ben, fuming, says that he *planned* to touch the water so as to brake the balloon and make a perfect landing on the beach.

The two men, friends for years and willing without hesitation to place their lives in each other's hands, almost never see things in the same way or remember what happens to them in the same light. They live on separate emotional planets — Ben, a man of quicksilver intelligence, quick to act, quick of temper, "straight ahead," as he says of himself; Max cool, remote, a ponderer, bedeviled by sly humors. Max thinks it has to do with genetics: he is the icy Nordic, Ben the son of the fervid Mediterranean. Both wonder why Max, who, as he admits, lacks Ben's physical agility and rapid reflexes, almost never crashes when he is flying alone.

Max realized, as night followed sleepless night, that he was driven to fly the Atlantic in a balloon. Probably he decided to do this, subconsciously at least, at the moment he read in the *Geographic* of

8

Yost's unsuccessful flight. But Max is not a man to act rashly on an impulse. Lying awake, he examined the situation. Why had Yost failed? Why had everyone failed who ever tried to make the voyage? Why had five transatlantic balloonists perished? Unmanned balloons made the trip at high altitudes as a matter of routine, and had been doing so for years. Therefore the balloon itself could survive the elements. The weak link in the system must be the pilot. Men in balloons over the North Atlantic were defeated by *themselves:* by yielding to fatigue, the cold, anxiety.

Max likened the conquest of the Atlantic to the climbing of Everest or to the four-minute mile: these things were thought to be impossible simply because they had not been done. Once done, they could be done again. But it required a Hillary and a Norkay, a Roger Bannister — heroes — to kill the fear by breaking the barrier. Men did great deeds by conquering themselves.

Thinking in the night, Max felt a stab of anxiety. What if some other man, somewhere else, was drawing the same conclusions that he was drawing from the flight of Yost in *Silver Fox?* After all, Yost had almost made it. He had shown, by going as far as he had gone, that the flight was possible.

Max had no interest in being the second man to cross the Atlantic in a balloon. He had read of a man who had flown from North America to Paris the day after Lindbergh; the man had just died in Connecticut, and nobody knew his name. To be first was everything.

Max has been on a winning streak for most of his life. Born in Oklahoma, the son of a roughneck genius who made a fortune in pipeline construction, Max grew up to be a southern gentleman. He acquired his combination of discipline and courtliness at Missouri Military Academy, where he was sent at the age of eight after the divorce of his parents. He rose to be a company commander, and was named "most valuable ROTC cadet" before he graduated at seventeen. He got his airplane pilot's license (by lying about his age) on his fifteenth birthday. At twenty, he closed a deal giving his father and himself effective control of the richest uranium mine in the United States. Before he was thirty, he was president of his own mining company and soon to be a millionaire in his own right. He was an old-style American, a westerner; he had defended what he had with his fists, and sometimes even with a show of hired guns, and he said what he thought when he felt like saying it. That was what Americans were supposed to do. That, and not being afraid to risk everything, was what made Americans Americans.

Max, raised in a military system from early childhood, had been cheated of a soldier's life: World War II had ended before he was old enough to fight. As a junior cadet, issued only a wooden rifle, he had risen at five to watch from his barracks window as older boys, members of the "Spartan units" at Missouri Military Academy, went through machine-gun and bayonet drill with real weapons. When these cadets graduated, they were commissioned directly from the school — there were solemn ceremonies in the presence of the whole dewy "battalion" — and fed into the war that had such an insatiable appetite for brave young second lieutenants. Says Max today, "It was an inspirational thing. I've never forgotten the feeling at those graduations. Those boys were going to die for their country, a lot of them. But the atmosphere, the feeling, was one of pride. I'd even say *happiness*." Max might have had a second chance for a soldier's happiness. He was a member of the ROTC at the University of North Dakota while the Korean War was on, but while fielding a punt in football practice he stumbled and fell on the ball — and its point, through some freakish bad luck, smashed into his right eye, detaching the retina. Eventually the loss of sight in that eye became total.

During the second week of February, Max decided to talk to someone about his plan. He chose a man he calls "my close friend and my Dr. Watson," an Albuquerque public relations expert named James Mitchell. As much as any man, Jim Mitchell is Max's confidant. He is a fellow Oklahoman, a farm boy who was a newspaperman before coming to Albuquerque to work for the biggest local industry, Sandia Laboratories. Sandia is operated by Western Electric as a nonprofit research center for the federal government; weapons and nuclear development and energy matters are its main business.

"Max and I were talking," Jim Mitchell recalls, "and he just shifted gears from one subject to the next, no particular change in his tone of voice, and said: 'You know what I'm going to do?' I said no. Max said, 'I'm going to fly the Atlantic in a balloon.' "

10

Mitchell never doubted that Max was serious. "Are you going to do it alone?" Mitchell asked.

Max replied that he did not think a man alone could make the flight. It was too much for the human body, too much for the human spirit. Nobody knew why that was true because nobody who had made the attempt had ever been able to describe the experience. Some punishments are too painful, too humiliating, to be put into words. Later, Ben Abruzzo would ask Ed Yost, a lionhearted pilot, if he would ever try it again. "Knowing what's out there? Never," said Yost — or so Ben remembers his words. Something "out there" made men long for safety. After he had seen for himself what it was, Max would make up an aphorism about the impulses it bred in a pilot: the temptation to choose safety is the greatest danger in an epic adventure.

"I'm going to ask Ben Abruzzo to go," Max told Jim Mitchell. "Ben's the luckiest SOB I know."

At this point, Max had not mentioned his idea to Ben. "I knew if I told Ben, Ben would be on it in a minute," he says. "When it comes to glory, there's some competition between Ben and me."

These two men, who a few months later were to come close to dying together in the numbing seas off Iceland, are vivid figures in each other's minds. Neither calls the other "he" or "him." To Max, in conversation, Ben is always "Ben," and, equally, Max is invariably "Max" when Ben speaks of him.

Max and Ben live for the experience itself, not for the memory of the experience, so they tend to get lost when they think about the past. They remember, each in his own way, what happened, but they don't necessarily remember when it happened. Neither is quite sure when they became friends. Max thinks it began as much as fifteen years before these events; Ben says it is more like ten. In fact, they met in 1966 while skiing on Sandia Peak, an isolated outcropping of the Rockies that rises to 10,447 feet on the eastern outskirts of Albuquerque. The northeastern outskirts of Albuquerque *are* the northeastern outskirts of Albuquerque because of Ben Abruzzo. He and his partner built the ski area on top of Sandia Peak, on National Forest land, and connected it to the bottom with one of the longest aerial tramways in the world. The lower slopes today are dotted with houses and condominiums, developed by Ben Abruzzo's Alvarado Realty Company on land that only a few years ago, when Ben and his former partner, Robert J. Nordhaus, bought it, was considered useless: wind-swept desert, too far out of town. Ben never saw it that way: he saw one of the loveliest mountain landscapes in the West, and he developed it with care, saving each tree and treasuring each outcropping of rock, so as to preserve its natural beauty. The result is a community that bears the mark of Ben's sensitive intelligence by preserving the stark beauty of the New Mexico high desert.

This land, and years of punishing work, made Ben a millionaire. When he was building the business, he would be so exhausted, night after night, that he would have to take a short nap in his desk chair in order to be able to drive home and go to bed. But when Ben was awake, he was wide-awake, supervising every detail, doing manual labor on the construction sites, cajoling, haranguing, sweeping obstacles aside. While inspecting a cable on the tramway when it was new, he was struck by the trolley of an oncoming cable car. So intent was he on what he was doing, and this is characteristic, that he did not hear the car until the last possible instant. His superb reflexes — and this, too, is characteristic — saved him: he leaped backward out of the way, not far enough to avoid being struck on the upper body, but far enough to avoid decapitation. He twisted his body in midair with a gymnast's skill (he was a trapezist in his youth), trying in the last flickering moments of consciousness to reach a steel ladder. If he missed it, he would fall sixty-five feet to earth and almost certainly be killed. In Ben, mind and body, thought and action, are one. His intelligence is not confined to his skull, but seems to run through his nerves and his muscles as well. He has been saved, and has saved others, by this gift. On this occasion, he reached the ladder, and safety, at the instant he lost consciousness. His body wedged in its rungs, and he hung, upside down, ribs broken, from the top of the pylon until rescuers reached him.

More, even, than Max Anderson, Ben Abruzzo is a risk seeker. He, too, is a light-aircraft pilot with three thousand hours in all sorts of weather. Ben would try anything that flew: skis on vertical slopes, sailplanes, hang-gliders, helicopters. He has crashed them all except the helicopter. His idea, when faced with an emergency while in the air, is to concentrate, to think, to *try* to the final instant. Once, after he pushed a hang-glider beyond its limits, it went into an uncontrollable dive and finally, carrying Ben with it, smashed into a neighbor's house. Ben kept his eyes open until the crash. He saw the wall of the house, then the part of it he was going to hit, then the boards in that part of it, then the grain in the wood, then the nails. The hang-glider crumpled; parts of it flew off. Ben observed that, too. "Finally," says Ben, "all I could see was one little square of wood, about an inch from my nose. I stopped right there, swinging in the harness. Wasn't hurt."

But Ben does get hurt: his friends are used to seeing him on crutches and in bandages. He pays no attention to injuries; he skied for years with torn cartilage in his knee before grudgingly giving a surgeon permission to make repairs.

Ben is not a tall man, standing an inch or so below the national average. He weighs, as he approaches fifty, almost exactly what he weighed when he was eighteen — 165 pounds. His head is classically Italian — broad brow, strong nose, firm chin. Moods travel across this face like weather across the Mediterranean sky. Ben Abruzzo belongs in America and New Mexico now, but he would look quite at home in a painting by an artist of the Italian Renaissance. His wavy dark hair is combed straight back from widow's peaks. Before he made his first transatlantic flight the hair was beginning to go gray at the temples; afterward the gray turned white. His eyes are intense and blue and they never leave the face of the person he is talking to. Ben rarely blinks. At the end of the day, perhaps owing to a lack of natural lubrication, the whites of his eyes are streaked with red. Sitting or standing, he is erect. He walks fast and talks faster. In his speech he often leaves out the pronouns. Not "I wasn't hurt," but "Wasn't hurt." He doesn't know whether this comes from his natural impatience (impatience is Ben's most noticeable quality, and according to his wife, Pat, has been so since she started going with him in his early teens) or the result of growing up in a household where Sicilian, a dialect that omits pronouns, was habitually spoken. Ben no longer speaks or understands this language. Sicily had its effect on him though. His father and mother both worked long hours in the family restaurant, and Ben was cared for in his childhood by a Sicilian woman, Serafina Rotolo, a distant relative who had been widowed early. Ben was the only son. To Serafina he was a prince. "She gave Ben his way on everything," Pat explains. "I tease Ben, I say, 'You've now taken my five percent.' He'll look at me. And I'll say, 'It's ninety-five percent your way and five percent mine, and now you've taken my five percent. I've had it. You're treading on my percentage and you'd better get off.' He usually does, but I'd have to tell him or he'd take it."

As for the chances Ben takes, his wife has learned to live with them. "I feel it's necessary to take risks," she says. "I don't feel you should do foolish things to prove yourself. But to be successful, no matter at what, you have to take risks. Ben has to be proving himself all the time and doing more than anyone else does and doing it greater and better. And he does."

Ben says of himself that he does not know how to be afraid. If he lacks fear, all his other emotions are intensified, like a blind man's hearing and sense of touch. Anger is an emotion he feels easily. In a furious argument with one of his partners, he overturns his presidential desk, creating a storm of papers like a ticker-tape parade inside his office. Playing backgammon on vacation with his friend Bob Bowers in a street café on a Greek island, Ben thought he had Bowers beaten. "There was no way he could win — no way! Then Bowers threw a double six, a double five, a double six and beat me!" Ben overturned the table — backgammon board, dishes and glasses and all. Thousands of dollars were involved, for Ben likes high stakes, but it wasn't the money — it was the defeat, the failure.

Ben is Sicilian without admixture, the child of a Sicilian immigrant, Luigi (Louis, in America) Abruzzo, and a mother, Mary, born in Chicago of Sicilian parents. When Ben was about ten, the family moved from a nice neighborhood in Rockford, Illinois, to a tougher one in South Rockford, where the Abruzzos' restaurant, The Three Trees, was located. Ben's father, who worked from dawn till midnight seven days a week in his restaurant, wanted to be closer to his work. "It was like warfare in South Rockford — those kids were beating me up at a rate that was just unreasonable; I had to fight my way back and forth to school." When Ben reached the sixth grade, he asked his parents for just two things — a set of weights and a punching bag.

"It was almost like a religious fervor," says Ben. "I punched that bag and lifted those weights every night and got my weight up to one sixty." Then, one by one, Ben Abruzzo beat up the kids who had beaten him up; the job took six years, until his last year in high school.

While still in high school, Ben met and fell in love with a Rockford girl named Patricia Steen. Pat was a young woman of almost ethereal beauty — blond and slim and shy, with dark eyes glowing in a golden face. The daughter of Swedish and Norwegian parents, Pat went to a different high school in Rockford, but she and Ben, after meeting on the beach where he was a lifeguard, were seldom separated for long. (Years later, after their marriage, Ben would pilot his own airplane back to Albuquerque in all weathers and at all hours, in order to avoid spending a night away from his wife and family.) While Pat and Ben were still in their teens and going steady, she fell overboard while they were sailing in a small boat on Lake Geneva, near their hometown. Though Pat was an expert swimmer — a member of her high school synchronized swim team — she panicked. Ben, with the seamless combination of thought and action that is the hallmark of his character, leaped instantaneously into the water. He saved Pat's life. The sailboat, with no one at the tiller, ran away from them before the wind, but the two young people swam side by side through the chilly waters to safety.

Ben went to the University of Illinois to please his parents. He switched majors often (dentistry, engineering, business) but ended with a degree in business administration. Immediately on graduation he and Pat Steen were married. This was in 1952. The Korean War was on, and Ben went into the Air Force from the ROTC. Two years later he was discharged as a first lieutenant and decided to stay where the Air Force had sent him: Albuquerque.

Ben, already the father of one child, went into the used-car business. The uranium boom of the midfifties (touched off by finds such as the one Max Anderson had made a couple of years before near Grants, New Mexico) was in full fever. Ben and his partner, Frank Alongi, bought a drilling rig and invested in some uranium claims. With a lot of other speculators of the time, they went broke. Ben lost his used-car business. He was twenty-three years old. He owed the banks $40,000. He refused to accept bankruptcy; he was determined to pay the money back. The bankers did not believe him. He put the small house he and Pat had built on the market and it sold in two days. They scurried to an apartment; Pat was expecting another child. Ben tried selling encyclopedias and pots and pans door to door. He tried to sell brooms; he would drive around in the old Packard the bank had let him keep for transportation with the brooms sticking out a broken window. He went to work as a carpenter's helper. Finally, he took a dull but steady job at Sandia Laboratories. Pat Abruzzo said, "It doesn't matter." But it mattered to Ben.

"I was in a terrible depression, I'd totally failed," Ben recalls. "The odor of failure is always there, always there, and still is. It's a tremendous lesson."

Ben paid off the $40,000 in debts to the last penny. He started the business that made him rich. "I'd been all the way down once," says Ben, "and that was enough." He never wanted another failure.

Max Anderson and Ben Abruzzo had always made decisions easily. They bought their first hot-air balloon, a Raven 50 called *Union Gas*, starred and striped red, white, and blue like the American flag, without even asking the price.

Their ventures often started with a telephone call. Two or three days after he had talked with Jim Mitchell, Max telephoned Ben. Both men, lovers of gadgets, have complicated telephone systems with speakers instead of receivers and panels of push buttons that dial numbers automatically, circuits whirring like science-fiction sound effects.

When Ben came on the speaker, Max said, "Did you read the story about Ed Yost in the new *National Geographic?*"

"Yes, I read it."

"Well," said Max, "I've been thinking about it. What would you think about you and me flying the Atlantic?"

Ben, the high-stakes player, likes to see another good player put a big bet on the table.

"Let's do it," said Ben.

Even before it was built, Max Anderson (with Ben Abruzzo's enthusiastic participation) named the balloon that would take them over the Atlantic *Double Eagle*. The name was an act of homage to Charles Lindbergh, the Lone Eagle, but had other meanings as well.

Because Ben and Max were planning to reconquer the Atlantic in the fiftieth anniversary year of Lindbergh's flight in 1927, they registered their balloon as N 50 DE — The "50" for Lindbergh's golden jubilee, and "DE" for *Double Eagle:* the second great crossing, the American Eagle, two Americans following in the flight path of the greatest hero in the annals of peaceful aviation.

The name had a lucky ring to it. Max, only half in jest, said that he and Ben would prang the Eiffel Tower. From the first day, without discussing it with each other, both chose Paris as *Double Eagle*'s destination. There could be no other. Paris, the birthplace of aviation, had been Lindbergh's goal, and it had been the unattainable dream of all who had tried before Lucky Lindy to fly from the New World to the Old.

Ben and Max nevertheless faced this sober fact: in 1977, less was known about flying helium balloons across the Atlantic (or anywhere else) than had been known in Lindbergh's day about airplanes. It was generally understood, in 1927, that it was possible to fly an airplane nonstop across the Atlantic. Two British flyers, John William Alcock and Arthur Whitten Brown, had crossed from St. John's, Newfoundland, to Clifden, Ireland, in sixteen hours and twelve minutes, on June 14–15, 1919. Lindbergh's feat was to do it alone and to reach Paris. Had he failed, or delayed, even by so much as a day, that forgotten man from Connecticut whose obituary Max had read might well have entered the history books in his stead. Many stood ready to do what Lindbergh did in 1927; the flying machine had reached a state of development, and men had reached a state of mind, where the flight was inevitable.

In 1977, on the other hand, almost nobody thought it likely that a balloon could cross the ocean. In truth, few had ever seen a balloon in flight. Besides, the seventies in America were a time when people had stopped expecting much from the human spirit. Daring was out of style.

Ed Yost, in the *Geographic*, had written that a manned crossing was only a matter of time. But Yost's was the loneliest of all voices — the voice of an enthusiast. Despite the fact that his flight took place during the nation's bicentennial year, it had received almost no notice. The balloon was a forgotten device — something primitive, something that had not worked out: "the worst way to travel," as a jovial French diplomat was to say a while later, on giving the balloonists a decoration.

The history of ballooning, it must be said, reads like the script for a zany movie. The balloon, it is believed, was invented in 1783 at Annonay, a town near Lyons, France, by the brothers Joseph Michel and Jacques Etienne Montgolfier. The brothers had observed that clouds, which are made of vapor, floated in the sky, and they reasoned that a lightweight bag filled with a similar vapor might rise into the sky and float like a cloud. They knew that smoke rose, and so they filled bags with wood smoke, and presto! the bags were carried aloft. On June 5, 1783, before a large crowd of spectators, the Montgolfiers inflated a linen bag 105 feet in circumference with smoke from a fire fed with bundles of straw. The balloon rose to a great height and traveled about one and a half miles in the ten minutes that it flew before the hot air within it cooled. This event caused great excitement in France and, subsequently, throughout Europe. Not until some time later was it realized that not smoke but hot air provided lift.

On August 27, 1783, the first hydrogen balloon, a sphere thirteen feet in diameter, made of thin silk varnished with elastic gum, ascended from the Champ-de-Mars in Paris. A throng of Parisians, including many fashionable ladies and gentlemen, stood in a pelting rain, watching the balloon rise rapidly to a height of some 3,000 feet. It flew for about forty-five minutes and fell in a field near Gonesse, about fifteen miles away. Terrified farmers attacked it with pitchforks and rakes and tore it to shreds. This balloon was built by two brothers named Robert according to designs by the physicist J. A. C. Charles.

In October of 1783, Jean-François Pilâtre de Rozier (1756–1785), superintendent of the natural history collections of Louis XVI, made several ascents in a tethered "fire balloon" — a balloon with a stove in the gondola. The next month, on November 21, Rozier, accompanied by the marquis d'Arlandes, made an ascent in a free fire balloon from the Bois de Boulogne. Feeding straw into a stove so that the heated air in the envelope was constantly renewed, the intrepid pair overflew the Invalides and the Ecole Militaire at 3,000 feet and landed, some twenty-five minutes later, about five miles away, on the outskirts of Paris. Rozier and Arlandes were the first men to fly, and live.

Ten days later, J. A. C. Charles ascended in a hydrogen balloon, accompanied by one of the Robert brothers, and flew about twenty-seven miles at a maximum altitude of 2,000 feet. He is regarded as the father of the gas balloon; he invented practically all the features basic to the design: the envelope itself, the valve at the top for the release of gas, the gondola suspended from a hoop supported by netting stretched over the inflated envelope.

A Frenchman, Jean-Pierre Blanchard, and an American physician, John Jeffries, crossed the English Channel in a free hydrogen balloon on January 7, 1785. After ascending from Dover, Blanchard and Jeffries found themselves, when about a third of the way across the Channel, descending at a frightening rate. To stop the "down," they threw out everything in the gondola. The balloon rose to a safe altitude, but as it approached the coast of France it began once again to fall precipitously. The pilots ballasted off anchor and ropes and most of their clothing. They considered jettisoning the gondola itself as a last resort and riding in on the rigging, but this proved unnecessary. The balloon ascended to "a magnificent height" and landed in the forest of Guînes. (For many years a legend existed, and was generally believed, that Napoleon Bonaparte had leaped into the gondola with drawn sword as Blanchard, the most famous of the early aeronauts, was about to begin his first flight on March 2, 1784, at Paris. The swordsman demanded to be taken along on the flight, but was wrestled out of the balloon. The intruder was not the future emperor, but a young man called Dupon de Chambon, and so far as is known, this was his only historic moment.)

Jean-François Pilâtre de Rozier, accompanied by P. A. Romain, attempted to cross the Channel from France to England on June 15, 1785. Rozier used a combination balloon — a fire balloon ten feet in diameter rigged beneath a hydrogen balloon thirty-seven feet in diameter. Rozier reasoned that he would be able to descend or ascend without wasting gas by increasing or decreasing the fire in the hot-air balloon. It was an unfortunate theory. After an uneventful ascent, the system burst into flames and fell 3,000 feet to the earth about four miles from its starting point at Boulogne. Rozier was killed instantly, and his unfortunate friend Romain survived only ten minutes longer.

It was not until 178 years later that the Channel was at last crossed by men in a hot-air balloon. Ed Yost and Don Piccard flew from England to France on April 13, 1963.

Sportsmen continued to make flights for a century after the death of Rozier, but the development of the airplane doomed the balloon as a practical device for transporting goods or people. Beautiful though it was to see on the breast of the wind, the balloon was a technological dead end. Its drawbacks were insuperable. In its hot-air version, it could remain aloft only a short time. The hydrogen balloon, as anyone who recalled the fate of poor Rozier knew, was likely to explode at the slightest spark and incinerate its passengers. Finally, and most damning, the flight of balloons could not be controlled in any precise way. The balloonist, on taking off, never knew where he was going to come down. That fact severely limited the number of men who were willing to go up in the first place. The number who were ready to invest the very large sums necessary to build a balloon was even smaller.

A balloon must always be built specifically for the flight it is going to make. It is not an item that can be bought off the shelf, like a pair of skis or a jet airplane. Balloon building is an art, and it is an art that made no significant advances — apart from the use of new materials and the substitution of helium for the nerve-shattering hydrogen — from the final year of the American Revolution until the 1950s. During that decade, research conducted under the auspices of the United States government resulted in such innovations as the use of lightweight plastic films for envelopes, the development of new kinds of ducts, and the introduction of the "natural shape" balloon.

In 1977, only one man in the United States was in the business of building transatlantic balloons — Ed Yost. Ben and Max went up to see him, after some preliminary talk on the telephone, in April of that year. Max was negotiating, at the time, for the purchase of a new company airplane, and the dealer, Bill Cutter of Albuquerque, offered to fly him and Ben up to Yost's factory at Sioux Falls in a new Beechcraft Kingair.

The world of ballooning is a quiet world, and Ed Yost is a quiet man — "a man of few words and those well chosen," as Max is fond of saying. Nevertheless, Ben and Max knew a good deal about Yost. Apart from his personal exploits as a balloonist, Yost was a key figure in the experimental manned-balloon program of the fifties and early sixties. In one of these programs, in 1960, Air Force Captain (later Colonel) Joseph W. Kittinger, reached 102,800 feet in the balloon *Excelsior III*. Bailing out of the pressurized gondola, he made a free-fall descent to 17,500 feet before opening his parachute and floating to a safe landing. (Ben Abruzzo, as a twenty-one-year-old second lieutenant at Kirtland Air Force Base, Albuquerque, had tried to transfer into this program but failed the eyesight test: his right eye is 20/200. "I envy Kittinger that jump," says Ben. "Eighty-five thousand feet straight down before opening his parachute!")

Ben and Max arrived at Sioux Falls in time for dinner, and Ed Yost conducted them to a restaurant that featured a harpist and two young women playing violins. They had seafood for dinner, and this was their first prolonged meeting with Yost. That evening, at his house, Yost showed Ben and Max his memorabilia — color slides of the flight of *Silver Fox;* a cable from President Ford, sent on the occasion of Yost's splashdown in the Atlantic next to a West German freighter. The freighter, streaked with rust, loomed very large in Yost's photographs, which he had taken from his gondola as it bobbed on the surface of the sea. Max was to remember that combination of images for a long time afterward: Yost, flying in a free balloon

21

where no man had flown before; and Yost, defeated, in the water with his balloon collapsed, the very symbol of impotence. Yost had been pulled south of his intended course and believed himself trapped in a weather phenomenon known as the Azores High. This is a great blue hole, a high-pressure area that is a more or less permanent feature of the Atlantic weather system. The Azores High is the reason sailing ships are becalmed in the waters west of the Azores, and it was the reason why Yost, venting and ballasting frantically, had had to abort his flight before the clockwise spin of the Azores High blew *Silver Fox* into the Caribbean. Neither Ben nor Max ever wanted to find himself in those circumstances.

In the night, Ben had been thinking about the sea, and landing in it. Like Max, he is an insomniac, and when he cannot sleep he wrestles with problems. The sea gave him problems. He knew what the odds were of ending, like Yost, in the water. "You've got to know — and if you don't know this you're just a damn fool to take off — that the chances are you will land in the sea," says Ben, describing his state of mind in April 1977. "Up to the time that we made it, all transatlantic balloons had landed in the sea. In your mind's eye you can see the Atlantic as an endless expanse of treacherous water. It's been that all through history — the treacherous North Atlantic, the cold North Atlantic, the vicious North Atlantic, the stormy. You just don't ever hear anything comfortable about it."

Ben, after tossing many nights in his imagination on its waves, decided that he could deal with the North Atlantic. He was an experienced sailor. "You have to cure yourself and decide you can accept a landing — a landing under any conditions you can think about — a high sea or a raging sea, black of night. The water is very cold. Without survival suits, your life expectancy is one to four minutes. With the survival suits you maybe have an hour or two — if you don't drown because of the wave action."

The only chance of survival was to be able to sail a tiny boxlike boat — their gondola would be fifteen feet long, with a six-and-a-half-foot beam, and would be five feet from keel to gunwale — perhaps for days, and somehow stay dry enough to live. Ben at last decided that he and Max could do that. "I decided I was comfortable with that," Ben says. "You have to. Otherwise you'd be a fool to go." Max never thought the gondola would survive in heavy seas. He thought it would swamp, sink, and leave them, with or without sur-

22

vival suits, in the waters of the North Atlantic. He was comfortable with that. "No risk," as Ben said, "no adventure."

Next day, they met Yost again to discuss the design and construction of their balloon. There was little to discuss. Yost builds only one kind of balloon for the sort of flight Ben and Max had in mind. His balloons come in different sizes, but they all look like his own *Silver Fox*. In engineering language, the design consists of a transected sphere placed on a cone at an angle of sixty degrees. When sketched on a piece of scrap paper, a balloon made in this way looks like an ice cream cone with an unusually large scoop of vanilla at the top.

The sphere-and-cone design is a time-honored one, going back to the very early balloons. It is very strong because the load tapes — immensely tough nylon straps — are stitched to the cone, or lower portion of the balloon, thus avoiding distortion of the sphere. The load straps are attached to a ring — J. A. C. Charles's "hoop" — from which the gondola is hung by cables.

The helium, expanding in the hours of sunlight, fills the entire balloon, stretching it taut when the envelope is inflated to full capacity. If the helium expands beyond the capacity of the envelope, it is vented overboard through a long sleevelike duct running down the side of the envelope; otherwise, of course, the balloon would rupture and plunge to earth. At night, when the helium cools, it contracts and rises to the upper portion of the balloon and the lower cone can be as slack as a sail in a calm. A balloon, while in flight, is *always* in a dead calm: it is, so to speak, within the wind and part of the wind, not an object driven through another element by the wind, as a yacht is blown over the waves. Therefore there is no sensation of motion and no movement of air within the gondola. A sheet of paper, laid on the open deck of a balloon moving with a fifty-mile-an-hour wind, will not even flutter. Nothing is ever blown overboard from the gondola of a helium balloon.

The balloon is equipped with a valve, fitted to the top, through which helium can be released in order to make the balloon descend. This is operated by pulling on a cord and carefully timing the intervals in which the valve is left open. Another line, the rip line, controls the rip panel. When the rip line is pulled, a triangular panel on the wall of the balloon is ripped out, spilling all the gas in the envelope. This is only done, needless to say, on landing.

Yost constructs his balloons of a special nylon material coated with neoprene. The fabric is cut with ordinary scissors on curved tables, some of these tables being more than a hundred feet long. The panels, once cut, look like the sections of an orange. Each is measured and marked at short intervals. The panels are then fitted together, mark against mark, and glued. Only the load tapes are sewn in place, for every needle hole is a potential hazard. A puncture the size of a pencil lead could, over the course of a five-day flight, permit the escape of enough helium to cause a disaster. Where the tapes are sewn, they are covered with the glued edge of the adjoining panel to seal the stitching. It is a tedious job and it can only be done by hand, and by people who realize what a mistake can mean to men in a gondola 20,000 feet above the Atlantic.

Silver Fox had had a capacity of 60,000 cubic feet, but it had been designed for a solo flight. *Double Eagle*, carrying two men and twice the gear, would need to be bigger. Ed Yost recommended a capacity of 82,973 cubic feet. The colors would be the same, silver at the top and black at the bottom. The silvery paint on the sphere is designed to reflect sunlight, so as to limit the expansion of the helium in the heat of the day when the sun is above the balloon. The black cone, conversely, absorbs heat in the early morning and late afternoon, when the angle of the sun is low.

The gondola, steel tubing and fiberglass, would be similar to the double catamaran carried by *Silver Fox*. It would be fitted with a sail and mast, a compass, ballast bags, a cover for heavy seas (Max smiled at that), a built-in toilet, cleats and fittings, and trail ropes.

The price, said Yost, would be $50,000 for the balloon. Ben tried, as any businessman would, to negotiate with Ed Yost. Yost simply repeated the figures: that was his price; take it or leave it.

Max said to Yost, "What about training? Will you teach us to fly the thing?"

Transatlantic balloons, for all their great cost, are flown only once. The dangers of damage are very great in inflating such a huge envelope — and, naturally, even the smallest amount of damage can mean disaster. Of the dozen attempts to launch a balloon across the Atlantic, four were aborted at or before takeoff because of rupture of the envelope.

Yost said he would teach Ben and Max to fly a smaller helium balloon — the principles were the same no matter what size the craft — for $3,000. Because they were already experienced hot-air balloonists, Yost thought they could learn all they needed to know about gas ballooning in one long training session.

The $3,000 included the helium, the ground crew — and the plastic-film balloon itself. After one use, the envelope would be discarded. Having been inflated and deflated, it would never fly again because of the risk that it might have been damaged or weakened. Ed Yost has only one standard of safety: one hundred percent. He added that he would guarantee *Double Eagle* to be free of defects for fifteen minutes after inflation and takeoff. If it was going to leak, it would leak in that period.

Would he include the cost of the training flight in the cost of the balloon?

"Nope," said Ed Yost.

Max and Ben stepped away and exchanged a sentence or two.

"Deal," said Ben to Ed Yost. The three shook hands.

Bill Cutter, the Beechcraft dealer, had been a witness to this conversation. With his brother, Sid, he is generally held to be one of the finest balloon pilots in the world. He looked at Max and Ben in amazement. He asked, "What did you say?"

Ben replied, " 'Build it.' We said, 'Build it.' "

"You're going to go — you're really going to do it?"

"It's a fair price," said Max.

"But that easily?"

"It's only a matter of placing the order for the balloon. We've made the decision to go," said Ben.

"By God, that *is* unbelievable," said Bill Cutter. "To do it so easily."

Of course, it hadn't been as easy as it seemed, with Ben and Max joking with Ed Yost on a sunny morning in April. Even for men of means, the investment was considerable. Before they were through with the flight, Max and Ben would have spent more than $100,000. There was little prospect of ever getting that money back. The flight was something they wanted to do by themselves and for its own sake. They have been asked if they were looking for the perfect adventure, challenging the Atlantic. Max laughs. Ben thinks about it and says: "I don't say things like that unless somebody helps me out — but, yes, maybe."

Patty Anderson says that Max had been thinking about a transatlantic flight even before he read of Yost's voyage in *Silver Fox*. He had mentioned it to her, in passing, earlier in the winter. "He asked what I thought about it. I thought, right away, that it was something he had to do. It made me fearful. I thought, 'Maybe it will pass, maybe he won't have the time, maybe it's just a dream.' "

Patty met Max the summer they were sixteen, when he was working for his father on a pipeline construction job. The pipeline passed near Bagley, Minnesota, Patty's hometown. Max was a cadet, an athlete, an airplane pilot. He was living a man's life; in a year's time, his father, Carl Anderson, would think he had enough muscle to handle million-dollar deals, and would send him off to look at mines and do the kind of backcountry roughneck business that had made Carl himself a millionaire. On one of their first dates, Max filled Patty's arms with teddy bears by shooting crooked .22's and throwing doctored baseballs at a carnival. From that time on, Patty never doubted his ability to beat the odds.

The following summer, though the pipeline had passed Bagley by, Max found a reason to come back. By the time he entered the University of North Dakota that fall, he and Patty were married. They kept the marriage a secret from their families until a year later, the bride living in Delta Delta Delta house and the groom at Sigma Chi, until the imminent arrival of their son Michael made it necessary for them to take an apartment. "It was a basement apartment," says Max, "and I decided right quick that I was never going to live in one of *those* again."

There are pictures of Patty as a sorority queen in the college yearbooks that the Andersons still keep, more than twenty years after their graduation, on the coffee table in their family room. They are people who hold on to their memories. No photograph is necessary to remind them of how Patty looked at eighteen. She looks almost the same today, except for a change in coiffure — blond hair, blue eyes, glowing smile. She is Norwegian on both sides and she is a Norwegian beauty. Her faith is Lutheran, and strong — church most Sundays and the charitable works of a good woman on other days. The proceeds, above expenses, from the flight of *Double Eagle* would be donated to St. Joseph's Hospital; Patty is secretary of the hospital's foundation board.

After Max returned from seeing Ed Yost, Patty knew that he

was committed to the flight. He told her so. "I've learned to take my husband seriously when he says he's going to do something," says Patty. "I knew what had happened before, that some had died. I lived with that thought for a while. I never said, 'No, I won't let you do it,' or 'You can't do it,' or 'I'm against doing it.' I'm not the type to say that to him about hardly anything. But the idea seemed frightening."

The fact that Max was going with Ben made Patty feel more comfortable. Ben was like a brother to her and to Max, and that was not a figure of speech: all the affection mixed with rivalry, all the generosity mixed with jealousy of real brothers was between them. "I know Ben has guts. Of course, I know that about Max. I've never known him to be frightened of anything," says Patty.

The idea of a balloon flight in itself held no anxiety for either Patty Anderson or Pat Abruzzo. Both had flown many times with their husbands, and had more often driven chase cars. Even the crashes were, when remembered, a cause for laughter. Ben, a few years before, had started a Christmas tradition; just before the holiday, he goes up in a balloon wearing a Santa Claus suit, and scatters candy to skiers on Sandia Peak and to children in school-yards. One year he made a very hard landing. The gondola tipped over and Ben was spilled out, his red suit disheveled, his false beard blown up over his face. Three very small Spanish-American children rushed to the deflated balloon and knelt by Ben's fallen form. "Sahnta Clauss! Sahnta Clauss!" they cried. "Are you all right?"

Max and Ben and Pat, having flown over Sandia Crest, once maneuvered the balloon among the ponderosa pines that grow on the western slope of the mountain, and drifting along at twilight with the burners giving out the little gasps that kept them at equilibrium, picked pine cones from the branches of the trees.

It did not seem strange to Pat Abruzzo that Ben, who has had a new plan almost every day for the twenty-six years of their marriage, should have decided on the spur of the moment to fly the Atlantic with Max. "Ben just told me they were going to do it," Pat recalls. "I thought, 'Oh, that sounds like a real challenge.' Also, I thought it would be a year or two in the planning and the assembly of the equipment and all, and six months later they were doing it. So that part was a shock and I questioned the success of the flight, the short preparation period. I really did."

It seemed to Ben and Max, when they returned from Sioux Falls to Albuquerque, that they had ample time to prepare for the flight.

"Money had changed hands, and that meant we were committed to go," says Ben. "We'd moved from the idea to the reality. At the time, we thought everything else — learning the weather, learning how to fly the balloon, communications, navigation, equipment, food, clothes — all those things were mere details."

The flight was just one element in their lives. Both had businesses to run and scores of employees to deal with. They planned to fly over Pikes Peak in a hot-air balloon race in July, and do some sailing together later in the summer. Ben and Pat had planned a trip to Europe with friends.

As casually as they had decided to go, they talked about how to get there. Max, in his methodical way, had drawn up a list of priorities. They divided the major responsibilities: Ben would work with Yost on the business of getting *Double Eagle* and its gondola built. Max would deal with navigation and weather. Neither man knew anything about celestial navigation. Neither knew much about weather patterns in the North Atlantic.

And, of course, neither knew anything about the subtleties of flying a helium balloon, beyond the scraps of technique they had been able to glean from Ed Yost.

Max and Ben had hoped to learn more from Yost than they did. In Sioux Falls they had peppered him with questions about the flight of *Silver Fox*. Yost's answers had been honest but brief.

28

"Ed was cryptic," says Max. "At the time I didn't really understand why. Now I do. You can't teach transatlantic ballooning. I did learn one thing from Ed — that he'd build us a hell of a balloon, but it was up to Ben and me to get to France in it."

Max and Ben never imagined they could do that without help, and as soon as they ordered the balloon they began thinking about assembling a ground support staff. Max had already had some telephone conversations about the behavior of weather systems over the Atlantic with his friend George Fischbeck, a former science teacher who had become the weatherman for KABC, a Los Angeles television station. Fischbeck's counsel was pointed: find the best meteorologist in the world and listen to his advice, because the success of *Double Eagle* and the lives of its pilots depended on that.

Max began the search for a meteorologist, and he asked George Fischbeck to help him find one.

A balloon cannot be maneuvered on the horizontal plane; it must go where the winds take it. But it can be maneuvered vertically: it can go up or down and find the winds that are blowing in the right direction, at the right speed. Max and Ben knew from their experience as airplane pilots that wind speeds and directions are constantly being reported by the swarms of aircraft that are over the Atlantic at any given time. Using this data combined with sophisticated forecasting techniques, why should it not be possible to steer a balloon as nobody had ever done? George Fischbeck saw no reason why it should not be possible; Max told him to continue the search for a man who was *positive* it could be done. This idea intrigued Max Anderson. He studied the altitude profile of Ed Yost's flight, and pondered the matter.

"My head was literally in the clouds at that time," says Max. "I knew the single most important thing for us to understand was the weather and how a balloon interacted with it. I didn't want to be distracted from that. Luckily, we had Doc Wiley."

W. C. Wiley, a retired Air Force colonel, was, among other things, the company pilot for Ranchers, Max's mining firm. Ben and Max never considered anyone else to head their ground crew. In addition to being an experienced airplane pilot, Doc Wiley was himself a balloonist and a sailplane pilot. He understood the problems and the romance of motorless flight. In nearly thirty years in the Air Force, Wiley had polished skills that would be invaluable in the months ahead: he knew how to organize, he knew how to improvise, and he knew how to talk to the military in its own specialized language. This last talent would, in the end, mean the difference between death and survival to Max and Ben.

Doc Wiley, in saving Max and Ben from distraction, brought a good deal of worry on himself. "We went up to Sioux Falls in April, and Ben and Max sort of winked and nodded at each other, which is their way of doing things, and ordered a balloon from Ed Yost," says Doc. "I knew right then it would be busy times ahead for old Wiley. It was already April, and they decided they wanted to fly in September, maybe even August."

The shortness of time disturbed Doc, but he knew it was useless to mention the matter: "Maxie and Ben don't take no for an answer when they decide to do something. When the die is cast, the people who work for them had better get things cranked up and going."

It is a principle of leadership with Max Anderson that a good man ought to know what to do without being reminded of the obvious. As things occurred to him, he would mention them to Doc Wiley. Ben did the same. But they left details in his hands. The details were myriad.

"They had *no* specific idea of what they wanted to take with them," says Doc.

"We trusted Doc," says Max, "and we did right to trust him. He knew what we ought to have — it was common sense. We had to eat, we had to keep warm and dry, we had to have some way of calling home, we had to have some way of knowing where we were. Doc knew all that."

Ben, when he had an idea, would give Doc a ring. Max would mention things to him as they flew from place to place in the company plane, or as Doc passed by the door of Max's office. "We want to be sure to have a good set of maps," Max would say. Ben would call: "We better get some dye markers, Doc, in case we come down on the ice pack."

Doc Wiley, in military fashion, did it by the numbers. He drew up categories of necessities, on paper and in his mind. The chief category in his mind was one he hardly ever mentioned to Max and Ben: rescue.

"I just kept turning *that* over in my mind," says Doc. "What do we do if we've got a damn balloon down in the Atlantic in a storm and the nearest ship or helicopter is two or three hundred miles away? I got them some survival suits. They liked the suits, but you're not going to get those guys to imagine themselves bobbing around inside a rubber union suit in thirty-foot seas."

Ben and Max planned to conquer the Atlantic. "Rescue" was not a word they applied to themselves.

Doc talked more often about mundane items. He started with food. Jim Mitchell's wife, Josephine, is a dietitian. She suggested that *Double Eagle* carry plenty of liquids, together with high protein, high-energy foods that were simple to prepare. Neither Max nor Ben is a cook, and it was thought that the flight would last at least five days, possibly ten. Nobody knew what effect long periods at high altitudes in an open gondola would have on the human appetite and human nutrition. Ed Yost, of course, hadn't said. It was taken for granted that some sort of special diet would be required. There would be no refrigeration; perhaps they would carry a simple stove for the preparation of soup and hot drinks. Jo Mitchell studied the problem. Other questions received less attention.

"One thing they completely failed to do was to make a careful analysis of the clothes they'd need," says Doc. "Both are skiers and they had lots of low temperature clothing. They just assumed that goose down would be the best thing up in a balloon, just as it was up in the high Rockies."

In the heat of the desert, Max and Ben joked about this. Max, the Norseman, was famous for his ability to withstand bitter cold with only the flimsiest protection: he would ski all day in subzero conditions without a hat, wearing only a Windbreaker over a light sweater. For some reason, altitude didn't bother him much, either — heavy exercise in the twelve-thousand-foot environment of Taos ski basin caused no shortness of breath in Max.

Ben, too, was inured to altitude. Both men had been living for years in Albuquerque, which lies at an altitude of almost five thousand feet, and had spent much time at higher elevations. They believed that they were better acclimated for a long flight at high altitudes than anyone who had ever before attempted the Atlantic. Ben was more susceptible to cold than Max, and he had a respect for the power of winter. At Sandia ski area, he had seen more than one healthy young person overcome by exposure. Death by freezing could be swift, and Ben knew the signs of hypothermia: the blurred speech, the shuddering discomfort followed by a sense of warmth and well-being, the loss of consciousness that could foreshadow death.

Ben didn't worry about himself. He had the right clothes, the best goose-down garments available, and he meant to take them all with him. He was sure they would protect him against any conditions he might encounter over the Atlantic in September.

Double Eagle would need a first-class communications system. Because of the need to limit weight, there was no hope of carrying a radio powerful enough to communicate directly from gondola to home base. Doc assumed, but he did not know, that the operations center for the flight would be somewhere on the New England coast. What was needed was a system that would permit Max and Ben, operating a relatively weak transmitter, to relay messages back to this base.

"The solution was pretty apparent," says Doc. "It's almost impossible to imagine the number of airliners and military planes there are in the air over the Atlantic at any given moment. We decided to use them as relay stations. Max and Ben would talk to the plane and the plane would pass on the message to us on the ground, or vice versa. We thought we might be able to use ships, too. What I really wanted was for the fellows to have a radio to call a ship if they went down at sea. They thought that was a great idea — there they'd be, bobbing around in the gondola and fishing when the *Queen Elizabeth* steamed up. Ed Yost didn't even have time to fish, that German freighter was under him so conveniently."

Though Ben and Max have been operating aircraft radios for years, neither of them is a skilled radio operator. In an aircraft, the pilot sets a switch to one frequency or another, presses the talk button on his microphone, and talks. Doc suspected that the procedure might be more complicated in a balloon, especially when the man operating the radio is suffering from fatigue and stress. He wanted to install the simplest possible equipment, but there were limits to how simple it could be and still serve the purpose.

In the end, Doc Wiley ordered, from commercial suppliers, three pieces of equipment. The first was a Very High Frequency (VHF) transceiver with a range of 120 miles, for talking to over-flying aircraft. The second was a High Frequency (HF) transceiver; under favorable conditions, it had a range of 500 to 1,000 miles, but it was a cranky device requiring fine tuning to punch through wavebands crowded with commercial cross talk. Finally, there would be a marine-band radio for communication with ships; its range was only about fifty miles. Ben also borrowed, from the New Mexico National Guard, a couple of surplus hand-held transceivers for emergency use. Ben and Max were confident they could operate all this equipment. Doc was less optimistic, but he was never able to hold them still long enough for the systematic familiarization and training sessions his military conditioning told him were advisable. The whole radio package would weigh about one hundred pounds, and, powered by another four hundred pounds of batteries, would be the heaviest single item, apart from the water supply, that the balloon would carry.

Doc Wiley, feeling that he ought to draw the attention of Ben and Max to the basic techniques of survival at sea, gave them a copy of the Air Force manual on the subject, 1969 edition. Both read it — Ben with more attention than Max. Ben was still in the process of getting comfortable with the idea of a sea landing, and the more he knew about the subject the better he felt. He became convinced that an intelligent man could live through the experience. Max continued to think that no amount of brains and preparation could save a human being plunged into midocean unless the water was dead calm and a rescue vessel was standing by.

Again and again, Max pored over the scrappy data relating to Ed Yost's flight. According to the article in the *Geographic*, Yost had never flown above 14,600 feet; much of the time, he had maintained lower altitudes, searching for winds that would carry him due east to Europe; he never found them. The belief grew in Max that an intelligent plan that would relate altitude to the movement of weather systems and the force of the winds, was the key to success. Ed Yost and all who went before him had made some fundamental error. What was the error? As a free balloon is a particle of the weather, like a raindrop or the nucleus of a snowflake, the solution must lie in the weather and its effect on a balloon.

Who, in all the world, was the leading expert on such matters? Max was determined to find him. He consulted experts in Washington and at the federal meteorological facility in Colorado. George Fischbeck, meanwhile, was sorting through the meteorological profession like an FBI agent through a drawer of file cards.

A single name kept cropping up — that of Robert B. Rice, chief meteorologist of Weather Services Corporation, a private forecasting company in Bedford, Massachusetts. This firm had handled the forecasting for Ed Yost's flight, and Bob Rice had been the chief meteorologist. Yost had made it plain to Max and Ben that he hadn't been satisfied with the results. That in itself was not enough to put Max Anderson off.

"I don't live by many unbreakable rules," says Max, "but there's one I believe in: never criticize a man for what he is, only for what he's done. Sometimes he would have done different if people had let him."

The only negative thing Max had heard about Rice was that he had been the meteorologist for Yost's unsuccessful flight. Max decided to find out if Bob Rice would have done things differently if he had had the chance. In late April, George Fischbeck told Max that, in his opinion, Rice was the best man for the job. Max called Weather Services and left a message for Rice.

The pink slip Bob Rice found next day on his desk listed Max Anderson's name and telephone number. Beneath that were scrawled the words: "Another balloonist!" Rice smiled the smile of the sorely tried. His experience as the principal meteorologist for Ed Yost's flight had not been a cheerful one. He was not sure he wanted to go through a similar experience.

Bob Rice had developed a revolutionary theory about flying balloons across the Atlantic. His problem, from the viewpoint of an experienced balloonist, was that he was a pure theorist; he had never been up in a balloon. Still, he knew as much about the behavior of the Atlantic weather as anyone knew. That, of course, was not very much. The atmosphere of this planet is, despite the great advances in the science of meteorology that have been brought about by weather satellites and other technological devices, almost as much of a mystery today as it was in the time of Aristotle, who wrote his treatise on the subject more than three hundred years before the birth of Christ. Man has, in the intervening centuries, learned a great deal about the composition of the atmosphere, and something about its behavior. But not even the most arrogant meteorologist — and this is a profession which instills humility — would claim that he knows what the weather is going to do, as a certain thing, even thirty-six hours in advance.

Of all meteorologists, Bob Rice would be among the last to make extravagant claims for his science or for himself. That was what Max Anderson liked best about him when first they spoke. "I heard this rumble coming over the phone," says Max — Rice has a bass voice with a current of humor running through it — "and I figured I must have an honest man on my hands."

The two men made an appointment to meet in Boston, and Max flew east a few days later. Max, who had been an altogether more lighthearted man since he had decided to fly the Atlantic, was surprised to discover how happy Boston made him. He had spent some weeks here at the Massachusetts General Hospital after injuring his eye in the football accident two decades earlier. He felt himself in familiar surroundings — the Common, the Ritz, the waterfront. He liked the smell of the sea in the onshore winds, and the old bricks of Beacon Hill. He went to lunch at Durgin Park, a landmark restaurant near Faneuil Hall where he had eaten as a youngster, and found the prime ribs of beef, his favorite, to be as good as ever.

Bob Rice is a bespectacled man with graying blond hair, neatly combed. He explained to Max precisely how he thought *Double Eagle* could fly from the United States to the European mainland. It was, he said, a matter of achieving the right altitude according to a plan worked out in advance. The balloon had to go out ahead of a high-pressure ridge, and maintain precisely the correct position.

"What you have to do," said Bob Rice, "is fly high, very high, all the way. You want to ride in or just ahead of a high-pressure ridge. Try to visualize this weather feature as a big wave, like an ocean wave. You'll ride it like a surfer. I think you can surf a balloon to Europe."

Max Anderson, hearing this, knew that he had found his meteorologist. That image — "surfing" — told him that he had been right in his instincts. He and Ben could *fly* the balloon; it was not a matter of surrendering themselves to the winds and the thunderstorms and hoping for the best. Just as a surfer, controlling his board with a combination of muscle and nerve, compels a towering wave to work for him, they could compel the invisible turmoil of the atmosphere to work for them. Moreover, they could be the first to do it. It was an irresistible challenge.

The sort of high-pressure ridge Rice was talking about formed in the Arctic, and then went out to sea, pushed by a following storm system and influenced by another weather system running ahead of it.

The ridge itself consisted of dry air; it was, in effect, a ridge of fair weather between two troughs of stormy weather.

The balloonist would wait on the coast for such a ridge to approach. At the precise hour, he would ascend into it. Meteorologists, using satellite photographs and other techniques, could watch for the formation of a good ridge, even predict within minutes when it would arrive at a certain point. They could tell, from day to day, how strong the winds associated with the ridge would be, and their direction. This data could be radioed to the balloonists from the weather station on the ground.

"It's very important to go to the highest altitude possible right after launch," Rice told Max. "Each day you go higher, so that by day three you're at what we consider a safe altitude — eighteen thousand feet."

"That means being on oxygen for half the flight," replied Max. It was generally agreed that a flight would take five or six days. Ed Yost said you either made it in that time or didn't make it.

"Longer," said Rice. "I honestly don't think that you can make a flight across the Atlantic at less than fifteen thousand feet for two thirds of the flight. No free manned balloon has ever been flown continuously at these heights. But if you're out to do something, you've got to do it the only way you can get it done."

From his years in airplanes, Max knew something about the weather. Bob Rice, in their conversations in Boston, at Durgin Park and at outdoor cafés filled with pretty girls taking the first soft sunshine of the New England spring, initiated him into its inner mysteries.

Weather in the northern hemisphere of the earth moves from west to east. This is the pattern: a high-pressure ridge sandwiched between two low-pressure troughs. The pattern extends all the way around the earth — trough, ridge, trough.

In the trough, the air moves upward. This is where clouds form, this is where storms take place, as moisture tends to form in air because of the vertical movement. Storm systems — "bad weather" — are created when air, cooled and condensed into cloud or rain or snow, is ejected out of the trough, as through a chimney. A balloon flying in a trough will get sucked into the storm and blown up the chimney, with results usually fatal to the flight.

On restaurant napkins, Rice drew the pattern — the high-pres-

36

sure ridge, a great wave of fair weather. It slopes westward, with its tip nearer to America and its base racing toward Europe. He drew a vertical line through the ridge and sketched a tiny balloon along this line:

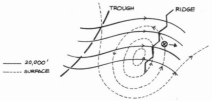

"You want to fly in the high pressure ridge *so* — climbing to stay ahead of it as it moves east," said Rice. "If you remain at one altitude, or don't climb fast enough, you'll fall behind the ridge and get swallowed by the storms in the trough behind and beneath it."

A balloon at 15,000 feet may be just ahead of the ridge. If the balloon dropped vertically, it would fall behind the ridge because of the ridge's slope.

In one vertical column there may be a cyclonic storm on the surface of the earth. Directly over it, at high altitudes, a balloon can be in sunshine with winds blowing away from the storm. Flying at anything less than 10,000 feet was to flirt with storms, and disaster.

It was, in short, a matter of maintaining proper altitude relative to the ridgeline. Like all great concepts, it was thrilling in its simplicity, and Max felt excitement and confidence mounting within him.

Max Anderson is a man who reacts to stimuli. He surrounds himself, in business and in everything else, with men and women who give off intellectual and emotional electricity. Himself a quiet man, he likes talkative, nimble companions who can activate his imagination with theirs. Rice, unlike George Fischbeck, *Double Eagle*'s ex-officio meteorologist, is not a raconteur. But when he discusses his specialty, he sends off sparks. These, in turn, fired Max Anderson with curiosity and new ideas. Another man's idea can give Max ten new ideas of his own.

Speaking to Rice, he began to think of new ways to fly a helium balloon. Rice's theories were opening up new possibilities. He had an idea, even that early, that the flight of *Double Eagle* might be more than pure adventure. It might break scientific frontiers as well, and discover new principles of flight.

Rice warned Max of the dangers. It is not possible to make a truly accurate weather forecast five or six days ahead. "You just don't get nice, big, fat weather systems that give you protection on all sides," he said. "That's why no one has ever flown the Atlantic."

As the high-pressure ridge, preceded by a cold front, moves across the Atlantic, it encounters two dominant features — the Icelandic Low, which sits in the northern latitudes near Iceland and Greenland, and Ed Yost's nemesis, the Azores High. The leading cold front tends to bog down under the influence of the Icelandic Low. The high-pressure ridge then starts to turn toward the south, into the great blue hole of the Azores High.

"The Azores High will look like it's reaching up and absorbing the weather system," Rice said. "The day goes by and it's vanished — disappeared into the Azores High."

But if a balloon is high enough — above 18,000 feet, it is still "surfing" on the remnants of the high-pressure ridge, above the storms and turbulence below. It can survive, turn toward Europe, pick up high altitude winds — and succeed.

In addition to flying high, another factor was essential. The launch had to take place in late summer or early fall, to avoid the worst of the Atlantic storm seasons. Rice and Max spoke of thunderstorms; Max had already had some conversations with a New Mexico scientist named Charles Moore, who had flown flimsy polyethylene balloons into thunderstorms. Moore had told him that a gas balloon caught in a thunderstorm could rise or fall at a rate of 1,500 feet per minute. In a hot-air balloon that would be dizzying. But Moore told Max that he had had absolutely no sensation of going up or down and was only able to tell what was happening by reading his barometer and altimeter. Max asked Moore what he *had* felt, and he was to have reason to remember the answer: "Very cold and very wet."

Ed Yost had told Max that, in his opinion, the thunderstorm season over the North Atlantic might last well into mid-September. Max discussed this with Rice; Rice didn't think any storm in those latitudes would push the balloon above 26,000 feet. Max came away believing, intellectually if not emotionally, that *Double Eagle* could fly through an oceanic thunderstorm. Once again, nobody knew for certain because nobody had ever done it.

As landings at sea preoccupied Ben, thunderstorms preoccupied

Max. He sought all the information about them available. In his mind, they were the greatest threat facing *Double Eagle*.

Back in Albuquerque, Max and Ben discussed Rice's theories. Ben grasped the concepts without difficulty. They decided to hire Weather Services as the meteorologists for their flight. They took the precaution of including a clause in the contract under which Weather Services agreed not to provide support to any other transatlantic balloon flight that might take place at the same time, or near the same time, as *Double Eagle*'s. Max felt that he had the secret of success in his hands; he wanted to keep it a secret.

Ben and Max began to condition themselves, each in his own way, for the rigors of the flight. They began to pay closer attention to diet. They went on playing handball, racquetball, tennis — Max, in some recess of his mind, thought it more important than ever to sharpen the competitive instinct, for soon they would be competing against the elements themselves and the desire to win would be of paramount importance. Ben swam for an hour five days a week, lifted weights, and did calisthenics every third morning; he lacked the religious fervor he had had in the sixth grade, but he knew himself better now. Max swam and ran. The two men did not discuss their regimens with each other, and they did not train together. Their schedules made this inconvenient, and neither saw any point in an excess of togetherness.

Max embarked on what he thought was an extremely important routine of self-discipline. He taught himself, painfully, to sleep. Where in the past he had permitted his mind to keep his body awake, he now controlled it, forced it to relax, slept in two-hour stretches. More than ever he was convinced that fatigue was the prime enemy he and Ben would have to overcome. They could understand the weather, master the balloon, and still fail if exhaustion destroyed their judgment and wore away their physical skills.

Ben agreed. In one of their passing conversations, they also agreed that their routine aloft would leave one man on watch for two hours while the other rested. The man off watch could be awakened in an emergency. But it was his duty to sleep as much as it was his duty to fly the balloon when he was on watch.

"Otherwise, we may kill each other," said Max.

Ben smiled at the grim joke. They never discussed it again.

Ed Yost, meanwhile, was making good progress with the construction of the balloon. Ben had been in constant touch with him by telephone. The training flight was scheduled for mid-May. Max and Ben looked forward to the flight. Yost had told them a little about it, and Max had got more fleeting images from Charlie Moore, the thunderstorm expert. Moore had said that a helium balloon was a puff of air, moving in the air. The silence was total; the conception Max had of the craft was that it granted a feeling of unbroken peace and serenity.

Still, he and Ben attempted to plan for the dangers they knew must exist. They called for books, and found none that told them the things they wanted to know. There is no technical literature of manned free ballooning.

"I was a little troubled all along that we had no data base for this adventure," says Ben. "Bob Rice made us feel better. But his field was weather, and that was just one of the things we had to learn. When we bought the balloon, we had no idea of the complexity of what we were getting into. It was the old story. If you don't know, everything seems straight ahead until you get into it and find out there's a lot more to it. And that's exactly what we found."

Ben and Max needed an expert on gas ballooning — someone to demystify the subject, teach it in plain language. At this point they did not know that such a person existed. Very soon, in one of the offhand encounters that marked their whole experience, they were to find the man they needed.

His name was Richard Schwoebel. He was a physicist at Sandia Laboratories, and twenty years earlier, before he earned his Ph.D. at Cornell, he had been involved as an engineer in developing and testing high-altitude manned balloons for the federal government.

In late February, Schwoebel and his wife, Jennie, happened to be looking at a building lot in one of the subdivisions owned by Ben Abruzzo's real estate firm. Robert Murphy, a vice-president of Alvarado Realty and Ben's right-hand man, had been showing the Schwoebels the homesite, which lay in the shadow of Sandia Peak amid the magnificent desert scenery Ben Abruzzo has been at such pains to preserve.

In chatting with Rich and Jennie, Bob Murphy said in passing that Ben and Max were thinking about flying the Atlantic in a balloon.

Rich Schwoebel's interest was aroused. He asked a number of questions, and after some prompting, mentioned that he had been engaged in balloon research.

"Would you like to talk to Ben?" Murphy asked.

Schwoebel said he would. Murphy returned to the office and told Ben Abruzzo of his discovery. Ben quickly learned that Max had known Schwoebel for some years. Schwoebel sang baritone in the choir at St. Timothy's Lutheran Church, where Max and Patty attended services. Schwoebel had done some consulting work for Ranchers, but neither Max nor Ben had known that he knew anything about balloons.

By coincidence, Schwoebel had been reading Ed Yost's *Geographic* article himself, and he realized that Yost had made certain assumptions about the effect of the heat of the sun on his balloon that were better applied to envelopes made of plastic film than to those fabricated from nylon and neoprene.

The next Sunday, during the coffee hour after services at St. Timothy's, Rich Schwoebel mentioned to Max that Yost may have miscalculated. Max questioned him eagerly, and before the conversation was over, he realized that Schwoebel knew more about balloons, and how men should fly them, than anyone he had ever talked to.

On the spot, Max asked Schwoebel to accept the post of technical director for the flight of *Double Eagle*. Schwoebel did so.

Rich Schwoebel is a quiet man, trained to speak in the unemotional vocabulary of science, but on his first meeting with Ben and Max he said something to them that remained ever afterward vivid in their minds.

"The question is," he said, "how many sunsets can your balloon survive?"

In sunshine, as we have seen, the helium in the envelope heats and expands, causing the balloon to rise. As it rises, helium is spilled from the balloon when the gas swells beyond the capacity of the envelope to contain it.

At sunset, the helium cools and contracts and loses some of its power to lift the balloon. The balloon falls, and if something is not done to arrest its descent, it drops all the way to earth.

Ballast is thrown overboard to stop the descent. At each sunset, a percentage of the remaining gross load of the balloon (fifteen percent in the case of *Double Eagle*) must be jettisoned to bring the balloon to equilibrium.

Throwing ballast overboard is like throwing away time: the more you jettison, the less time you can remain aloft. The loss of helium, as it vents under the influence of superheating by the sun in daylight hours, enters into this equation. Loss of gas is loss of time aloft, also.

Schwoebel discussed this with Max and Ben over lunch at the Airport Marina Hotel in Albuquerque. He had never met Ben. He was immediately impressed by his verve and by the quickness of his mind. Schwoebel had known Max Anderson as a genial businessman whom he had met at coffee hours after church services. This Max

Anderson, half scholar and half reckless adventurer, was new to him.

The blithe self-confidence of both men worried Schwoebel a bit. He knew how chancy manned balloon flights into the unknown could be. He had resigned from the Navy's Stratolab project partly to escape from the tensions of a program in which human lives were put in hazard. Yet the idea of a flight across the Atlantic intrigued him. At least partly because of the many times Schwoebel had seen Max and Patty and their children all together in church, he decided that he would volunteer his services out of friendship. Neither he nor Jim Mitchell accepted any pay.

Schwoebel did not expect that the flight of *Double Eagle* would make any significant contribution to human knowledge. He did think, watching Ben and Max in their enthusiasm on that first day, that they were the sort of adventurers who, if they succeeded, might uplift the human spirit. The fact that Yost was building *Double Eagle* reassured Schwoebel. After he had asked some questions about the size of the balloon and its gross load, however, a doubt formed in his mind. It was designed for a flight lasting five days. It was Yost's opinion, as expressed to Max and Ben, that a balloon would make it across the Atlantic in five days, or not make it at all.

Schwoebel did not hold the same view. A high-pressure ridge of the kind Ben and Max expected to ride can be expected to move at thirty to forty miles an hour. If it does move at that speed, and no variables distort the flight plan, then *Double Eagle* could "surf" the three thousand miles to Europe in four to five days.

Schwoebel worried about the variables. The weather forecast might break down. In fact, it would almost certainly do so, because, as Bob Rice had pointed out, it is impossible to make a wholly accurate forecast over a period of even four to five days. The winds might be slower than those forecast. The balloon might not achieve ideal altitudes because of other unforeseen weather conditions or miscalculation of ballast, or for other reasons.

It was essential to design a safety margin into the balloon system, a margin that would permit *Double Eagle* to remain aloft for six or seven days if necessary. It was better to land in Europe with excess helium and unused ballast than to survive one sunset too few and plunge into the sea.

Schwoebel's calculations showed that the balloon Max and Ben had ordered from Ed Yost was too small. He recommended that they ask Yost to increase the size to at least 100,000 cubic feet; 120,000 cubic feet would be even better.

Yost, when Ben got in touch with him, grunted. He respected Schwoebel's expertise, but he did not agree with his conclusions. The balloon would be big enough. Besides, there were practical considerations: construction had begun, Ben and Max had already invested $20,000 in the cost of material and labor. All that would be thrown away.

Ben and Max looked at Schwoebel's calculations and listened to his arguments, and could find no flaw in either. "If you're going to throw away something," as Ben said later, "it's better to throw away money than your life." They continued to press Yost to abandon the original design and change to a larger one. Yost resisted.

In mid-May, Ben and Max were scheduled to meet Yost at Amarillo, Texas, for their training flight in a helium balloon. When Doc Wiley flew them down to this rendezvous, they took Rich Schwoebel along. He and Yost, they figured, could talk as expert to expert.

"I didn't want Ed Yost to think there was any Nervous Nellie factor in our decision," says Max. "I just believed Rich; so did Ben. We understood the principles he was expressing. Rich is so damn brilliant you'd be a fool not to believe him."

Rich Schwoebel had known Yost by sight, and by his already considerable reputation, when both were working in the manned-balloon program at General Mills in St. Paul, Minnesota, in the late fifties. He remembered, with the grin that Yost's swashbuckling style brings to the lips of his acquaintances, their first "meeting." Schwoebel, a young engineer, was helping to hold down a fully inflated balloon on an airport runway. A small plane taxied to the end of the runway, which was, of course, closed. The plane revved its engines and began a takeoff run directly at the balloon. The plane's undercarriage cleared the balloon by only a few feet, and then the aircraft vanished into the clouds in a steep climb.

"Who," asked Schwoebel in amazement, "was *that?*"

A companion replied, "That was Ed Yost."

At Amarillo, Ed Yost listened to Schwoebel's arguments with what seemed to Max and Ben to be half an ear. Schwoebel, in his late forties, retains the innocent looks of a choirboy, but he is as tenacious as a priest discussing theology when he is defending numbers he believes in. "Rich was very determined, Ed was very terse," says

Max. "I was surprised that even Ed could resist the logic of Rich's arguments."

But Ed Yost insisted that the sunset loss was on the order of ten percent a day, not the fifteen percent Schwoebel had calculated. Schwoebel believed that *Silver Fox* would have failed to reach Europe if it had encountered any trouble at all. Yost had asked Bob Rice for a weatherless flight — no storms — and he had had such a flight. One of the results of flying in sunshine, at altitudes below the faster windflow of the upper skies, was that he had had to drop to low levels in search of winds to carry him away from the Azores High. Yost had never found those winds, and he had used precious time in his fruitless search.

Ben thought, watching the two men talk, that he saw the light of respect kindling in Ed Yost. "That was the day Ed began to be willing to listen to Rich — no question about it," says Ben.

Nevertheless, Yost could not be convinced, on that day, that a bigger balloon was necessary. As always, he had an advantage: he had been there, and had flown farther into the Atlantic than any man before him. Ed Yost's experiences and the conclusions he drew from them weighed heavily with Ben and Max. It was impossible not to respect and admire Yost, unthinkable not to rely on his judgment. Still, they thought that Schwoebel was right.

"Ed was an experienced gas balloonist, and he'd had trouble," Max says. "How much more trouble could a couple of inexperienced pilots expect? I wanted that cushion of a bigger balloon, that margin for error." They left Amarillo without getting it.

Nor did they take their training flight — the ground winds were too heavy to make a takeoff practical, or to permit the several practice landings they hoped to make. It was a bitter disappointment; the night was moonlit, and Ben and Max were eager to fly. Ed Yost, describing flight in a gas balloon, came alive with pleasure. His eyes glowed as he described the delicacy of the helium balloon, the way in which altitude could be altered by casting out a single handful of sand, the serene silence of the flight. Max was amazed to see emotions rise to the surface of this taciturn man. It only increased his eagerness to find out what made this sport so thrilling.

Next morning, Ben and Max made a final effort to persuade Yost to compromise. If he would not accept Rich Schwoebel's arguments, would he accept more money to redesign *Double Eagle* and give it a greater capacity? Yost replied that this was impossible — the spherical top of the balloon had already been cut. It had to be sewn and sealed in its present shape. There was no way to make it larger except by starting over again and building a new balloon. That, Yost repeated, was unnecessary; he wouldn't do it. It would mean waste and delay — possibly such a delay that Ben and Max would miss the launch window in early autumn and be forced to scrub their flight.

Ben and Max saw that it was useless to pursue the argument further. Yost would not yield; they would fly in the smaller balloon or not fly at all.

Max and Ben began about this time to meet regularly with Schwoebel and Doc Wiley and Jim Mitchell, who would handle press relations and act as moderator and recording secretary of the group. The moment had come, both men felt, to approach the flight more systematically, to eliminate surprises.

Rich Schwoebel brought another man into the group. His name was Sydney Parks, and he was an expert in electronics who worked, like Schwoebel and Mitchell, at Sandia Labs. Syd Parks was to communications what Rice was to weather and Schwoebel was to balloon design and performance. He had built his first crystal radio set as a schoolboy in his native London, and had been among the first radar technicians in the Royal Navy in World War II. After emigrating to the United States in 1957 and taking American citizenship, he had worked on some of the most sophisticated electronics gear ever devised by the defense establishment. Syd Parks knew all about missiles and rockets and how to communicate with them; talking to balloons was new to him.

Sydney helped the group to refine its approach to the problem of communications. Given the limits on weight, time, and money, he believed that Doc Wiley had recommended a good radio package. After talking to Syd and Rich, the pilots decided to take two additional pieces of communications gear. Syd would build, in his home workshop, a homing beacon. This device, which emits an internationally recognized signal on assigned frequencies, would automatically broadcast the call letters of *Double Eagle* — 50 DE. Used routinely, it would permit aircraft and ships to home on the balloon, using their automatic direction-finding (ADF) equipment, from distances up to five hundred miles. This would also permit overflying aircraft to make navigational fixes on the balloon and transmit its position to the pilots and also back to the control center ashore.

It was decided also to add another automatic beacon that would communicate with Nimbus, a NASA earth satellite. This device would give precise navigational fixes by processing the signal from the balloon's beacon through the computers at the Goddard Space Flight Center at Greenbelt, Maryland.

Max, meanwhile, had pointed out to Ben that neither of them knew anything at all about celestial navigation. There are not many people in the deserts of the American Southwest who are expert in the use of the sextant, but Max found one, after considerable searching. His name was Richard Reif, and he was a teacher in the Albuquerque public schools. The schools have a small planetarium, and Reif, projecting a simulation of the September night skies over the North Atlantic on its dome, taught Max and Ben how to recognize Vega and several other fixed stars besides the familiar North Star. With the aid of computer printouts, Reif devised a system for plotting longitude and latitude. It was a good system, and Max was sure that it would work.

He had less luck with the sextant Reif lent him. The instrument had been purchased from World War II, Air Force surplus, and the oil in its bubble — a vital element in the instrument — was discolored by age. To use the sextant, one looked through the bubble of oil into a small mirror in which the image of a fixed star was reflected. For Ben and Max, each of whom had only one fully usable eye, this was a difficult task. It was made more difficult for Max because he had been born with a hand tremor. Still, the two of them persisted, shooting stars in their back yards at night until they were satisfied they had mastered the technique. Max wondered how much more difficult it would be to use the sextant from the unstable gondola and under oceanic skies that might not be so clear as those over the New Mexico desert, but he was certain that he would find a way.

The more Max and Ben studied the problems of the voyage, the more convinced they became that Rich Schwoebel was correct. They needed the larger balloon. Every bit of information that came to them confirmed this. Max was talking frequently on the telephone to Bob Rice and to George Fischbeck. From the two meteorologists he derived a growing understanding of wind velocities and directions. "Bob and George sort of drew a map of the Atlantic sky in my mind,"

Max says. "I'd been flying around in aircraft since I was fourteen without knowing exactly what was up there. Now I knew — the atmosphere may be invisible to the human eye, but it's as real as rocks. Flying into some of those invisible features is just like flying into a mountain. We had to have time to go around obstacles. The only way you could do that was to have a bigger balloon, more helium, more ballast — more time."

Ben called Yost, who told him again that the construction of *Double Eagle* was beyond the point of no return. "Maxie and Rich Schwoebel and I agreed that we ought to have that extra day of insurance. Ed Yost felt that the extra day wasn't necessary. His opinion never changed: if you don't make it in five days you're not going to make it anyway."

Ben called Max and said, "Ed Yost says it's impossible to change." Neither man liked the feeling of impotence this gave them, and perhaps for the first time they felt an intelligent doubt, like a current running between them, that they could make the flight. Skill and nerve could not compensate for what they had come to believe was inadequate equipment; by now, both Ben and Max believed that Rich Schwoebel was the most brilliant man they had ever met, and he had become their talisman. As no man before him, Schwoebel showed them what their limits were.

"I remember thinking," Max says, "that if Ed Yost, or anyone who tried the Atlantic before us, had had Rich Schwoebel, he would have made it. Well, we *had* Rich, and Ben and I sure knew that we had to listen to him if we wanted to land with dry feet and happy hearts. You don't often find a fellow like Rich, half genius and half Christian."

As Doc Wiley had realized, Ben and Max are not men to take no for an answer. Ben kept talking to Yost on the telephone. He made it plain that dollars were not a problem. Ed knew that; he insisted that time *was* a problem. There was the suggestion, in an undercurrent, that Ben and Max were creating a problem where none existed. It was an impasse. Even if they had wished to go to another balloonmaker, and they did not, they could not have done so. There was only one Ed Yost.

Three weeks after the initial meeting at Amarillo between Schwoebel and Yost, Ben and Max went back to Texas to make their training flight. This time, weather conditions were good. Ed Yost had provided a 16,000-cubic-foot balloon made of clear plastic material. To Ben, as this balloon was inflated with helium, it looked like a gigantic Baggie with a rainbow inside it as the last light of the prairie sun shone through it. In addition to learning to fly, Ben and Max were, in this single flight, to pass the federal requirements for a gas-balloon pilot's license. Yost was inspector as well as instructor.

They took off after sunset, and flew through the night over the undulating treeless plains. Yost was a consummate pilot; they watched him and learned by observing. Ben was astonished at the way in which the balloon responded to the slightest controlling touch. It was true in practice, as he had learned in theory, that even a handful of sand poured overboard would cause the balloon to rise by several feet. The most subtle valving would produce descents. Ben had never imagined that any balloon could be so responsive.

They rose to 10,000 feet. It was a moonlit night and darkened ranches lay below them. For the first time, Ben and Max became aware of something that would thrill them in all their flights. They could hear every sound on the ground, thousands of feet below them. Dogs barked, somehow sensing the passage of the balloon though it was too high to be seen even by human eyes. Cattle lowed. Max heard a screen door being opened and the twang of the spring before it slammed shut, and then the footsteps of a man on wooden porch steps and his truck starting; even heard the change in pitch in the hum of the pickup's tires as they passed from dirt road to blacktop. Something about the balloon seemed to capture and amplify sound; it was a fascinating experience. Max had no sensation of movement, lateral or vertical, and both he and Ben watched the altimeter and the barometer carefully as they maneuvered the balloon, searching for some sensation in their own bodies that would confirm the readings on the instruments. There was no such sensation. Here, above the Texas panhandle, it occurred to Max that they were experiencing the closest thing to weightlessness it was possible to achieve without going to the moon. He understood in a flash of intuition why gas balloonists had always been intoxicated by the sort of flight he and Ben were making now.

They practiced a number of landings in barren fields. Yost showed them how to use the trail rope as a rudder to bring the gondola in for landings that were astonishing in their smoothness. The trail rope was invented in the 1870s by the English aeronaut Charles

Green, and it is the most important control, apart from gas and ballast, in a balloon of this type. Usually about 150 feet long, it is tied to the gondola at one end. When the balloon is close to the ground, the rope is spilled over the side. As it drags over earth or water, it acts as a rudder, and the balloon will fly a steady course ahead of the rope. In large balloons, several ropes are used: *Double Eagle* would have five.

The trail rope can be used to adjust the altitude of a gas balloon in a very sensitive way. Because the rope has weight, it acts as recoverable ballast. If a foot or two of rope drags on the ground, the balloon is relieved of that much weight, and will rise. If the rope is hauled in, the balloon becomes heavier by the addition of the rope's weight, and will sink. No expenditure of ballast, no valving of gas, is necessary.

Ed Yost showed Ben and Max how to fly the balloon at twelve inches above the ground. The trail rope guided it over the terrain like radar. For Ben, it was a kind of piloting he had never imagined. He felt at home from the first instant in this strange device, and it claimed his concentration. He heard the sounds coming up from the ground, noted the absence of physical sensation, remarked on the way in which the gondola constantly revolved. But it was the balloon system itself that fascinated him. Ben, after months of hearing theory, had an actual apparatus under his control. He understood how to fly it so quickly that Ed Yost, after only a short period, turned over control to him.

When Ben tired, after putting the balloon through all the maneuvers of which it was capable, he sat down in the gondola next to Yost, and watched Max fly. Max, too, found the technique easy. He took the balloon up and down, and finally descended to a very low altitude to try controlling the flight with the trail rope. The balloon, glistening like a great teardrop against the face of the moon, rode above him. He was flying east, toward the flush of dawn.

"The birds woke up," says Max. "All at once. From dead quiet we went to a place where it sounded like all the songbirds of North America began to holler. I'd never heard anything like it. I just listened and forgot everything else. I thought, maybe I'd better wake up Ben and have him listen to this. It was beautiful."

At this point, Ben woke up. "We're just skimming over the ground," he recalls. "We're like ten or fifteen feet above the ground,

50

doing about thirty knots. I look over the side — it's light enough to see the terrain, but the stars are still out. Boulders — great big boulders! Max was looking at the stars."

Ben, as much amused as alarmed, waited for Max to notice what was happening. Max was still looking at the stars, with his head cocked like a man listening to a faraway song.

Ben said, "Max, how close are you going to get?"

Max came to with a start: "What? What?"

"Well, take a look down. Look."

Max looked downward. "Golamighty, Ben," he said. "Maybe we ought to throw out a handful of sand."

Ben did so, and the balloon rose. "Old Max was listening to the birds," says Ben. "Meadowlarks, they sounded like. Max was looking at the stars, and studying them, and listening to the birds, and we're almost pranging those boulders swooshing by . . ."

The flight lasted about twelve hours, but covered only about fifty miles from point to point because the balloon had flown in a great half-circle. Max and Ben had hoped that they would learn more from Ed Yost about his own flight, and about gas ballooning in general, than they had learned before. After all, there were just the three of them, alone in a gondola. Two sat on a webbing strap slung from one side of the gondola to the other while the third controlled the balloon.

"We thought Ed would be a vast storehouse of information and good advice," says Ben, "but in fact we learned very little from him about his own flight because he is just a man of very few words. He didn't refuse to answer our questions. He just gave short answers. Like I'd say, 'Ed, tell us about the ballasting sequence.' That can be quite a detailed answer. Ed, not because he's trying to keep anything from you but because that's the way he is, he'd just say, 'Well, I compute my ballast about midday and when evening comes, I just ballast it off. That's it.' I'd say, 'Well, Ed, isn't there a little more to it than that?' And Ed says, 'Nope, I just ballast it off, and do a little maintenance ballasting during the night.' "

Ben discovered that he had to be careful how he asked even simple questions. "You might not get an answer if he doesn't think your question is worthy. But if you listen to Ed carefully, what he does say has a great deal of value and it's up to you to figure out all the pieces that go in between, in his pauses and silences. Ed's a master at his business of design and manufacture. No question about that. But he isn't the best communicator in the world and I don't think he intends to change that."

As dawn broke, the balloon came over a series of swelling hills and began to pass over ranches. Ranchers were already up and working, and Max and Ben talked to them from the gondola. Ben thought it must have been an eerie and beautiful sight for the people on the ground — "to see this ghostly shape come over the hill, just the top first, and then the whole balloon, and then the gondola, and then us." They landed twice and took some of the ranchers for rides. At last they came upon a farmer's field, with a father and his two grown sons working with their backs to the approaching balloon. Ben shouted, but the men below didn't hear. He shouted again, and this time got the attention of those below. The older man leaped in surprise, but his sons, following Ben's shouted instructions, seized the trailing drag rope and pulled the balloon to earth.

"Want a ride?" Ben asked the older man.

"No *sir!*"

But both boys — one in his teens and the other not much older — went up, and when the balloon was landed, the pilots deflated it. Yost gave the polyethylene envelope to the farmer. "You can cover your haystack with it," said Yost. "It'll last you forever."

Ed Yost's chase crew found them at the ranch. They loaded the wicker gondola into the back of a truck and raced back into Amarillo for a celebratory breakfast. With pickups rattling and war whoops sounding in the sabbath hush, they arrived just as the city's many churches were concluding services. One of Ed Yost's men, seated in the open back door of a van, dragged his foot on the pavement and smoke curled from the sole of his boot.

Doc Wiley was sent into the best restaurant in town. He asked for a private room, and the maitre d', after accepting Doc's invitation to peep through the window at what Wiley had outside, quickly arranged for one.

Ed Yost, whose noble thirst had impressed Ben and Max on earlier meetings, ordered five Bloody Marys. They thought Ed was treating his crew to an eye-opener, but Yost drank all five Bloody Marys himself. He had three more with breakfast, before the champagne.

Max and Ben decided that they would once more approach the subject of changing the size of their balloon. Yost seemed mellower now than he had been the last time they broached the subject.

"I wonder, Ed, if you've thought any more about Rich Schwoebel's calculations," Max asked. He does not remember that Yost made any answer to his question.

Ben said, "We've got to the point, Ed, where we think we've really got to have a bigger balloon. What we'd like for you to do is build us a new balloon, of at least a hundred thousand cubic feet."

Max and Ben were prepared to repeat Rich Schwoebel's arguments. "I was going to make our case if it took all day," says Max.

It took no time at all.

Ed Yost said, "Okay, if that's what you want. Fine. I'll do it."

Could he have it ready for a September launch?

No problem. The delivery date would be the same.

How much more would it cost?

"Ed just started computations for the new balloon — its size, the material needed — on the spot," says Max, "and of course he came out with the same figures as Rich."

The price would be about $5,000 more — for the cost of materials. Ben and Max were amazed. They had expected to pay for a whole new balloon.

"Just like that," says Ben. "Three weeks earlier, it was impossible. That morning it was no problem. We said, 'Deal,' and went home happy. So did Ed, as we found out later."

On the way back to Albuquerque in Max's plane, Max and Ben talked over this sudden turnabout.

"You know, Ben," said Max. "There's something strange about that."

Ben laughed. "It's just Ed's way," he said.

Back home, word was beginning to spread that Max and Ben were going to try to fly the Atlantic. Few doubted they would try it; fewer still believed they would make it.

Patty Anderson, by this time, was convinced they would make it across. She had been helping Max with the sextant, listening to the planning sessions with Ben and Schwoebel and Doc Wiley around the swimming pool. She saw that Max was approaching the voyage as he approached everything: with foresight, planning, intelligence. The new men in the picture, especially Rich Schwoebel, added to her confidence. She liked the idea of the new, larger balloon. "The more I understand something, the less I fear it," Patty says. She had always understood why Max was going to attempt the Atlantic; now she was beginning to see clearly how he was going to do it. She had never seen him happier with a project.

There was, however, a small cloud on Max's optimism. What was going to happen to the old balloon now that Ed Yost had so unaccountably agreed to make them the new one they wanted? Ben told him not to worry about it. But Max had thoughts in the night.

"Everyone who attempts to fly the Atlantic," Max said later, "has an unseen ghost chasing him. Lindbergh had the ghost right behind him, and so did Ben and I. It's the fear that someone else will steal the impossible dream and beat you across. I feared the hell out of that."

When Max Anderson wanted to protect his uranium deposits in Grants, New Mexico, from claim jumpers in the 1950s, he hired a fellow named Gus.

Gus had clear gray eyes and he wore a big black Stetson that is called a Mormon hat in his part of the world, and he had a sheared-off trigger on his .38. Gus had killed three men before he came to work for Max, and after he left Max's employ he killed another one who made the mistake of walking toward him a little too fast while holding a knife in his hand.

Gus did not have to kill anyone for Max's mining company. People just stayed away because they knew he was there. A couple of fellows who had not heard about Gus's presence wandered in, and Gus took away their guns and chained them up to a tree for the night.

Gus had died in bed by the time Max was ready to fly the Atlantic in *Double Eagle*, and in any case Max realized that there is no way to protect an adventure with an armed guard. Still, as spring progressed, he worried about the unseen ghost that might be pursuing him.

Ben understood Max's concern but was less bothered by it. He had come to believe, after only one night in a helium balloon over Texas, that he could pilot one of these devices as well as anyone. From the moment he took control of the flight, Ben felt that he was *the* pilot. He and Max were equals, of course, but Ben, in his own mind, was the first among equals where piloting skill and instinct were concerned. This was not, necessarily, a belief that Max shared.

"Does somebody else want to go?" said Ben. "Fine. We'll have a race. Tell 'em, just like that — okay, put it on the line. Winner takes all."

Max did not know for certain that they had any competition; he just knew that competition was a fact of life. As an eighteen-year-old, he had left Patty at home in the first summer of their marriage and gone prospecting in the Canadian Arctic. He and a college friend found an outcropping of uranium and filed a claim. The thrill of that first discovery hooked Max forever on the romance of mining. But he never exploited that particular find, and a decade later he learned that he and his friend Bo Dunsworth from the Sigma Nu house had been within a hundred miles of the richest uranium field in the world and had blundered by it. Somebody else found it because Max and Bo had looked in the wrong place. Max tried never to let that happen to him again, and he remembered that you did not have to see, or even know about, a rival to have him beat you to the mother lode.

Max had no need of more uranium, but he did need to be first across the Atlantic. He and Ben set up a formal timetable. By the first of September, the balloon and all the equipment would be at the launch site. They would insert *Double Eagle* into the first suitable high-pressure ridge that rolled out of the Arctic and over the coast of New England after that.

Bob Rice would have preferred takeoff from a point above the 50th parallel, which passes through Newfoundland, because it is the shortest and most direct route over the British Isles and into the European continent. But Ben and Max were Americans, flying the American flag on an American balloon, and both were determined to take off from American soil.

Max assigned one of his engineers at Ranchers, Dave Hogan, to set up a flow chart. This would show the state of readiness of all elements, broken down by individual responsibility — how Doc and Syd were coming with the radios, how Jo Mitchell was progressing with food supplies, how Rich Schwoebel was acting on his own ideas and the dozens of others, some practical and some zany, that Max and Ben were flinging in his direction. The whole group met every two weeks, usually in bathing suits beside the swimming pool at Ben's house or Max's.

Doc Wiley kept worrying about clothes. He urged Max and Ben

to take along waterproofs. Procuring such gear was no problem: Max's miners, working underground in water up to their armpits sometimes, were equipped with rubber boots and overalls and coats and hats. Why not take a couple of those outfits along? Max and Ben did not think such heavy gear would be necessary; it would impede their movements. Ed Yost was building a rain skirt that would cover the gondola like a tent. Besides, it was believed that rain falling on the balloon would not reach the gondola: it would, instead, pour off the spherical portion of the balloon, which had a broader diameter than the gondola. The balloon itself would act as a gigantic umbrella, leaving Max and Ben dry inside a curtain of water.

"I'll bet," said Max at one point, "that'll give us some super rainbows — Ben and me, looking through the falling water at the sun."

They weren't convinced that they would see any rain. Ed Yost had not, and none of the other transatlantic balloonists who had written about their journeys had mentioned getting wet. Only Charlie Moore, flying into thunderstorms over Socorro, New Mexico, had got wet, and he had done it on purpose. Max and Ben intended to avoid thunderstorms. Max went on studying this problem all through the summer; he wanted to understand it.

In June, Max flew to Boston for more talks with Bob Rice and others at Weather Services. It was decided that Weather Services would serve as flight control center for *Double Eagle*. Doc Wiley and Rich Schwoebel and Jim Mitchell and Syd Parks and the wives and the rest of the crew would wait there while Max and Ben flew. When success seemed certain, Pat Abruzzo and Patty Anderson would fly to London by commercial jet and proceed from there to the place where their husbands had landed.

Schwoebel and Rice would tell Ben and Max, from the ground, how best to fly. Rice would furnish precise meteorological data — the speed of winds aloft at every altitude, the behavior of the high-pressure ridge that was their onrushing surfer's wave, the proximity of storms.

They would need to have contact twice a day — before sunset, when the balloon cooled and began its daily descent, and in the morning, when it was superheated by the sun and began its ascent. Those were the periods of crucial decision. A single miscalculation permitting the balloon to fall too far or rise too high would require heroic corrections that could leave them short of ballast or short of helium — and, very likely, short of their landfall.

Schwoebel's job was to make sure *Double Eagle* used its ballast and helium to maximum efficiency. He had already drawn up charts and graphs — a flight profile showing the ideal altitudes for the day and night portions of a projected seven-day flight. A chart showed exactly how much ballast should be expended at each sunset to achieve the ideal altitudes. If the balloon went too high, the extra helium would be vented, shortening the planned duration of the flight; if it went too low, too much ballast would be expended to bring it back to altitude. Adjustments would have to be made, naturally, but Schwoebel reminded the pilots over and over: "Ballast is time. Helium is time. Each time you expend either, you throw away time."

Ben's attention was fully engaged by this concept. With Schwoebel, he worked out the arithmetic of sunset survival. The subtleties continued to grip his imagination: one degree Centigrade of heat on the envelope of the fully loaded balloon was equal to about twenty pounds of weight. If the sun heated the helium by one degree, that was equivalent to throwing over twenty pounds of ballast. The figure varied as the weight of balloon, gondola, and ballast changed from day to day. The balloon, in theory, could keep going up forever in such circumstances unless it vented gas and came back to equilibrium — that is, found an altitude and stayed there. The same was true in reverse: one degree of cooling at maximum weight was like the addition of twenty pounds of weight; the balloon would go down until ballasting a like amount arrested its fall. Ben set about a program of weighing everything that would go into the gondola and labeling it. Pat Abruzzo and Patty Anderson and some of their children helped in this. Ben even weighed the gondola. He told Doc to include a saw and an ax among the expedition's equipment.

"What for?" asked Doc.

"If I run out of everything else, we'll chop up the gondola — there's eight hundred pounds of ballast right there — and ride into France on the load ring in our skivvies," said Ben, cheerfully.

Rich Schwoebel raised his voice, a once-a-year phenomenon. "You do that, Ben," he said, "and you won't come back — either of you."

Ben grinned. He began to think about harnesses, like parachute harnesses, that could be attached to the load ring. He and Max could maybe land with something like that. He asked Doc to look into that.

Doc had devised a survival kit — a parachute for each man, with a one-man life raft attached; it was equipped with a light and other signaling devices. He had rigged a small helium balloon to which the distress beacon could be attached in case of a crash at sea or on the ice pack, or even on some remote spit of land. Quietly, Doc Wiley was investigating the procedures for the rescue of downed balloonists by military air-sea rescue units in the Atlantic. Max took no great interest in these activities. Neither did Ben; in his conscious mind, he was at peace with a sea landing. But he still dreamed of such a landing, and when he did, he always saw Max and himself going down at night, in pitch darkness, into heavy seas. The dream would wake him up, and that gave him quiet time to think. Ben wasn't training himself to sleep; he'd always got by on very little sleep, and he thought he could do so in *Double Eagle*. What he did, in the night, was to construct imaginary situations, both routine and emergency, and put himself through a drill to control them. If the rate of descent is 300 feet per minute, how much ballast is needed? And if the rate is seven hundred fifty feet? He would choose items to be jettisoned, and in his imagination throw them overboard and watch the altimeter as the balloon corrected itself.

Max knew nothing of this, but, speaking into a tape recorder at about this time, he said: "I am most fortunate to have a partner like Ben. He not only has personal courage, he has a tough mind and he doesn't quit. I guess that's worth its weight in gold because the willingness to see a thing through to the end under any circumstances is the margin between success and failure."

In Boston, Max revisited the Durgin Park, revealing a taste in restaurants that Bob Rice never fully understood. Why should such a rich man like such a plain place? With Doc Wiley and a local pilot named Ted Rider, Max and Bob Rice overflew the Massachusetts coast in search of a suitable launch site. Max and Ben had agreed that Massachusetts was a good place to launch from — Max had friends at the Perini Construction Company, a huge firm with headquarters in Framingham, who had agreed to let *Double Eagle* be hangared and outfitted in their work yards after it was brought east from Sioux Falls. Bob Rice was in Massachusetts, with all his instruments and charts. And, finally, Boston was a media center. Max realized that the press would be interested in the flight and he wanted to be as good a host to the reporters as possible. At this point, neither Ben nor Max imagined that there would be anything more than superficial interest in what they were doing. The inflation of a balloon, they knew, always drew a crowd. But Lindbergh had taken off in loneliness, and they expected to do more or less the same.

Rice had abandoned his arguments for a more northerly launch. The bigger balloon gave them extra time: he was sure they could ride a north wind up the coast, across Maine and the Maritimes, and catch an eastbound high-pressure ridge on the 50th parallel or thereabouts. It meant wasting a whole day to reach the jump-off point, but he understood the symbolic importance of launching from American soil.

After a day of exploration, Max narrowed the choice of launch sites to two — one a baseball field north of Boston on Cape Ann, on the outskirts of Rockport, and the other some thirty miles due south of Boston, at Marshfield. Of the two sites, Marshfield seemed the more practical — *Double Eagle* could be inflated in a large gravel pit, fifty feet deep and surrounded by large trees, that would shield it on all sides from shore winds which might damage it. Right next to the gravel pit was a large school, and Max was pleased by the idea that the children would be able to watch the launch. Then, too, Marshfield was only ten miles from Plymouth Rock. Max liked that — launching *Double Eagle* from the place where the Pilgrims established their first settlement in America.

Ben wasn't altogether happy with Marshfield as a launch site, and some of the others had reservations as well. It was too far south. Ben did not like the idea of beginning the flight with a long run northward over woods and mountains. They would begin the flight in darkness, as they would wish to save a sunset by launching after the sun went down, and that would mean floating across Boston Harbor through swarms of aircraft taking off and landing at Logan International Airport. Max talked about the view, and chuckled. He believed that the Logan tower would steer air traffic around them. The discussion went on all summer, and not until late August was the question resolved. They would launch from Marshfield. The choice was Max's responsibility, and in this, as in all things, he and Ben had to trust each other's judgment, or fail.

On July 1, Ben and Max went to Colorado to fly hot-air balloons in the first Pikes Peak balloon race, and Max's unseen pursuing ghost at last became visible. His name was Dewey Reinhard, and he was a respected balloonist. His name had cropped up several times as that of a man who might be thinking of an Atlantic crossing, and the rumors had become more persistent since Ed Yost had surprised Max and Ben with his sudden change of heart about building them a bigger balloon.

Ben won the Pikes Peak Balloon Race by flying directly over the highest point of the jagged mountain. Fifty feet below, the starter waved a black checkered flag. Ben called down to him: "If any SOB says he beat me, you tell him he's a damn liar!" Ben believes that he was only the second balloonist ever to fly over Pikes Peak, and he pronounced himself, on landing, "the granddaddy of mountain flying." Over drinks Max passed the jocular word that he had, in fact, pulled Ben across the finish line (they were flying in separate balloons) by attaching a thin nylon line to the gondola of Ben's balloon. Ben did not think much of the joke. "I'm going to have to listen to the winner all the way across the Atlantic," said Max, "and I want him to start off with *some* humility." It was the usual Anderson–Abruzzo formula: win at any cost, and then make a joke of it.

After the race, Dewey Reinhard invited all the balloonists who had taken part in it to his workshop, a garage in Colorado Springs. There he unveiled a gondola, obviously designed for a water crossing. It was a catamaran basically identical in design to the one Ed Yost was building for Ben and Max. To Max, it looked somewhat more seaworthy than *Double Eagle*'s gondola. Reinhard's gondola was much heavier. It was fitted with a number of mysterious devices — winches and lines with scoops and what seemed to be an anchor affixed to them.

Ben took Max aside. "What do you think of that Rube Goldberg outfit?" he asked.

"It's for flying the Atlantic," Max replied. "Dewey's going to try to do it the way *Small World* did — fly low, pull up water for ballast, anchor and sit on the surface and let storms go by." (*Small World*, a 53,000-cubic-foot hydrogen balloon, lifted off from the

Canary Islands in 1958. Its crew of three, planning to ride the trade winds east to west across the South Atlantic, landed it at sea after a flight of twelve hundred miles, and then sailed the gondola an additional fifteen hundred miles to landfall in the Caribbean.)

"It'll be a long trip, if he makes it," said Ben.

"*Small World* didn't make it, and those folks were flying in the South Atlantic in the calmest season of the year. Dewey's going to have to face waves up to twenty feet high in the North Atlantic in the fall."

Ben and Max, wedded to Rice's philosophy (and Schwoebel's logic) that the way to survive the North Atlantic weather was to fly high above it and breathe oxygen, believed that Dewey Reinhard was making a basic error in logistics.

He and Ben did not think that they could honorably ask Reinhard any questions about his plans without revealing that they, too, planned to fly the ocean. They did tell him about *Double Eagle*, and they believed that this was the first moment when Reinhard knew that *he* had unseen ghosts in pursuit of *him*. Ben had just won the toughest hot-air balloon race of the season, not a fair omen, and of course Reinhard knew the reputation of Anderson and Abruzzo as a ballooning team. He knew, too, what their financial resources were. These were not so great as Reinhard may have imagined, or as the world later came to believe, but they were certainly greater than Reinhard's. His wife had mortgaged some property to help him finance his flight.

Reinhard said he had been considering this flight for a couple of years. Ben and Max did not press him for details; his methods were his secret. They did learn that he was going to use an 83,000-cubic-foot balloon, and, smiling, they were pretty sure they knew where he had got it. Ed Yost had two customers for transatlantic balloons, and Dewey Reinhard was going to attempt his crossing in the original *Double Eagle*. He would, when the time came to name it, call it *Eagle*. It had a black cone and a silvered spherical top, just like all of Ed Yost's balloons.

Ben and Max believed so strongly in the correctness of their own approach that they did not see how their rival could possibly succeed, using a method that had already failed — *if* that was Reinhard's system. "Dewey made me wonder in the night," says Max. Ben, too.

62

They stepped up the pace of preparations. A launch in early September was a necessity.

More than ever, Doc Wiley felt the pressure of time. Ben and Max would have sudden brainstorms. Max awoke wondering what would happen to their drinking water if they made a hard landing at sea. Suppose, against all his expectations, they *did* survive? They would need water. Would the plastic containers Jo Mitchell had found for them survive the crash? Tests were needed.

Jim Mitchell and one of his sons climbed to the roof of their house and threw several jugs of water to the concrete drive below. There was no damage. "If we're at a high altitude," said Max, "that water's going to be frozen. What then?" The Mitchells put containers in their home freezer, and when they were frozen, threw them off the roof. Again, there was no damage. Max was glad to have that question resolved.

Jo Mitchell worked out their diet. The balloonists, she thought, were disappointed that she did not recommend esoteric foods. She anticipated a loss of appetite from fatigue and disorientation, and believed that Ben and Max would be more likely to eat their favorite foods than to consume unfamiliar rations. Her shopping list included bread, meat, and cheese for sandwiches, and a variety of palatable, high-protein foods such as peanut butter and eggs, some raw and some hard-boiled. The gondola would be equipped with a small cooking stove to heat soups, tea, and hot chocolate. Anticipating intestinal problems, Jo included cereals and other bulk items. Pat and Patty added favorite foods: salami for Ben, sardines for Max; the makings for peanut butter and jelly sandwiches. The gondola would carry a thirty-day supply of Army C rations as emergency supplies. Rich and Jennie Schwoebel made Ben and Max the gift of seven kinds of wine, one for each of the countries they might land in. Jo Mitchell told the balloonists that nutritional requirements at high altitudes, in conditions of extreme cold, would not be significantly greater than in temperate conditions on the ground. So long as the body was warmly clothed, it required only a normal intake of calories. Both Ben and Max, perhaps remembering boyhood tales of lost explorers, thought that they ought to take along a lot of chocolate, and a friend of Max's from Hershey, Pennsylvania, provided them with a whole case of enormous one-pound candy bars. Jo Mitchell had her doubts about the value of chocolate as a survival ration, but thought it might have some psychological value. Ben and Max set great store by the chocolate.

Max got Ben a pair of custom-made, rose-colored glasses with a painting of the Eiffel Tower on each lens.

At the biweekly meetings by the pool, the brainstorming went on. Most of the talk centered on the balloon, the weather, the ballasting and valving. It was, in effect, ground school, with Rich Schwoebel as instructor. "We played the game of 'What-if?' " says Rich. "There was no structure — after all, we were sitting around in our bathing suits and Pat and Patty would bring us things to eat and drink in that wonderfully hospitable way of theirs. But I thought, after I got used to Ben and Max — a conversation with them when they're enthused is like tacking on a sailboat in a squall instead of plowing a furrow straight toward the horizon in a powerboat — that we really were covering an amazing amount of stuff. They're both superintelligent in their own ways. They don't just want to excel — they take it for granted that they will do so."

Ben would return to the subject of the gondola from time to time. Neither Schwoebel nor Wiley had much faith that Ben could sail it in a storm. Ben realized that Max felt as they did. "I guess Maxie was willing to die just to fly the Atlantic," he says. "I wasn't. I *knew* I could land it in any sea and that it would sail better than a big boat; it wouldn't corkscrew or broach like a larger craft might. In the end, I was right." So he was. At the time, Max, grinning before he plunged into the pool, told him not to worry, he had learned to identify all species of sharks. "If I see one that's gonna eat us, Ben," he said, "I'll pass you the word."

Early in August, the town fathers of Marshfield confirmed that the gravel pit by the school would be available to *Double Eagle* for launch the following month. Max and Ben had been pressed for time — Ben had taken two weeks off for a cruise of the Mediterranean with Pat and their friends Billie Slade, the Daileys, and Bob Bowers, and Ben and Max had had business deals to attend to. They had spent a few days on their sailing boat, *Mariah*, in waters off La Jolla, California.

While aboard *Mariah*, they had had another of the freak accidents that plague their relationship. They had been running up on the anchor, with Max at the helm with the auxiliary engine running, and Ben coiling the rope. A loop of the anchor line got tangled around Ben's foot. Max did not notice what had happened; perhaps Ben was on his blind side. Ben felt his foot being crushed against the gunwale as the boat moved past the anchor, which was jabbed into the sand at the bottom of the cove where they were anchored. The pain was excruciating, but Ben had no time to cry out. He was being snatched overboard. He knew that he would go into the water upside down, and drown in moments. To prevent that, he leaped for a stanchion and wrapped his arms and legs around it. The immense weight of the onrushing boat bent the stanchion as the anchor rope hauled at Ben's captured foot. Max saw what was happening, eased off on the controls, backed up, and freed his friend.

No bones were broken, but Ben discovered on returning to Albuquerque that his foot had been bruised and crushed.

After Ben's accident, Max consulted a physician friend, Dr. Edward Murphy, recently retired from the staff of St. Joseph's Hospital. Dr. Murphy gave Max a crash course in the treatment of catastrophic injuries. Max learned how to use a tourniquet, how to apply an inflatable splint to a broken leg, how to sew cuts — gut thread for internal injuries, nylon for lacerations of the skin or severed veins and arteries. Dr. Murphy's supplies — splints, bandages, pills for pain, pills for diarrhea — were packed into a waterproof kit by Patty Anderson.

Max passed on his newfound medical knowledge to Ben, who already knew about first aid from his days as a teenage lifeguard and from his experience in the ski area. "I really got all this stuff so Ben can sew me up and set my bones," Max told friends, in Ben's presence. "I'm trying to get in touch with a veterinarian who can tell me how to take care of Ben, but there don't seem to be any in Albuquerque who know how to treat gorillas."

That got a laugh from Ben, who said he would sew up his own wounds if the choice was having Max do it. Max had long since given up taking the medicine that controlled his hand tremor; the drug slowed his physical reactions and affected his eye-hand coordination. Ben, who suffers from high blood pressure, planned to take his pills as usual while flying in the balloon. He did not investigate the possible effect, if any, on his condition of high-altitude flying while consuming oxygen. It is known that stress raises blood pressure. Ben believed that he would not be seriously affected by stress during the flight. Exhilaration is what he anticipated.

Ben spent a few days in bed, and then on crutches and a cane. He was still limping a little in mid-August, when he and Max, accompanied by Doc Wiley and Max's college-age son Kristian, went back to Sioux Falls to have their first look at the newer and bigger *Double Eagle*. Ed Yost was right on schedule, and the balloon was near completion. So was Dewey Reinhard's *Eagle*, formerly Max's and Ben's original *Double Eagle*. The gondola was about seventy-five percent complete, and Max and Ben worked with Ed Yost in getting it ready. Yost, who had slept in the gondola of *Silver Fox* and gone through numerous dry runs and drills before taking off, believed that familiarization with this open boat that would be their home for a week or more was essential.

Max and Ben spent five days in Sioux Falls, helping to braid the five trail ropes the gondola would carry, filling sacks with lead shot for use as ballast, and packing this shot along the keel, where it would provide stability in case of ditching. Everything was weighed and labeled — a task that Ben took seriously.

Ben is a furious, fast worker. He concentrates on what he does, and concentrates completely. Max found plenty to interest him in the casual conversation of Ed Yost's balloonmakers. There were no men with their skills and experience anywhere in the world. Max drank in all they had to say. He wanted to know as much as he could about the balloons Ed Yost made, and about Ed Yost. "I figured our lives were linked to Ed and his product," recalls Max. "To make things worse, I was getting a lot of phone calls from the office. There was a certain amount of squabbling, with Ben thinking I wasn't working up to capacity."

This was the first surfacing of serious irritation between the two. Ben did not see anything unnatural in it. "Max and I weren't used to doing this kind of manual work, and maybe we felt that." In the end, Ben enjoyed it. Touching the ropes, weighing the bags of lead shot, getting in and out of the gondola, seeing *Double Eagle*, still slack as a sail but all the same the greatest balloon he had ever laid eyes on — nine stories high, fifty-two feet in diameter at the equator, and as beautifully made, in its way, as a spacecraft, gave Ben a feeling of

66

confidence. "I *liked* that balloon system, learned to like it, in those five days," Ben says, "as you learn to like a person. I wouldn't have gone up in the thing, at least not happily, if I hadn't got to know it first. Ed knew that this process was necessary."

While in Sioux Falls, they made an important decision about the gondola: half of it would be decked, the other half left open, for easy access to stowed supplies and ballast. They measured the space beneath the front deck and decided that the radios could be fitted there quite conveniently; stowing them under the top of the deck would, they thought, provide whatever protection from wet weather might be necessary.

Max's sister-in-law, Cleone Lunseth, who had been coping with Minnesota winters all her life, advised Max to wear layers of light wool on the voyage. Even when wet, wool retains its insulating properties. Max heeded her advice and avoided the goose-down clothing he had intended to wear. Mrs. Lunseth's suggestion, as it turned out, was vital, but she was never to know this; she died only days before the launch.

Max and Ben gave no serious thought to constructing a shelter for themselves. They would have sleeping bags and ponchos. And the balloon, they went on believing, was a natural umbrella. No water could come into the gondola.

"Hell, Ben," said Max, "I think if we wear long handles at high altitudes, and get us some good, down sleeping bags, like the kind they use on Mount Everest, we'll have everything we need."

"With that and the rain cover, we'll be fine," agreed Ben.

If it did rain, Yost said, it might be a good idea to pull the valve a couple of times to make sure no water had leaked in around it and frozen.

"What if it doesn't seat exactly right?" asked Max. "We'll have a leak."

"It'll seat," said Yost.

"I've been wondering about something else, Ed," Ben said. "What about icing? We might get icing . . ."

Yost said, "The balloon won't ice."

Max and Ben saw no reason not to believe this, and by now they had stopped asking Ed Yost to explain things beyond a simple statement of fact.

Before leaving, they watched Yost test the valves for their balloon and Dewey Reinhard's. This was beautiful work, and it was a pleasure to watch a consummate craftsman like Yost do it.

Max and Ben thought of leaving a note for Dewey Reinhard: "We've checked out your valve, Dewey, and except for a slight hissing sound it looks all right to us." They decided against the joke — they wanted to beat Reinhard to France, but they didn't want to make him nervous.

As proof against the cold — although they hadn't confided this to Yost or anyone outside their team, they thought they might fly at 25,000 feet or higher — they laid in a supply of Bushmill's Irish whiskey and a bottle or two of cognac. Ben decided to take his warmest après-ski boots. His crushed foot bothered him more than he mentioned.

Both Ben and Max had, by August, reached a state of mind that Ben later described as serenity. To Doc Wiley it more closely resembled euphoria, but so great was his affection for both men that he found himself, between spasms of realistic fear in which he saw them in distress hundreds of miles from any rescue vessel, that he entered into the joyful spirit of the adventure. Nevertheless, he was spending a good deal of time on the telephone, getting acquainted with the men who ran the Air Force Rescue Center at Scott Air Force Base, Illinois. He didn't talk much to Max and Ben about this activity of his; his instincts told him they didn't want to hear about it.

Both Max and Ben had lost weight. They were trimmer than they had been since their teens, and that alone made them feel confident. The physical conditioning conditioned the mind. Max had believed in the connection between hard muscles and a tough mind ever since military school and those cold mornings when he had looked out his barracks window at the Spartan units moving through the snow and rain at the double. Ben, as a sixth grader, had saved his pride with his punching bag, his weights, and his fists.

By late August, Ben had, or so he believed, considered all the possibilities, gone through all the drills. "I knew I had thought it all out — all the things that can happen to you, and I knew I could survive all those kinds of experiences. By doing that, you condition your mind to the point that when it's time to take off, you have no problem at all — none; no anxiety, no stress, no fear, no nothing. You've already made your mind live through that before you fly. The last two weeks you have a very serene feeling, a very nice feeling of no anxiety at all."

During their cruise in the Mediterranean, Ben and Pat Abruzzo were caught in a terrific summer storm. Pat is a sound sleeper, but the pitching of the Greek ship in which they were passengers awakened her and she went to the porthole.

"Angry, dirty waves were battering the ship," says Pat. "They were like hands trying to rip open the ship and pull you out."

Pat woke Ben and made him come to the porthole. "Take a good look at that," she said. "Are you ready to come down in that, Ben? Because that's what's happened to everyone else. Are you really ready for that?"

Ben looked at the sea with only mild interest and got back into his bunk. He had to pull up the sides, barred like an infant's crib, to keep from being tossed onto the deck.

Flying home, a few days later, he went into the cockpit of the TWA airliner and told the pilots what he and Max were planning to do. Ben had never been quite certain in his mind that overflying commercial airliners would take the trouble to talk to a balloon in flight.

The pilots assured him that they would be glad to chat on VHF, pass on messages, give *Double Eagle* navigational fixes.

Ben asked the pilot what radio frequency the airlines monitored. The pilot told him, but suggested that *Double Eagle* use 121.5 megahertz.

"But that's the emergency frequency," said Ben.

"That's right," the pilot replied. "You guys are going to be in a state of emergency all the way across the Atlantic."

The pilot said, "You're really going to do that — cross *that* in a balloon?" He pointed at the sea, bright as a mirror 30,000 feet below.

From the windows of a jet, with its machinery solid as the earth itself beneath his feet, the ocean seemed calm, beautiful, welcoming. In a balloon, thought Ben, we'll see it even better; he imagined spotting ships below and shouting down to the crews as he and Max had called to the farmers outside Amarillo.

6 Not long before they left for Massachusetts to launch *Double Eagle*, the Abruzzos and the Andersons were invited to a bon voyage party at the home of their friend Billie Slade. Most of the people they knew best in Albuquerque were there, and it was a joshing, prankish evening. Ben is warmed by good company and by Scotch whiskey, and he was having a fine time at the center of attention. He didn't notice, though the others did, that a woman, a friend of the hostess whom he had never met, spent much of the evening staring at him. There was, Max said later, a stricken look on her face when at last she approached Ben.

Ben took her hand in his cordial way and told her his name. Because he didn't know her, he sought to put her at her ease by asking her questions about herself, but she interrupted him.

"Don't go," she said.

Ben and the woman were standing in a circle of chattering people, and he had to strain to hear what she was saying.

"I said, 'Don't go.'" The woman paused and looked away. Her embarrassment was obvious. "I know you'll think I'm crazy, but the minute you walked into the room I had a very strong premonition," she said. "If you go in that balloon, you won't come back."

Ben tried to make a joke of it. "What about Max? Is he going to die, too?"

"No — Max will come back. But you won't."

The woman was completely serious. Ben thanked her for the advice and made more jokes. Later, he asked Billie Slade about her.

"What is she, a fortune teller or something?" he demanded.

70

"Yvonne Johensen?" said his hostess. "No, she's not a fortune teller. She's a professor at the University of Albuquerque."

Ben shrugged off the incident, but it lodged in his mind.

As Ed Yost had promised, *Double Eagle* was ready to fly by the end of August. Just before Labor Day weekend Yost delivered it, the envelope packed in a special case and the gondola loaded by his own men, to Perini's yard in Framingham. Then he went to California to complete a job for the Navy at its testing grounds at China Lake. He would be out of touch, unreachable, at the Navy installation. But he would come to Boston on September 9. He gave Doc Wiley his flight number and time of arrival at Logan International Airport.

In his garage workshop in Colorado, Dewey Reinhard continued to tinker with his bizarre gondola. Doc Wiley reported to Max that Reinhard was approaching a final state of readiness. He could fly at any moment.

The prospect that Reinhard and his copilot, Charles Stephenson, might be first off the mark was intolerable to Max and Ben. In interviews with the press, they wished Reinhard luck, and meant it. Max made his wry jokes about it in private.

"Dewey and Stephenson were the tortoise and Ben and I were the hare," says Max. "I knew we were taking risks, hurrying the way we were. Everybody knows what happened to the hare in Aesop's fable. But this was real life, and if there ever was an unbeatable hare in real life, it's got to be Abruzzo."

Max and Ben had, besides, their secret weapons — Bob Rice and Rich Schwoebel. Earlier, Reinhard had approached Bob Rice to act as meteorologist for his flight; Rice had refused on grounds that he and Weather Services were under exclusive contract to *Double Eagle*. As further insurance, Max considered the undeniable truth that Ed Yost could not be in two places at the same time. Only Yost could supervise the inflation of his balloons, make the final adjustments to the valving systems, get the balloons into the air. Ben and Max believed that they had first claim on Yost as launchmaster because they had got to the coast before Reinhard.

Rice had cautioned Ben and Max that they might have to wait for as much as thirty days for a suitable high-pressure ridge. Neither man believed in his heart that they would have to sit around quite that long. Rice was watching the Canadian latitudes where migratory

71

polar highs of the kind *Double Eagle* wanted to ride to Europe were formed. As soon as the baby was born, he would tell Max and Ben. In his cautious way, he mentioned that the conditions in the early days of September seemed to be favorable.

On Wednesday, September 7, Rice called Ben and Max, who were staying at a hotel in Boston, and asked them to come to Weather Services. On arrival, he showed them satellite photographs and other data. The sort of weather system they wanted would form over the Canadian coast. Rice had spotted a departing high-pressure system in the region of the Gulf of St. Lawrence. The high-pressure ridgeline — that all-important "surfer's wave" that could carry *Double Eagle* to Europe — would extend northward from the high-pressure center along longitude 60 degrees west, an imaginary line running north and south inland of the coast of Labrador. A cold front, forming in the region of the Great Lakes, was rushing along behind the high-pressure ridge, and would push it with exceptional velocity from west to east.

It would be possible to launch *Double Eagle* just after sunset on Friday, September 9. But there were risks. The speed of the storm blowing out of the Great Lakes might push the high-pressure ridge out to sea before the balloon could reach the coast of Labrador. In that case, *Double Eagle* would be swallowed by the storm and might not be able to escape from it. Second, tropical storm Clara was centered off Cape Hatteras; Rice believed that she would remain where she was and have no effect on the flight. Still, he believed it was a dangerous policy to release a balloon into the North Atlantic while a tropical storm was present anywhere in that ocean.

The swift southerlies blowing up the coast would carry *Double Eagle* across Maine, New Brunswick, and Quebec, and they would enter the high-pressure ridge just as it passed over the coast of Labrador. They would turn into the Atlantic over Goose Bay, just as Lindbergh had done fifty years earlier. The system was moving very fast; timing was vital — delay, even a delay of a very few hours, would put them behind the high-pressure ridge, in the trough: in the storm.

"It's a calculated risk," Rice told them. "If you get off late from Marshfield, or if you hit local weather, or if you get behind the ridge for some other reason, you'll be in the storm. It's dangerous, but it's possible."

"The wind was really cooking," Ben recalls. "The direction was good. Max and I both knew, after we talked to Bob, that the launch window was open. It was just a matter of flying out the window. We knew that another window mightn't open for thirty days or longer. That had been the experience in the past."

"Bob Rice gave us the data," says Max. "He was calm and scientific. It was our decision. I didn't see anything to do but go."

To Ben he said, "Maybe we ought to just take her up."

Ben looked at the photographs of the earth, the swirling masses of cloud, representing such unimaginable forces.

"As far as I'm concerned," said Ben, "it's a go."

Says Max, "I made no historic statements. I thought it would be better to call up Doc and tell him to get her ready."

It was nightfall before they got hold of Doc Wiley to tell him of their decision.

Doc said, "You want to go at six o'clock Friday evening, and it's Wednesday night now?"

"Yes," said Max. He explained the weather situation, and Ben saw in his face the old Andersonian mixture of enthusiasm and stubborn determination.

"There ain't no way you're going to make it," Doc said. "We haven't even started to load the gondola. The long-range radio is on the West Coast, being repaired; we can't get that back in time."

"We'll go without the long-range radio," Max said. "We've got the others. It's the weather, Doc — we have to catch the weather just right."

Doc, calmly, outlined the problems: they had to get the balloon to the launch site. They had to label everything that was going to go into the gondola — hundreds of separate items — as well as load it. Syd Parks was still wiring the radio system. Ed Yost was in California.

"It's impossible, in my opinion, to put all that together in less than forty-eight hours," Doc said.

Ben snapped, "We're going to go whether you've got this thing put together or not."

Doc Wiley knew that the argument was over. Ben and Max had decided to do something, and it was his job to make it possible.

Ed Yost was due to arrive on Friday afternoon, only hours before the liftoff. He could not be reached in the meantime, and Doc was just as glad. It required hours for Ed to prepare the balloon for launching. Before his own flight, Yost had gone through days of rehearsal, hours of careful examination of checklists. Doc thought Ed Yost would believe that Ben and Max had lost their senses. You simply did not spend almost $100,000 for a balloon system to which you were going to entrust two lives, and leap aboard at the last minute, like a tourist late for a plane. But Yost had promised to come, and nobody doubted that he would be there.

The flight, thanks to Jim Mitchell's easy expertise, had attracted a great deal of attention from the media. Mitchell's philosophy from the beginning had been that no flackery was necessary. The event would sell itself. He made no attempt to create artificial enthusiasm, but merely let the wire services and the papers know, through some of the most low-key press releases ever issued, that Ben Abruzzo and Max Anderson were going to attempt to be the first human beings ever to cross the Atlantic in a balloon.

The result was that Max and Ben spent the greater part of their time in Boston talking to reporters. Doc Wiley, attempting to work against what seemed to him an impossible deadline, found himself talking into microphones instead of attending to the dozens of tasks facing him. For help he had Pat and Patty and their children, Syd Parks, and whoever else he could press-gang into running errands, weighing ballast, shopping for last-minute necessities. He had no time to consult with Max and Ben about such matters as the operation of the radios, the function of the Nimbus navigational system, the use of the homing beacon, the maps that would guide them across the Atlantic, the emergency procedures to be used in case of a landing in the sea. In Albuquerque, they had skimmed the surface of all these subjects, but the sort of in-depth briefing that Doc, the retired colonel, thought indispensable had just never happened.

Doc was philosophical: "You just aren't going to get those guys to listen. They didn't have a minute *to* listen. Every time I saw them, some guy had a microphone stuck in their face and those lights were on, blinding you to the real world."

The real world, to Doc, was getting the balloon into the air and getting the pilots back safely. Finally, he could stand no more intrusion by the media, and on Thursday evening, when it was time to truck the balloon and the gondola from Perini's yard in Framingham to the gravel pit in Marshfield, he went along. Syd Parks was staying in a motel there, and Doc moved in with him. By rising before dawn, he and Syd managed to get the radio equipment — the VHF sets, the marine band radio, the Nimbus transmitter, and the homing beacon — wired and installed. At the last minute, the high frequency (HF) long-distance radio arrived and they installed that too. Doc, in moments snatched from everything else he was doing, had got hold of the factory in California and cajoled them into shipping it by air express.

By midday, the press was swarming over the launch site. Ben and Max chatted equably with the reporters. Pat Abruzzo and Patty Anderson, with their blond good looks, were to spend a good deal more time before the cameras than their husbands before the flight was over. Later, in England, the wives would be recognized by strangers who had seen them on the telly; Ben and Max, inaccessible in their gondola, were famous names but unknown faces.

Pat Abruzzo felt a warmth toward the press from the beginning, and her transparent sincerity caused the cameras to love her. "Of course," says Pat, "I knew from the start that in case of a rescue, the media would be the ones who could help our men. To me, they were friends I could turn to."

No ropes or restraining devices of any kind had been erected, so that the considerable crowd that had gathered wandered at will over the site, gazing with curiosity at the balloon and the strange mixture of space-age equipment and homely items (an ordinary camping stove, a portable toilet, with plastic bags to catch and contain waste; Ben planned to save these sealed sacks for extra ballast) that lay in a jumble on the gritty floor of the gravel pit.

The Anderson and Abruzzo children were busy filling sandbags and organizing the items to be placed in the gondola. Rich Schwoebel and Doc Wiley, with Ben's advice, had worked out a sequence for loading so that the items needed from day to day would be uncovered at the right time. Each item was weighed and labeled — everything aboard, except Max and Ben, was expendable as ballast. Pat Abruzzo and Patty Anderson were in general command of this operation, and keeping busy eased their minds. Patty had just returned from Minnesota, where she had attended the funeral of her sister.

Patty's mother, famous in their family as a cook, had sent a huge

German chocolate cake to Max. September 10, the first day of the voyage of *Double Eagle*, would be his forty-third birthday, and this particular sort of cake was Max's favorite.

Doc was helped in the more technical tasks by Rich Schwoebel, who has mechanical as well as intellectual skills, and by Syd Parks. Stephanie Anderson Nennicker's husband Werner, a graduate engineer, was a help too, as were Max's older sons, Michael and Kristian and Timothy, and Ben's sons Benny, Richard, and Louis, the last a blond version of his supercharged father. It was a pleasure to Max, standing a little apart talking to a group of children who had wandered down from the local grammar school, to see all that activity. Max loves his own children, and there are few things he enjoys more than chatting with youngsters. As he explained to the schoolchildren how he was going to fly *Double Eagle*, while watching over their bright heads the diligent work of his own bantering offspring, he felt a great wave of contentment run through his heart.

A light onshore breeze was blowing, and again Max smelled the salt of the sea. He watched the breeze with interest, but with no concern. Days before, he and Ben and Schwoebel and Rice had released small test balloons inflated with helium and watched how the eddying sea winds affected them. They had, by this method, found a launch site that, Ben and Max believed, would permit *Double Eagle* to make a smooth ascent, untroubled by downdrafts that could spell embarrassment, if not disaster. He was anxious to make a perfect liftoff. Partly this was for the beauty of the thing: Max is an impeccable dresser (cowboy boots with engraved sterling silver toe caps, glove-leather sports jackets, handsome rings on his fingers and tangles of gold chains round his neck). It's very unlikely that you will find a brave and well-trained cadet inside an untidy uniform. Max was interested, too, in giving as much reassurance as possible to the people on the ground. He was beginning to sense a current of nervousness in the air.

Ed Yost had not arrived, and he was the key to everything. The helium truck was at the gravel pit, waiting to inflate the balloon. But only Yost knew how to install the valve and supervise the inflation.

The delay played on Ben's nerves, and Doc Wiley was agitated as well. They realized, in the rush, that they had made no arrangements to meet Yost at Logan Airport when he arrived from California.

"No helicopter?" said Ben. "No *car*, even? How is Ed supposed to get here?"

It was a long drive from the airport — a couple of hours even in light traffic.

There was no sure method of getting in touch with Yost, who might or might not respond to a page at the airport when his flight arrived. Nevertheless, Doc tried to procure a helicopter to collect Yost at Logan. A local man, Carl Peterson, who had loaned *Double Eagle* crew two mobile homes and performed many other kindnesses, tried to reach F. Lee Bailey, the criminal lawyer, who lives nearby, in an attempt to borrow Bailey's helicopter. This effort failed.

Yost arrived by midafternoon, having stopped by Perini's to get his truck. Doc Wiley told him, as he surveyed the chaotic scene, that *Double Eagle* was going to launch at the first possible moment after sunset.

"It *is?*" said Yost, derisively.

"Ed couldn't comprehend it," says Doc. "Who could blame him? He looked around, sort of shrugged, and went to work. Ed is a maestro at this kind of thing. We'd never done it before. I mean, we didn't know how to take the balloon out of the packing box."

Yost arrived, as well as anyone remembers, at about three o'clock. In minutes, he had the launch crew jumping. The balloon, immensely long, was spread on a sheet of canvas to protect it from sharp objects on the ground. Yost, squatting with a cigar clamped in his teeth, fitted the valve to the top. Ben watched this operation, as he watched all the others, with keen interest: if the valve leaked, if Ed Yost made the slightest error in installing it, the helium would leak out and *Double Eagle* would fall like a stone into the sea. Yost does not make such mistakes. But Max could never, either then or later, bring himself to trust the valve. He knew it would open when its cord was tugged. But would it seat properly again? In mines, he had seen valves on pumps stick, leak, fail completely, and had seen how helpless such mishaps left the men who were at the mercy of the valve. He had great faith in Ed Yost; but he did not trust valves, and would never, in any balloon, be able to bring himself to open one. There were too many reasons why it might not close.

By now, television crews and print reporters were multiplying like mosquitoes at evening. Ben and Max, courteous hosts, talked to all of them. They had earlier signed an agreement with CBS to carry one of their cameras along on the gondola, and network technicians were installing this equipment. It added weight to the payload. That pleased neither Yost nor Rich Schwoebel, but both were confident that the new *Double Eagle*, with a capacity that finally measured out to 101,000 cubic feet, would carry the load.

"Everything down to the last thirty percent of the payload is expendable as ballast," Rich Schwoebel told Ben as they went over the ballasting tables once more.

"Please include Max and me in the thirty percent," said Ben.

Max and Ben were wearing their flight suits — coveralls of blue double-knit material, beautifully tailored. Onto the chests and backs and arms and legs of the flight suits, Pat and Patty had sewn all sorts of patches, symbols of past ballooning triumphs. Ben wore the black Greek fisherman's cap Pat had bought for him on their Mediterranean cruise. Max, as usual, was bareheaded, relaxed, chuckling. Ben, when he was not speaking into a television camera, was making banter with friends from Albuquerque, but there was anxiety in the chaffing voices of his companions. He felt tension building in the crowd, too. More and more people were arriving, many of them with lawn chairs, to watch the launch. It seemed to Ben that thousands of pairs of eyes were fixed on him. The gravel pit was something like an amphitheater; he was surprised that there should be so much interest.

To strangers, Max might have seemed relaxed. Patty Anderson detected anxiety beneath his smiling exterior. She understood the importance of timing. Max and George Fischbeck had explained the weather pattern. She knew the dangers of launching late. Across the gravel pit, she watched as Max talked intently with Bob Rice and George Fischbeck. Already the sun was falling toward the western horizon, and moment by moment the shadows of the spectators standing on the western rim of the gravel pit were lengthening. Patty wondered if Ben and Max might simply scrub the launch if time ran out. She didn't ask him; she knew they must have some zero hour in mind, and she was confident he would not violate his own intelligence by taking an unacceptable risk. Preparing Max's personal effects had reminded her of packing his suitcase for one of his trips, except that it was vastly more complicated. She had tried to think of everything: for example, she had wrapped each of Max's garments — wool shirts, wool socks, long underwear, sweaters, even handkerchiefs —

in separate, sealed plastic bags. If it rained into the gondola (though everyone said that could not happen) nothing would get wet. The feeling she had was like the one she had had so many times before: Max was going on a long trip. She had packed for him and seen him off hundreds of times. When he returned, she would unpack for him and make him southern fried chicken, his favorite dinner.

Max sauntered up to his wife. "Patty, I sure would like to have some fried chicken," he said. "For tonight."

Patty realized he meant for his supper aboard *Double Eagle*. Patty gave someone some money and sent them to the nearest Kentucky Fried Chicken outlet to buy a barrel of the stuff. That way there would be enough for Ben, if he wanted some.

Patty noticed, for the first time, that there were no seats of any kind in the gondola — these things had just been overlooked. Good heavens, she thought, the men are going to have to *stand* all the way across!

There was little enough room even to stand, with only half the bottom of the gondola decked. The other half was a V-shaped depression, the inside of one of the catamaran's double keels.

Patty went to a woman who was sitting in a lawn chair not far from the gondola. "I know you're going to think I'm crazy," she said, "but will you sell me your lawn chair?" She explained.

"Look, take it," said the woman. "I won't sell it to you, for land's sakes. I'd just be proud to have your husband take it along!"

Patty found another chair, and put both aboard.

Ed Yost was now ready to attach the balloon to the load ring. He asked for his crimping tool, a large pair of pincers specially designed to do this vital job. The crimping tool could not be found. It had been left behind at Perini's shop, forty-five minutes away. A car was sent into the rush-hour traffic to fetch the crimping tool. This meant, everyone knew, a further delay of at least an hour and a half, perhaps longer. In the end, it cost two hours.

While they waited, Max and Ben continued to talk to Fischbeck and Bob Rice. The high-pressure ridge was still moving fast across northern Canada. As predicted, the weather in front of it and behind it was stormy. They could expect to hit some rain before they climbed to altitude the first night after they crossed the coast of Labrador. Rice said again that it was difficult to make a forecast that would stand up for more than a few days, especially in such a volatile situation. But he believed that the speed of the system they were going to enter was so great that they might make a very quick crossing. All depended on timing. He didn't like the delay. He had hoped that *Double Eagle* would be in the air and sailing north by six-thirty at the latest.

So had Ben and Max, but they now realized that their timetable was abandoned. Once again, they didn't discuss the matter with each other; there was no need. Each knew what the situation was.

The feeling of foreboding was such that someone, one of the youngsters, made a remark to Ed Yost about the risks Ben and Max were facing.

"Do your job," said Yost, gruffly. "Getting sentimental won't help."

Ben was blaming himself and Max for not having arranged a faster way to bring Ed Yost from the airport; it was their responsibility; they should have seen to it. Then there was the matter of the crimping tool. Delays, omissions, acts of stupidity — all infuriated Ben. He had forgotten, in the excitement, to take his blood-pressure medicine that day, and he would forget to do so throughout the flight. He felt the tension and the anxiety in others very keenly. He sensed them, even, in Max. His friend had stopped making jokes; he was off by himself, looking out toward the sea.

Among the friends from Albuquerque who had come to give Max and Ben a send-off was Bob Bowers, winner of the high-stakes backgammon game in the Greek restaurant. Ben and Bowers were warm friends, and their competitiveness was an expression of affection. Now Bowers took Ben aside, away from the reporters, and talked to him. Bowers is a hard-faced, rawboned man with a rasping voice. He looks like a middleweight contender who quit while he still had all his brains.

Double Eagle was fully inflated; the crimping tool had come and all was ready for the launch. The balloon was a beautiful sight, rising into the darkness, washed by the harsh television lights. For the first time, seeing the balloon in that way, Ben understood, emotionally, that he really was going to fly the Atlantic. *Double Eagle* was a reality — his and Max's. He saw Pat's bright blond head near the gondola and wanted to go to her. The launch was no more than fifteen minutes in the future. He thought: I may never see Pat again. What the hell does Bowers want with me?

He looked at Bowers and saw tears in his friend's eyes. Ben looked around in his darting way and realized that almost everyone was crying, even total strangers.

Bowers grasped Ben's hand. "Here is this big burly guy," says Ben. "He was teary-eyed. He said, 'Ben, buddy,' — it's always 'Ben' when we're not betting money against each other, but 'Abruzzo!' when he's mad at me — anyway, Bob said something like, 'Ben, you know, I'm really, you know, *worried* about this flight. It's so damn dangerous. Why don't you just take off, fly fifteen or twenty miles, set down, call it good? You know, just trying is a lot. Tell the world you had a big leak. Why don't you do that?' "

Ben said, "No way. We're going as far as this dude will go."

He clapped Bob Bowers on the arm, shook hands, and strode off toward the balloon. The sea breeze had died with the sunset, as the sands on the beach cooled, and there wasn't a breath stirring. *Double Eagle* thrust upward into the night, straining at its moorings. The ground crew was still scurrying around the gondola. Ben looked for Pat and his children. He pushed his way through a circle of people, friends and strangers, smiling to reassure them. Inside the circle, Max, looking to Ben as bemused as he had looked while listening to the awakening birds over Texas, was standing quietly while the weathermen talked to him.

Ben knew that the irrevocable decision, to go or not to go, would be made in the next few seconds. Whatever he had said to Bowers, it was still possible to change plans if there was a good reason to do so. Rich Schwoebel, watching Ben as he approached, saw a somber and pensive man. Max wondered, with a rush of fondness for his partner, if Ben was remembering the woman at the party and her premonition about Ben's death. He thought of making a joke about it, but then thought better of it. Actually, Ben was weighing the situation.

"I had a great and heavy reservation about the weather, and what we were going to face," says Ben. "We were facing the great unknown. We imagined the worst." Ben gave no thought to the woman at the party, or to fate or luck; only to the realities. "I don't think a person has a foreordained destiny," he says. "None. A person who leads a certain kind of life, one in which he is willing to accept challenges of any kind and new things of all kinds as they come along — well, then, that person *is* going to have a much higher chance of being involved in something that's revolutionary, something that is new, something that is first, something that brings recognition to that person."

Ben believed that he was that kind of person. To Max and Rice and Fischbeck, he said, "What's the weather?"

The meteorologists had reservations. They had lost two precious hours; the high-pressure ridge, their surfer's wave, was moving at sixty miles an hour toward the beach, a phenomenal speed. They might come in behind it, and be sucked into the following storm. If that happened, they would have to climb fast, to break through the weather, pierce the slope of the ridge, and get ahead of it. That would mean a prodigal expenditure of ballast, and the loss of a day's endurance: they would have to throw away time at the very start of the flight.

Max said, "I think we can fly that sucker. If the present velocities hold, how quick can we get across?"

Rice and Schwoebel agreed that it was possible, barring the unforeseen — which could never be barred — that *Double Eagle* might sweep across the Atlantic in four days or less. Schwoebel was analytical and calm; it was a technical problem, a matter of adjusting to new conditions.

Schwoebel had worked out a flight manual for Ben and Max. It suggested how much ballast to expend at each sunset in order to attain the ideal altitudes set forth in the flight plan. Ben and Max, and especially Ben, who found the ballasting process fascinating, understood what to do.

Dark was falling. Rice told them again that they would have to decide whether to take a calculated risk. In no case should they go after 9 P.M. Rice had been checking by telephone with technicians at Weather Services, tracking the high-pressure ridge. If *Double Eagle* launched later than 9 P.M. it would almost certainly fall behind the ridge — and there were thunderstorms behind the ridge.

"The launch window is still open," said Rice, "but it is getting very narrow."

Rice expected that the trajectory would take the balloon north from the launch site. When Ben and Max reached the Labrador coast, they would hit clouds and rain. Once again, Rice and Rich Schwoebel emphasized the importance of climbing rapidly through this local storm and into the dry, fair air of the high-pressure ridge. To stay low would be fatal to the flight, because low-level winds would drive the balloon north, away from Europe and toward the Arctic ice pack.

"Remember," said Rice. "Down is north. Up is east. When in doubt, climb. That's the way to France."

Max turned to George Fischbeck. They were old friends; Max believes that Fischbeck, a man who throbs with good humor and intelligence, has better sensory apparatus than most people, that he has the gift of the smart guesser.

"George," Max asked, "you've heard Bob. He has reservations. How do you feel?"

Fischbeck looked long at his friend, and realized that he was going to go no matter what he said to him.

"Good," said George Fischbeck. "Not wonderful, Max. But good."

Schwoebel felt that launching conditions were ideal. He had some misgivings about the weather off Labrador, but the weather was not his field; he had no reservations about the balloon system.

"Ben?"

"Go," said Ben.

But he had the feeling that he would never see his family or anyone he knew, except Max, again. He took Rich Schwoebel by the arm and led him aside.

Ben, speaking in a low voice, said to Schwoebel, "Rich, I want you to document all your expenses, and you should talk to Pat about this in the event Max and I don't survive, and she'll take care of everything."

Schwoebel was taken aback. "Ben, I appreciate your saying that," he replied, "but I don't think we have that difficult a situation."

Ben nodded and went off to join his family.

Doc Wiley, meantime, was attempting to explain the radio system to Max. After the long-range HF sets had arrived from the repair shop on the West Coast, Doc and Syd Parks had tested them. The radios worked for twenty minutes and then quit. All that was left was the VHF transceiver for communicating with aircraft and with airport control towers, and the marine-band, balloon-to-ship radio. The homing beacon and the Nimbus satellite apparatus were automatic. Doc Wiley gave Ben and Max twenty minutes of instruction on the use of the radio equipment, and this was all the training they had.

Wiley handed Max a portfolio of charts for the Atlantic, and for the land masses they would overfly. The maps were stowed in the gondola.

"I tried to talk to Max about the maps, and the radio transmission schedule, and the rescue plan," says Doc, "but I could tell he wasn't hearing a word. I felt we'd done what we could. They'd decided to go. I knew the facts. If that balloon went down fifty miles off the coast, there was no one there to pick them up. Even that soon we just wouldn't be able to reach them. Max knew it; I didn't have to tell him."

Before the last goodbyes began, Ben came near again. Lying on the ground beside the gondola were the two parachutes they had planned to take along. Max had never wanted to take them. Aloft, they could not be worn because they were too bulky; in case of a catastrophic failure of the balloon, there would be no time to buckle on the harnesses; once in the water, the billowing silk would make swimming impossible. A man could only live for minutes in Atlantic waters in any case. Better, thought Max, to ride the balloon down and die without making a fuss.

"Ben, I'm not going to take that damn thing," said Max, giving the parachute a kick. "It's just extra weight."

"Let's leave 'em," said Ben — another dare taken.

Doc Wiley detached the survival suits and the one-man life rafts from the parachute rigs and stowed them in the gondola.

Max kissed his children, one by one: Stephanie; Michael and his wife, Kaye; Kristian and Tim. Ben embraced Benny and Louis and Mary Pat and Richard; Benny had been married to his young wife, Kelly, only a month before. Pat Abruzzo, tears welling, kissed Ben repeatedly.

Mary Abruzzo, Ben's mother, was dry-eyed as she kissed her son goodbye. Of all the people there — and there were dozens of Ben's relatives from Rockford on hand — his mother was the strongest. Often in his life he had felt her calm strength and love flow toward him; he had never been more grateful for it than now. While Mary Abruzzo stood holding hands with her daughter Terry, Ben's other sister, Marie Turiciano, lifted everyone's mood by draping a necklace of garlic around Ben's neck and another around Max's. The garlic strings are an ancient Sicilian charm against devils and evil spirits. Ben's was interwoven with Italian red, white, and green ribbons and Max's with the blue and gold of Sweden.

Max and Ben got into the gondola. Patty handed Max his box of Kentucky Fried Chicken, and the German chocolate cake his mother-in-law had made for him. She said, "Happy birthday, Max," and gave him her wonderful slow smile.

Then Patty went running to the microphone that Doc had somehow managed to have set up, and sang, "Happy Birthday" to Max. Hesitantly at first, and then in full voice, the crowd joined in. Pat Abruzzo, as she sang, stood near the gondola, gazing intently at Ben. His eyes were roving over the whole crowd and there was not so much as the shadow of a smile on his face. Max, holding his cake, seemed pleased.

Doc Wiley stepped up to the gondola, meaning to help Yost and Schwoebel cut loose the sandbags from its rails so that the balloon could rise.

"There'd been a lot of emotional kissing the wife goodbye," says Doc. "Now we had about fifty seconds remaining before the launch. I shook hands with Maxie and we looked each other in the eye and I know that both of us felt that we were saying goodbye forever. I can't help but say that I think Maxie knew, in that instant, that he might never see any of us again."

Yost began to cut the sandbags loose, and the great balloon began to rise. It was 8:16 P.M. — they were more than two hours late. Ben heard a flapping sound and looking up, realized that the American flag, hanging vertically from the equator of *Double Eagle*, was rippling in the wind of the balloon's movement. "The Star Spangled Banner" was being played, on a phonograph record, over the loudspeaker system. Children, hundreds of them, were swarming below, shouting and skylarking. The air was filled with cheering. Max, crouched over the radios inside the gondola, saw nothing of this, and Patty couldn't see him; he was hidden inside the balloon system.

Ben, looking down from the gondola as it rose into the darkness, gazed into a pool of brilliant light cast by the television equipment. It seemed to him that tears were glistening in the eyes of everyone he saw; it was no trick of the light — five thousand people were crying.

He looked for Pat. "I was looking down, I couldn't see her right away, and then I did. I was looking down and saying to myself that I might never see her again."

Pat Abruzzo was running beneath the gondola, looking up, weeping. She saw Ben plainly. Though she did not know if Ben could hear her, she called to him in a strong voice, "I love you. God be with you both. I'll see you in France." As she spoke these final, hopeful words, Pat smiled brilliantly, and Ben saw that, and the tears shining on her cheeks.

As *Double Eagle* disappeared from sight, Patty Anderson and Pat Abruzzo stood together, embracing.

Ed Yost got into his truck and drove away. Later, he told Doc Wiley that he went to church, for the first time in years, and prayed.

 As *Double Eagle* rose from the gravel pit, Max was seized by a violent fit of shivering. This happens to him sometimes in moments of excitement, or when he has had a cold drink; it is a side effect of the condition that causes his hand tremor. Normally it passes quickly, but this time it persisted for several long moments, and Max could do nothing to bring it under control.

Ben noted the shivering. He was used to seeing it, and gave it no more notice than Max gave to Ben's flashes of temper.

Though it was a balmy night, Max felt cold to his bones. He tried to understand what was happening to him. He felt no physical fear. In fact, looking down at the pool of light in the gravel pit, with the doll-like figures just barely visible, Max realized that he had never in his life been so happy. Yet apprehension stabbed him, and he put it into words.

"Ben, of all the things that can happen," said Max, "the worst would be to splash this balloon. I don't want to go no damn two hundred miles and go into the ocean."

Ben, grunting, went on with his work. He was stowing the gear that had been left loose on the floor of the gondola. Its interior was lit by the soft glow of eight small lights powered by a single D-cell flashlight battery. Max did not know if Ben was answering him with his grunts or making the little noises of a man at work.

"If that happened, if we splashed like damn fools, I couldn't go home," Max said.

That did get Ben's attention. Max was telling him that embarrassment was worse than death. Ben remembered what Bob Bowers had said to him: "Fly fifteen or twenty miles and bring it down; tell the world you had a big leak." He decided this wasn't the time to tell Max *that* story.

As soon as Max voiced his anxiety, his fit of trembling passed. Ben was still depressed, and the realization that Max would rather drown than fail, while it didn't surprise him, did nothing to lift his spirits. He thought again of all his friends, just barely able to say goodbye. They were, all of them, as manly as Bob Bowers. Ben himself would use the word *macho* to describe their attitudes; what other attitudes could they have and still be his friends? Jack Hammack, his close friend, a man who sometimes irritated Ben by looking after him like a mother hen, had been there, and Jack Dailey. Both had helped with the launch and kept control till the final seconds. Then they had got weepy. Ben shook his head and clenched his teeth in a mixture of exasperation and gratitude.

He thought: If you were going to jump out of an airplane into a combat zone, they wouldn't all cry. They'd say "good luck," and away you'd go. That's how you get people to go, keep the music playing and roll the drums. That gives you confidence. The way we went was *terrible*.

Double Eagle, in lifting off at 8:16, had beaten Rice's final deadline by only forty-four minutes. Their margin of safety was razor-thin. They would need a perfect flight to Labrador in order to hop onto the high-pressure ridge.

The night was black, with only the sliver of a pale northern moon on the horizon. Max was talking on the radio, trying to raise the Logan tower. Ben, ballasting carefully, brought *Double Eagle* quickly to its initial planned altitude of 2,000 feet. The balloon responded beautifully to his touch; he felt that he was stroking a living creature, something that already was beginning to return the affection he felt for it. The lights of Boston and its suburbs sparkled inland from the black teeth of the shoreline with its wharves and capes.

Ben called to Max. "Look," he said. "Look down at that. What a beautiful sight!" Max stood up and gazed overboard. Behind him, the VHF radio crackled with the voice of the controller in the Logan tower, asking *Double Eagle* to identify itself. Because the balloon was so large, and because it moved so slowly, it returned a bizarre image on the radar screen — a great slow burst of green light, like a flower opening in a series of time-stop photographs.

"Sir," said Max, who so addresses all unseen presences, including the people he talks to on the radio, "this is Five Zero Double Eagle." This was the first time Max had spoken the call sign of the balloon and doing so gave it as much identity for him as Ben had felt when he had first made it fly.

"Five Zero Delta Echo," replied Logan control, using the correct phonetic forms of the letters D and E. "We have you twenty-five miles southeast. Maintain two thousand feet. Do not progress over the field."

"Five Zero Double Eagle, Roger. Sir, we don't know if we can control our direction of flight in relation to the field, but at this time we are progressing due north."

A pause, and then the toneless voice of Logan control came over the loudspeaker again. "Five Zero Delta Echo — you say you cannot control your direction of flight?"

Max pressed his microphone button. "Only by wind direction, sir. Five Zero Double Eagle is a transatlantic balloon."

Another long pause. "A transatlantic balloon. Roger."

To Ben, Max said, "I think they're a little skeptical, Ben."

Ben laughed. He saw fun to come as they progressed up the coast, being handed from one incredulous flight controller to another. A balloon! They were floating in the darkness over Boston Harbor, showing a steady white light and a flashing red strobe, at something like twenty-five miles an hour; at that speed, any known flying machine would fall out of the sky. But there they were, pinging on all the radars on this side of the horizon. The tension was broken.

Max, grinning with each exchange, talked to the Logan tower again, asking for bearings and navigational fixes. They were headed straight for Gloucester on Cape Ann. Max could see the golden lights of the old fishing port dead ahead. To the right of the balloon there was nothing but forbidding black ocean. We'll see a lot of *that* in the next few days, thought Max. This voyage would represent the longest period he had spent without seeing the glow of electricity since he and Bo Dunsworth had gone prospecting for uranium in the Northwest Territories twenty-four years before.

The flight path of *Double Eagle* was slightly east of true north.

Except for the changing perspective of the lights on the shore, they had no sensation of movement. *Double Eagle*, with everything aboard, weighed sixty-six hundred pounds — minus the three hundred pounds of ballast Ben had used to bring her to altitude. Yet she was part of the wind, and so were Ben and Max. The sensation was pure freedom — a greater freedom than any airplane could give, with its straining mechanical parts.

Max stopped looking at the compass after the first few moments, and relied on landmarks. He began to feel hunger. Smells do not escape from a gondola, and the aroma of his mother-in-law's chocolate birthday cake, and that of the Kentucky Fried Chicken, was delicious in the motionless air. Max, busy laying the balloon's first course, decided to eat as soon as they were clear of the harbor. They could see the landing lights of jetliners and hear the shriek of their engines, but neither man felt threatened by these hurtling machines. In the brief intervals of silence, they heard sounds, even human voices, rising from the ground below.

As they approached Cape Ann and Gloucester, Logan control came on the air again. By now the controller and Max were on friendly terms. Max had the feeling that the controller was happy to be shepherding a balloon, and had perhaps been told by someone that *Double Eagle* was real, and in the Boston newspapers.

"Five Zero Delta Echo, Double Eagle balloon, this is Logan control. One of the fellows working here in the tower, his wife lives in Gloucester, and she thinks she can see your strobe."

"Roger, Logan. We're mighty pleased that the lady can see us, sir," said Max.

"She wonders if you can see *her*, Double Eagle. She's switching her porch light on and off. If you can see her porch light would you show another strong light to acknowledge her signal?"

"Roger," said Max. Looking down into the shoal of bulbs 2,000 feet below, he saw nothing that resembled a porch light being flicked on and off, but Max could not disappoint a lady.

"I see her light," he said into the radio, "and I'm blinking our call letters in Morse with a high-power flashlight . . ."

"She sees it! She sees it!" cried a voice in the background. It was the woman's husband, talking to her on the telephone.

A few moments later, *Double Eagle* passed over the two small islands that mark the boundary of the local controller. The balloon was passed to the next controller, at Pease Air Force Base, the first of several invisible hands that would lead *Double Eagle* up the coast. Very soon, they had left the lights behind them. Pease radar, by taking fixes twenty minutes apart, was able to tell Ben and Max that they were moving at approximately thirty miles an hour: the technicians had some difficulty, for they had never tracked so slow a target. Ben and Max were delighted with their speed — Bob Rice had forecast an initial velocity of twenty to twenty-five miles an hour.

Max and Ben had done all their housekeeping, deployed the long aerial for the homing beacon that trailed below the gondola like a tail, and started their log. The balloon was flying perfectly. Ben kept a watchful eye on the gauges, but *Double Eagle* seemed to have no temperament. They ate some fried chicken and cut Max's cake. Max's appetite was excellent; he didn't really notice what Ben ate. In the mild light inside the gondola, the two men appeared to each other as dark silhouettes. Ben had put on the lighter of his goosedown jackets, and he was a husky figure, standing over the instruments, with his peaked fisherman's cap square on his head.

Max was comfortable in a sweater and an unzipped Windbreaker. He put on his glasses and by the beam of a flashlight plotted their course. Their present drift would take them within a few miles of Bar Harbor, Maine, the place from which Dewey Reinhard and Charles Stephenson planned to launch their *Eagle*.

Through a mouthful of chocolate cake, Max said, "Ben, maybe we ought to drop a note in a bottle to Dewey, and tell him to look for us in Paris."

"Dewey's still in Colorado." The men from CBS had told them that before they lifted off from Marshfield. *Double Eagle* was first out of the gate.

It was, however, a long steeplechase. Midnight was approaching. Max, true to his plan to force himself to get the necessary amount of sleep, decided it was time to rest. He asked Ben how he was.

"Fine. I'll take the watch."

"Good. Then I think I'll sleep for a while."

"Fine." Ben was speaking in monosyllables, his usual style when aloft with Max. After unrolling his sleeping bag and crawling into it, Max looked up for a few moments at the black bulb of the balloon. It was ghosting over deep woods in utter silence. He closed his eyes, commanded his mind to cease forming thoughts, and went to sleep. Before his mind shut down altogether, he noticed that some cirrus clouds were forming higher up; they sailed across the cuticle of the moon.

Most of the tension had drained from Ben, but he found it difficult to comprehend how Max could simply lie down and go to sleep as he had done. In all the years of their friendship, he had never seen Max asleep; it changed him somehow. Ben never quite got used to this, in all the time they flew together afterward. Ben himself was wakeful, alert. He could get by on three hours of sleep or less and work a full day. He did not imagine that being in a balloon would change his requirements.

While Max slept, *Double Eagle* flew over the White Mountains of New Hampshire, carried by the windflow over the peaks as a boat is carried by water over submerged rocks. Ben didn't see them, or much of anything else, for there was ground mist and broken cloud all around. He watched the formation of the cloud and fog with interest, but with no great concern. Bob Rice had told them to expect it — they would be flying in weather part of the time. He hadn't expected to encounter such thick clouds so soon.

There was no point in contacting base; they had regular times for such conversations, and the next scheduled transmission would not come until after sunrise. Once again, he worked out the ballasting figures in his head: total ballast on takeoff, 3,400 pounds; amount expended, 300; amount remaining, 3,100. The sun, when it rose and superheated the helium the next morning, would take them to their planned altitude of 6,000 feet by midday. Then there would be the stepped climb — ballasting at sunset to stay ahead of the high-pressure ridge. He had absolute faith in the flight plan. He had absolute faith in Rich Schwoebel, the author of the flight plan. He had absolute faith in Bob Rice.

But he was flying through thick clouds while Max slept, and he had no particle of trust that the weather was going to be good to them.

When *Double Eagle* had taken off from Marshfield, the cold front associated with the low-pressure trough was 483 miles to the west. It was gaining on the balloon at a rate of about twenty miles an hour, and it was filled with cloud and rain, thunder and lightning. There was no way to tell the speed of the balloon except by radar fixes from the ground, but Ben knew, from radar data, that *Double Eagle* was flying almost exactly along its planned trajectory. Pushed along by very fast south and southwesterly winds below 5,000 feet, it was making almost forty miles an hour — an extraordinary speed for a balloon. Ben can do complicated sums in his head — multiply five- or six-digit numbers, spitting out the correct answer almost as fast as a calculator can do it. The trick pleases him. Now, in the glow of the instrument dials, he calculated that the balloon would reach the coast of Labrador in about twenty-four hours, with the storm still 140 miles to the west. Then the balloon would pivot right and climb in front of the ridge. That, at least, was the hope and the plan.

Back in Bedford, at Weather Services, the flight path of the balloon was being plotted on a chart. Doc Wiley and Rich Schwoebel were in touch by telephone with the control towers along the flight path, and they had a better idea than the balloonists of how splendid the flight profile looked. Doc Wiley, speaking to Ed Yost on the telephone, cried, "Man, Ed, old buddy, we're going like a speeding bullet. We're going to be there in three days!" Any good news was wonderful news to Doc. He kept remembering that the Nimbus transmitter had not been properly tested, that Max and Ben had not had the training they should have had on the radios, that too much had been left undone and unsaid. He thought that Ed Yost had thought them all mad, to go as they had gone. Yost deserved some good news. "Ed had kicked these guys out of the nest," says Doc, "and of course he felt responsible for them. He kept in real close touch with me on the phone." That Ed Yost was worried enough to let it show by making telephone calls did nothing to quiet Doc's nerves. But the atmosphere in the control center, in the flight's first hours, was happy. "Not euphoric, but happy," says Doc.

Bob Rice was elated by the wind velocity that pushed the balloon up the edge of the continent, but worried by the clouds that were forming over the mountains.

As fixes came in and were recorded on the chart, it became apparent that *Double Eagle* was headed directly for Mount Katahdin (5,268 feet), the highest mountain in Maine. Doc Wiley, who considered it part of his job to protect Pat Abruzzo and Patty Anderson from undue worry, tried to divert their attention from the red line on the map. But Pat and Patty read what was happening. Patty turned to Rich Schwoebel, and in her expression, a mixture of worry and, he thought, amused memories of earlier hairbreadth escapes by Max and Ben, he saw that she realized the danger.

"If that's a mountain or anything in the way," Patty said, "they'll hit it. I know they'll hit it!"

It was two o'clock in the morning, on Saturday, September 10, Max's birthday. He was sleeping peacefully with the zipper of his sleeping bag drawn down to let some of the heat of his body escape; Ben could hear the quiet sound of his friend's breathing. He had forgotten it was Max's birthday, though he still had the sweet taste of chocolate frosting on his teeth, and he promised himself that he would brush his teeth when he finished his watch.

The balloon, lifted by warm air associated with what was left of a warm front over central Maine, was flying at 2,700 feet. The clouds had closed in around the balloon and Ben could see nothing; even the supine figure of Max, a stride away on the floor of the gondola, was blurred by wisps of clouds. Visibility was zero.

Ben had a chart of Maine spread out on the deck above the radios, and he was talking to Bangor control. As Bangor gave him their speed and the direction of their flight from radar fixes, Ben, too, was drawing a red line from point to point along the chart; and at the same time that the people at Bedford saw Mount Katahdin looming up on the map, Ben realized that this peak must be dead ahead of the balloon. Mount Katahdin is a stone monolith, rising out of the deep woods of Baxter State Park like a half-buried Indian war ax. Two other mountains, North Brother, 4,143 feet in elevation, and North Turner, 3,323 feet, flank Katahdin to the west and east.

Ben had done a great deal of mountain flying — he had just won the first Pikes Peak balloon race, after all — but he had done most of it in the limpid, dry air of the Southwest, in daylight, where the eye could see for a hundred miles or more. Over foggy Maine, he couldn't see three feet, and he didn't know whether this moisture-laden air (he felt it on his skin, clammy and cold) would behave as desert air behaved. He knew *Double Eagle* was very close to the mountains. Should he fly on in hopes of missing their stony ribs, which could slash the envelope to shreds, or ballast off enough weight to rise to an altitude that would take them over the top?

There were dangers in the latter course — air flowing over a mountain often spills down the far side like a waterfall, creating what flyers call a rotor. *Double Eagle* could tumble down the other side of Mount Katahdin with Ben and Max inside like two men in a barrel going over Niagara. That would mean wasting more ballast to bring her back to altitude. They would be throwing away time — at least half a day, perhaps more.

Ben decided to wake Max. Neither man was captain, even on watch. All vital decisions would be taken by both men: they had equal amounts of money invested and an equal chance of dying should bad judgment kill them. This method of command by consultation arose from no formal agreement. It was the way they had always done things, and Ben did it now, over the Maine woods.

Max heard Ben's voice, calling him awake. He was deep in sleep and did not rouse easily. There was no note of urgency in Ben's words; he simply said, "Max, wake up." Max felt, inside the warm goose-down sleeping bag (*too* warm; he was sweating a little), that he was pulling himself back into the world. He had a brief dream, just before he woke, that he was climbing something, perhaps a rope, toward Ben. Then he was wide-awake. He felt utterly refreshed, and knew at once where he was. It surprised him, when he looked at his watch, that he had been asleep only two hours. He, too, forgot that it was his birthday. He was vaguely pleased with himself that he had looked without hesitation at the watch on his left wrist, which showed eastern daylight time. On his right wrist he wore a second watch, showing Greenwich mean time, the official time — "Zulu" time in aeronautical parlance — of the voyage.* Ben also wore two watches, and they had made jokes about getting the two mixed up because of their bad eyes.

Ben was talking on the radio to the control tower at Bangor. Max, pulling on his boots and shrugging into his jacket, paid no close attention to the squawking loudspeaker. For the first time it occurred

---

* Both *Double Eagle* flights were clocked according to Greenwich mean time, the standard measure of time for ships and aircraft. Greenwich mean time is the same as London standard time, which is four hours later than eastern daylight time. The balloonists and their ground crew used the term "Zulu time" to mean Greenwich mean time, and this usage has been retained in these pages. It would of course be difficult to gain a clear picture of time elapsed if "local" times were cited as the balloon moved across the ocean: it passed through five time zones. Zulu time uses the twenty-four-hour clock, dispensing with the terms A.M. and P.M. Thus 0000 is midnight, 1200 is noon, 1800 is six P.M., and so on.

to him that it would have been a good idea to bring along a couple of headsets — the noise of the radio might disturb Ben when he was off watch; Max knew his partner was a light sleeper.

"We've got a problem," Ben said. "We're completely blind. Bangor has lost us on radar because of the terrain features; we're flying under their screen. The last track they gave us showed us heading right for this." He tapped Mount Katahdin on the map.

"A mountain fifty-two hundred feet high?" said Max. "That's a big piece of rock."

"You'll think so if we hit it," said Ben.

Max and Ben knew what the options were. Both were reluctant to use ballast so early in the flight. Max, remembering the hurricane off Cape Hatteras, feared that they might be blown east, into the influence of that storm, if they flew higher. Rice had warned of that.

"I got a message from Rich," Ben said. "He says our track is good and we ought to stay low and avoid ballasting."

Rich Schwoebel had telephoned the Bangor tower, and he and Ben had talked to each other through the man on duty. It was a system that seemed to work well; throughout the early stages of the flight, Ben and Max were amazed and grateful over the willingness of air controllers and pilots to act as relay stations for their messages to base.

Schwoebel, after consultations with Rice, believed that air currents would carry the balloon *around* the mountain. The flow of air in mountains is such, says Bob Rice, that "in my opinion, you couldn't run into an isolated mountain with a balloon if you wanted to." On the night of September 10, that remained an untested theory, and he did not pass it on to Max and Ben.

Nevertheless, that was Max's opinion, and Ben's as well. Max reminded Ben that he, Max, had lost the Pikes Peak balloon race because he had delayed his ascent moments too long and got too close to the mountain. Instead of flying over the top, he had been caught in an air current that swept him around its side. Ben, burning gas and climbing while farther away from the peak, had risen above its summit before his balloon came under the influence of the winds that had captured Max.

Both men believed the same thing would happen at Mount Katahdin. If they stayed down, the winds would carry them past.

96

"I believe we can just do-si-do right through the passes," Max said.

"It *sounds* good," said Ben.

"If we're wrong, we're in for one hell of an anticlimax," Max replied.

Max laughed; he didn't know why. Hitting a mountain in the fog and cloud, he thought later, would have made a comical story. Such an accident would be bad luck. But plunging into the sea just off the coast would be bad flying. One was a joke, the other a disgrace.

Ben was rummaging around in the hold while Max had these thoughts, and when he straightened up he held a brass megaphone in his hands. It was the hailing horn from their boat, *Mariah,* and Ben had brought it along thinking that he might be able to talk to men on land, and perhaps to ships at sea. Lindbergh at one point had flown close to a fishing boat, turned off the engine of *The Spirit of St. Louis,* and shouted to an astonished but unhearing fisherman, "Which way is Ireland?" The idea of Ben's doing the same tickled Max. Ben thought it was a sensible precaution, bringing the hailing horn.

Now Ben, who is a yodeler of almost professional quality, clapped the hailing horn to his lips and began to yodel through it. He would yodel, pause and listen, move the horn, yodel again, pause and listen.

Max, watching the gondola lights glisten on the brass horn, waited for a period when Ben, head cocked, was listening.

"Ben, what the hell are you doing?"

"Yodeling. The sound bounces off the mountain. If my yodel comes back, we can count the number of seconds it takes and find out how close we are to Mount Katahdin." He waved the hailing horn. "This'll give us an edge on the SOB. We can go up before we hit anything."

Ben yodeled every few seconds for the next fifteen minutes. Both men listened as intently for the returning echo of his yodel, but neither heard it. At the end of a quarter hour, at about 0700 Zulu, almost seven hours into the flight, they decided that they had passed around the three peaks. They never saw them, but on the other side, the weather cleared, and Max, looking over the edge, saw the lights of a village in the vast dark woods. Consulting the map, he decided that the town must be Shin Pond, because he saw light glinting in a small body of water nearby.

Both Ben and Max felt that they had handled their first crisis as well as it could have been handled. Though they said nothing to each other about it, both liked the mild electricity that had resulted from rubbing intelligence and experience against risk and the unknown. They were reassured, too, that they had been able to consult Rich Schwoebel with such ease. If the radio system was going to work as well as that all the way across the Atlantic, they would have the continual benefit of Schwoebel's learning and judgment. They never doubted that the radios would work. Getting around Mount Katahdin and its sister peaks seemed a good omen.

Max suggested to Ben that he try to sleep. Without demur, Ben went aft and unrolled his sleeping bag. Max, remembering the yodeling, smiled as Ben, with the brisk movements that are so characteristic of him, put his feet into the sleeping bag, jerked it around him, and shut the long zipper so fast that it whistled. In moments, to the surprise of both men, Ben was asleep.

Max stowed the hailing horn and checked the instruments. The track was between 20 and 25 degrees true north — right on the money. The wind held steady, as Bob Rice had said it would, out of the south-southwest.

The sky was clear again; even the few scudding clouds that had hung around the north face of the invisible mountains had disappeared. Max thought that the enormous expanse of the North Woods was wonderful; he had never imagined that such a wilderness could exist in the overpopulated East. In the feeble light of the little moon, the myriad ponds beneath the balloon glittered like a handful of coins flung down on a rumpled velvet dress. Up above, the stars were out in their billions. Max drew in his breath at the beauty of the sight.

It was the last time he would see stars on this voyage.

8 Running silent, with all radios except the homing beacon switched off to conserve battery power, Max felt an occasional tremor run through his body. It was cold; the terrain over which they were passing seemed to radiate damp, frosty air upward. Max was catching his first scent of the tundra, and it was thrilling. Afterward, remembering the moment, he would wonder if the joy he felt in the predawn dimness of his forty-third birthday had anything to do with the Norse blood that ran in his veins, if the cold and the loneliness and the idea of a voyage over the sea stirred some racial memory deep within him.

His thoughts at the moment were entirely focused on the four-hundred-odd cubic feet within the gondola, and the balloon above it, drawing a mitten across the stars. He had no thoughts of the past or the future; only of the present moment. Ben slept peacefully; Max stooped to determine whether he could see Ben's breath, though the thermometer registered around forty degrees Fahrenheit. No cloud issued from Ben's mouth; that accorded with what Max had read on the instruments, but he was not prepared to trust instruments entirely. Already one of the VHF radios was acting badly. It had begun to sputter and fail even while they were over Boston Harbor. The other one seemed to work well.

At a little after 0800 Zulu, eight hours into the flight, the stars began to fade. Max remembered, with a twinge of annoyance, that he had neglected to take any star shots with the sextant. There had been no need to do so since *Double Eagle* had been receiving extremely accurate position reports from ground radar. That would end in a matter of hours, when the balloon crossed the coast and put out to sea. Max realized that he could have used the practice, and smiled to remember that the first shots he had taken in Albuquerque with the sextant had told him that he was standing near Phoenix, Arizona.

Double Eagle was at 2,800 feet or a little less, and from that altitude Max could see the first signs of dawn in the east. Amid the blacks and purples of the night, he discerned the shades of salmon that are the sailor's warning. That didn't surprise him, for Bob Rice had told him to expect rain as they passed into Labrador. He still believed, as Ben did, that in six or seven hours they would fly out of the bad weather that lay ahead, and that the sun, superheating the helium, would lift *Double Eagle* into a region of perpetual sunshine.

At about 0900 Zulu, nine hours into the flight, Max switched on the VHF transceiver. The crackle of the set awakened Ben, and Max heard him stirring behind him, wriggling out of his sleeping bag. The control tower at Loring Air Force Base, near Presque Isle, Maine, came on the air almost at once. The voice on the transmitter was strong and youthful, and, to Max's momentary surprise, female.

Abaft the balloon, Max saw a broad river glinting in the first light. He looked at the map and thought that it might be the St. John, which runs along the Canadian side of the Maine–New Brunswick line.

"Have we crossed into Canada?" Max asked the young airwoman.

"No, sir. You have about fifteen miles to go. Our radar shows you tracking over the ground at forty-five miles per hour."

"Terrific! Forty-five over the ground. Thank you, ma'am."

Once again, Ben and Max had a bit of fun with the ground station.

"You're a *balloon*, Double Eagle? You're flying to Europe, nonstop?"

The two men, chuckling with the good feeling that it gave them to chat with a girl as they woke up, checked their maps again. They decided that the river they had seen was the Aroostook, a tributary of the St. John. Both were anxious to cross over into Canadian territory. Max thought, Once that happens, the international leg begins; the Atlantic is next, and we're going for it.

At 1020 Zulu, more than ten hours into the flight, *Double Eagle* crossed the St. John River near Grand Isle, on the northernmost tip of Maine. Max broke out the Canadian flag. Ten minutes later, the nearest Canadian air traffic controller passed on a message from Bedford. Bob Rice estimated the velocity of winds at 7,000 to 8,000 feet to be fifty knots (57.5 miles an hour), at 230 degrees — a remarkable speed and precisely the right trajectory. Rich Schwoebel added, "Altitude increase with sunrise will be satisfactory and no additional ballast recommended."

This news cheered them. Ben had long since recovered from the fleeting sadness of the liftoff, and once again he loved the idea of the flight. He was puzzled that the balloon was not climbing more swiftly, especially in the light of Rich Schwoebel's reassurances. Evidently Rice and Schwoebel expected *Double Eagle* to go to at least 7,000 feet during the morning. That had not yet begun to happen, though the sun had been showing its full disk above the horizon for about half an hour.

There were clouds below the balloon, and to the west for the first time they saw cirrus clouds — it was the storm system Bob Rice had described to them. Ben got out his camera and took some pictures of it. They sipped hot chocolate, heated on their camp stove, and ate some cereal. Their milk, stowed with their other perishables in picnic ice chests, was cold; Max had another piece of cake but did not quite finish it. Neither man felt hungry; Max supposed it was the excitement, the adrenalin.

The storm to the west did not trouble them. They knew it would be there. Canadian air control gave them more radar fixes, and Max, laying their course on the map, measured and remeasured their progress with calipers. They were well ahead of schedule. If they were going to climb into a fifty-knot wind they would outrun the storm with ease.

While Ben was taking his photographs, Max spotted the first visitor of the flight, a single-engine Cessna. The plane flew to within a mile of the balloon, and the pilot, putting down his flaps, hung the little aircraft on its propeller. Max supposed he was taking pictures. He scanned the horizon for some glimpse of the CBS helicopter. Before leaving Marshfield, the producer, Ed Gorin, had told them that the helicopter would fly by and film *Double Eagle* early in the morning. Max had been amused at how many times Gorin had warned Max and Ben not to wave at the television camera.

Stephanie Anderson Nennicker had made signs that said HELLO, MOM, and HELLO, ED, and WHICH WAY PARIS? and WHICH WAY TO BEER?" Max had them ready in the gondola, and could hardly wait to flash them. But, owing to the danger posed by the approaching storm, the helicopter from CBS never appeared. It was a disappointment; Stephanie and Max would not have their joke, and Max is not a man who likes to deny his only daughter the things she enjoys.

As *Double Eagle* progressed northeast across New Brunswick toward the Gulf of St. Lawrence, Ben was once again in less jovial spirits than Max. It seemed to him, gazing at the high cirrus to the west through binoculars, that the weather was gaining on them. Also, for the first time, *Double Eagle* was not behaving as theory said it should. The sun was shining on the envelope — on the black cone, designed to absorb heat. Ben checked the thermometer and saw that the temperature had risen some three degrees. That should be the equivalent of sixty pounds of ballast, and *Double Eagle* should be commencing a steep climb. Yet by 1105 Zulu, more than an hour after full sunrise, and the eleventh hour of the flight, the balloon had climbed only 200 feet, to 3,000 feet, and was venting a little helium.

Ben put his head overside and inhaled the escaping gas. This has a comical effect on the human speech apparatus, and when Ben turned to talk to Max, he sounded like Donald Duck.

"We ought to be getting more superheat, Max."

"We're getting it," said Max reassuringly. He tapped the altimeter glass. "We're climbing." He showed Ben the map; Ben had already memorized it, but he looked again. "There's rising terrain ahead, so the timing is good," said Max.

Max noticed a sawmill below in the woods, with golden sawdust lying all around it, and great stacks of logs and lumber. It seemed to him a beautiful sight. He looked forward to seeing the Gaspé Mining Company on the Gaspé Peninsula; he calculated that their track would take them right over this famous installation at about noon. Because it was Saturday, there was virtually no work going on below, and the vast country was silent and empty. Where the leaves in Massachusetts had still been green, here in New Brunswick the maples were touched with scarlet and the birches with gold.

At 1145 Zulu, *Double Eagle* passed over Campbellton, New

Brunswick, and crossed Chaleur Bay onto the Gaspé Peninsula. The balloon was still at 3,000 feet, but soon afterward, venting helium, it rose to 3,600 feet. The sun, obscured by windblown clouds, had begun at last to lift the balloon; there may, too, have been some heat rising from the surface of the bay.

The Gaspé Peninsula is mountainous, with ranges of hills running east and west like the long rib cage of this remote and empty land. *Double Eagle*, though the altimeter read 3,600 feet, was actually only some 1,700 feet above the mountains — altimeters register the height above sea level, not the distance above a land mass. The balloon was not far from the Gaspé Mining Company, and Max was looking eagerly around the horizon, trying to spot it.

The balloon fell out from under them.

Ben said calmly, "We're in a down."

Ben watched the instruments. He called off the rate of descent: 300 feet per minute. That meant they would hit the ground in a little over five minutes if the balloon maintained that rate of descent. Both Ben and Max knew the laws of inertia — the balloon, all three tons of it, if it continued to fall, would fall faster.

Ben heard a flapping sound above him and looked up, wondering if somehow a strip of fabric had been ripped from the balloon. The two flags — the Stars and Stripes and the Canadian maple leaf, were standing straight out. Ben thought: That's a good thing to know, that the flags flap when we go down. It's kind of an alarm signal. Then he thought, Ride it out; the balloon will recover. Ballast only if absolutely necessary.

Ben and Max did not understand what was happening. Because they were so close to the terrain they had, for the first time, a physical sensation. Max felt his stomach rise, as if he were in a fast elevator. Ben, looking down, saw the trees rushing upward; with each passing second, more detail became visible to him. It was something like crashing the hang-glider into the house: he saw branches now, he would see leaves in a matter of moments, and then he would see veins in the leaves and the texture of the bark. By then, *Double Eagle* would be lost. They were going to crash. Such a thing wasn't supposed to be possible, but Ben knew it was happening, and so did Max.

The altimeter was unwinding now at a rate of 500 feet per minute, and increasing. Ben cut loose a bag of sand hanging from the side of the gondola and they heard it crash with a splintering noise in the trees below, followed by the impact, a second later, of a second bag cut loose by Max. The descent slowed. Ben and Max, more cautious of their ballast now, poured sand over the side.

The balloon by now was very nearly into the trees. They had fallen almost 2,000 feet, into a ravine between two spiny ridges. The descent had taken less than four minutes.

Double Eagle reached equilibrium — that is, stopped — less than a hundred feet from the treetops. It started back upward, after a pause and a barely perceptible bounce, like a yo-yo at the end of its string.

As the balloon rose, Ben and Max heard a tearing sound beneath the gondola. *Double Eagle* hesitated, then surged upward. The ripping sound beneath was deafening. It sounded to Max as if a branch were being torn from a tree, and with his keen sense of smell he detected the odor of crushed vegetation and of sap running from a break in a limb.

Ben said, "It's the homing beacon antenna!" And when he looked over the side, he saw that several yards of the antenna cable had been ripped off and left behind, tangled in the splintered branches of a treetop.

Relieved of all that ballast — Ben and Max had already calculated that they had thrown over 120 pounds of sand — *Double Eagle* ascended rapidly.

Max said, "I wonder what the hell *that* was."

"I don't know." Ben was busily checking for damage, and anxiously watching the altimeter. He feared that the balloon, relieved of so much ballast, would rise too high; he believed more than ever in her sensitivity.

"You know, Ben, I believe that was some kind of rotor."

Ben thought, and nodded. They had been in scores of rotors in hot-air balloons, usually after flying over the crest of a mountain. The air on the other side, flowing over the peak, caused a whirlwind. A hot-air balloon, in such conditions, whirls like a top, gondola swinging, and can be brought under control by burning gas. *Double Eagle* had fallen straight down, as if a shaft had opened beneath it.

They climbed quickly to 4,000 feet and held that altitude. Max judged their speed over the ground to be what it had been — forty miles an hour or better. The weak sun was no help to them; plainly, they weren't going to attain their planned altitude of 7,000 feet by noon.

In fact, with the sun directly overhead, and shining on the reflective silver top of *Double Eagle*, the balloon seemed to be sinking slightly. That, too, was a mystery.

Ben pulled the homing beacon aboard and discovered that they had lost about twenty feet of it, together with the lead fishing weight that had been attached to its end to keep it perpendicular. There seemed to be no other damage. Ben began to repair the antenna. Without it, no aircraft or ground station could home on them by radio. Radio was, of course, their means of calling for help in case of disaster. And the notion of disaster, after what had just happened to them, did not seem so remote as it had only a few hours before, at sunrise. To the west, the cirrus that marked the storm front kept approaching.

Max worked at the VHF transceiver. He wanted to reach Bedford and talk to Rice and Schwoebel. There must be an explanation for what had happened. Ben, working with flying hands on the damaged antenna, watched the weather to the west and the dials of the instruments with equal attention. He wondered if Max, who seemed so cool, realized how close they had come to a crash. Max, owing to the loss of his eye, has faulty depth perception, *zero* depth perception in Ben's opinion. He had seen Max hit the ground before with a total lack of concern. Guts played a part in Max's sangfroid, but so did the fact that he did not know he was on the deck until he hit it.

"Kind of an exciting few minutes," said Max. Ben made no reply.

Double Eagle flew steadily for fifteen minutes, and the northern coastline of the Gaspé Peninsula came into sight, with a blacktop road winding along its cliffs. Directly ahead, Max saw a car on the road; the vehicle was slowing down, its driver having spotted the balloon.

Double Eagle began to fall again. From 4,000 feet, it dropped at a rate of at least 500 feet per minute. Max and Ben ballasted off more cautiously this time, waiting till the last possible moment to see if the balloon would recover by itself; they hated to give up ballast, to throw away time. They were in sight of the sea — the

Gulf of St. Lawrence was less than five miles away. The terrain ahead rose steeply, and each had the same thought: we're in a rotor wave, it will lift us over the rising land. But they were falling so fast that Max thought he could hear the wind of their passage in the trees a hundred feet below the keels of the gondola, which was traveling forward at forty miles an hour even as it fell toward the earth, and he cut loose a bag of sand.

As Max let go the sandbag, he saw that the car he had noticed earlier was parked on the coastal highway directly in the path of the balloon. The driver stood beside his automobile, with a camera lifted to his eye. Max watched the sandbag falling, plummeting nose-first like a bomb, and it seemed to him that it was going to make a direct hit on the motorist. He shouted a warning. Ben, meanwhile, had jettisoned a second sandbag, and it, too, was plunging toward the man and his car. It was a brand-new car — Max noticed that.

The motorist must have seen the objects falling toward him because he snatched open the door of his car, leaped in, and sped away. Max and Ben heard the screech of his tires and the changing of gears as the automobile careened around the curves of the highway.

Double Eagle recovered and climbed, lifted on the wind flowing up the mountains ahead, as its pilots had anticipated.

"I think we're all right now, Ben," said Max.

"Let me compute the ballast," Ben said. "We used a hundred and twenty pounds that time. This has got to stop."

The balloon crossed the coast at an altitude of about 1,000 feet, and as it passed over the edge of the land it went into another sickening plunge. Max had the feeling that they had fallen off the cliff. The fall this time seemed uncontrollable, and Ben and Max ballasted off furiously, cutting loose sandbags. The balloon stopped within 150 feet of the water.

Double Eagle rose sluggishly. Though they did not immediately notice it, Ben and Max had flown beneath a solid cloud deck. As no sun penetrated the clouds, none could heat the helium and add lift to the balloon.

Max said, "Oh, Christ. I wonder how many more of these are coming. This is eating up our ballast at a hell of a rate."

"It sure is," said Ben grimly. He marked the amount thrown overboard on his chart; it was vital to keep accurate records.

Ahead, they could see Anticosti Island, a long green strip of land lying diagonally across the mouth of the St. Lawrence River. Max saw two ships ahead, one leaving the river and the other entering.

"We were going down at at least seven hundred feet per minute on that last one," Ben said.

Max switched on the marine-band radio to the emergency frequency and tried to contact the ships. One of them, the freighter *Akron,* came on immediately.

"Are you in distress?" asked the freighter's radioman, in a heavy Hispanic accent.

"Can you see us?" Max asked. The radioman confirmed that he had the balloon in sight. "If we get in any trouble we'll call you. We've passed through a pretty rough period, but it seems like we're back in control of the airship."

Double Eagle was back at 1,000 feet and scudding over the water at thirty-five knots (forty miles an hour). *Akron* was capable, Max judged, of no more than fifteen knots, so he counted little on help from the ship. They would simply run away from her.

The balloon went into a fourth down, and this time, despite frantic ballasting, both men were certain that they were going into the gulf. Max thought: I hope to hell we don't hit the water because that will show up on the barograph and it may disqualify us for the record. You're supposed to stay in the air the whole way across the Atlantic. (The barograph, carried on all record-seeking flights, is an automatic recording barometer activated by clockwork; a stylus marks a constant trace of the aircraft's altitude and time of flight on a revolving drum.)

When the plunge stopped, the gondola was no more than eighty feet above the water. The sound of the sea and its smell, a mixture of salt and oil and other matter disgorged by the river and by passing ships, was very strong.

Ben and Max put out two trail ropes. The ropes would prevent the gondola from broaching if they did go into the water. Without the ropes, the gondola might go in sidewise, scooping up water like a cup on a string — not a pretty prospect. They almost decided not to deploy the ropes for fear they might become tangled with the radio antennas hanging below the gondola.

A few minutes later, the balloon crossed the coast of Anticosti Island. They were at minimum altitude, under 1,000 feet, and the

107

balloon immediately went into a mild down. Max and Ben did nothing to correct it, and soon the craft began to climb again. Ahead of them, over the island, they saw rain falling. Ben rummaged around in the storage space and unpacked the rain skirt, a sailcloth cover for the gondola that was their only protection from the elements.

At this point they heard a mild pattering sound.

"What's that?" Ben asked.

"I hear it. I don't know."

Ben listened, meanwhile trying to unfold the pink rain skirt with Max's help; it was a difficult task in the narrow confines of the gondola. Ben looked upward at the envelope, now a little slack because of the helium that had been vented earlier in the day.

"It must be the helium inside the envelope," he said.

Max paid no attention. He was absorbed with the rain skirt. But the sound they heard was not helium. It was a misting rain, striking the envelope. In a moment or two, Max felt wetness on his face, and he opened his bag, in which Patty had so carefully packed his changes of clothes in waterproof plastic, and smiled when he found that she had even sealed up his poncho in this way. He put on the poncho and a sheepskin hat.

Ben, struggling with the rain skirt, was wearing the great puffy goose-down parka that Max had seen him wear many times when they skied together. Because the parka was made of a shiny material, Max had assumed that it was waterproof. So had Ben. His parka had protected him from snow in the Sandias, and he assumed that it would shed the misting rain for the few minutes it took to install the rain cover. But the installation took longer than a few minutes.

The rain grew heavier. Ben and Max struggled with the rain skirt. They did not know how to put it up; Ed Yost had never had time to tell them. By the time they figured out how to attach it to the load ring and spread it, like a tent, to the rim of the gondola, they had spent an hour and a half in a driving rain.

Max, in his poncho and his sheepskin hat, was dry. Ben's goose-down clothes, despite what Max had assumed, were not waterproof, and he was soaked to the skin. He felt terribly cold, but he did not mention this to Max, and Max did not notice. He was talking into the tape recorder they had brought along to record their thoughts and their conversations.

"After forty-five minutes over the water, hanging on to survive and throwing over all kinds of stuff, it's become so quiet and peaceful we don't know how to act," Max was saying. "We've put up the pink rain skirt . . . and are kinda going along fat, dumb, and happy. Our number one beacon is eating power."

Ben, in the pink glow cast by light falling through the rain skirt, was trying to discover why the beacon was draining its batteries at such a rate. He decided to shut it off, to save power.

They had a talk about their situation. Ben thought that by falling below the clouds the balloon had experienced the equivalent of a sunset. Max agreed.

Ben asked, "You don't think we'll get any superheat the rest of the day?"

"No, I don't."

As they spoke, it was just before noon, local time, or 1500 Zulu — fifteen hours into the flight.

"Then we're going to have to make a tough decision as to our weight and ballast," said Ben. "We'll have to reconsider our total ballast and the weather situation. There's a cold front moving up the bay."

Ben was already wet and cold. His voice had lost some of its firm timbre. Again, Max did not notice, but he was surprised when Ben, in the next breath, made a mistake in arithmetic. He had never known him to do such a thing, in all the hundreds of hours they had spent facing each other across card tables and backgammon boards.

Ben said, "It's fifteen hundred Zulu into the next day, so we've been flying nineteen hours, is that correct?"

"No, Ben," Max replied gently. "It's fifteen hours."

Ben studied both his watches, then nodded.

"We took off at eight, went to twelve, went twelve more to this point in time — fifteen hours. Right."

Max suggested that they eat. He had been munching cake most of the morning, and so had Ben, but they had had nothing warm. Ben nodded his agreement. Rain was still drumming on the rain skirt; as it had no windows they couldn't look out; they knew they were somewhere over eastern Quebec, approaching the southern border of Labrador.

Max put some soup on the stove and noted how calmly the liquid lay in the pan; it might have been sitting on the burner in his kitchen in Albuquerque.

"We're very stable now, Ben," he said.

Max spoke into the radio and contacted Gander control. With Ben feeding him the data concerning ballast, he passed this message to Bedford: "We have offloaded fourteen hundred pounds and are now under clouds at fifteen hundred feet."

The meaning of the figures registered on Max as he spoke them. They had started with thirty-four hundred pounds of ballast — enough, they thought, to survive seven sunsets. Fifteen hours into the flight, without having passed through even one true sunset, they had lost more than forty percent of their ballast. The four great downs over the Gaspé Peninsula and the Gulf of St. Lawrence had cost them three days of flying time.

The real meaning of what Ben had said earlier about making "a tough decision as to our weight and ballast" flashed for the first time across Max's conscious mind. Ben was saying, calmly and professionally, that they might have to abort the flight, bring *Double Eagle* down before they reached the Atlantic.

Max again contacted Gander air control. The radio operator gave them their position and speed. He asked the usual question: "What are you?" Max told him. "Understand, Polaris Double Eagle. You are a Polaris missile. Roger, Roger." Ben and Max guffawed — *Double Eagle* was the slowest "missile" in the history of flight.

Max asked for the weather report for Goose Bay and eastbound.

A cold front was moving into the Goose Bay area. There were embedded cumulus — thunderstorms — behind the front. The ceiling was going to zero-zero; wind speed sixty miles an hour; freezing level, 6,000 feet.

"Oh, dandy," said Max. "Do you have a telephone? Will you call our base at Bedford, Massachusetts, and give them that weather report, sir? Call collect."

"That fellow just gave me," said Max to Ben, "the worst weather report I have ever heard since I started flying, and I got my pilot's license twenty-eight years ago today."

Ben took over the microphone. The radio was malfunctioning — incoming messages were garbled and their transmissions were barely understood at the other end. Ben contacted Goose Center — the air traffic control tower at Goose Bay, Labrador. The tower asked, over and over, for their position and condition. Ben, over and over, responded. The tower could not hear him.

110

Finally Ben said, "Oh, shit! This is Fifty Double Eagle. Condition okay." To Max he said, "They'll get the message back to Schwoebel."

Max finished his cooking. Ben did not eat much. Max wondered, in passing, if Ben had remembered to take his blood-pressure medicine. He did not feel that he ought to mention it.

Max said, "If we don't get back in the sun, it's going to be bad."

In the Bedford control center, Rich Schwoebel and Bob Rice and Doc Wiley read the message from *Double Eagle* describing its series of downs over the Gaspé Peninsula and the Gulf of St. Lawrence, and they could not forgive their own lack of foresight.

"Here we were, a bunch of pilots," says Schwoebel. "We simply ignored the terrain conditions. I couldn't believe that *all* of us had missed this."

No one had reported, in the scientific literature, the effect that had nearly crashed *Double Eagle*, but it was known to exist. The ground crew had been reading charts, not topographical maps. They had simply forgot to warn Ben and Max that they would almost surely hit rotors as they passed over a steep coastline in a high wind.

"That got by me," says Bob Rice. "We were looking at the high winds as benevolent — look how fast they're going, get 'em out in front of the cold front. Doc is a sailplane pilot. He knows all this stuff, and I should, too. I just wish I'd told them to fly higher — to be ready for it."

Rice believed, and still believes, that if the balloon had been flying higher as it crossed the Gaspé Peninsula it would have been all right. It still would have encountered rotors, but it would have had many thousands of feet of open space beneath it, and it would have ridden the torrent of air down and then up again with no loss of ballast. It would have been a fun-house ride instead of a terrifying experience.

To Doc Wiley, the message after the Gaspé downs was the first rude awakening of the flight. "Maxie said they had severe damage and might have to ditch," Doc recalls. "We were apprehensive until we got the data on ballast. That was the first hollow feeling; I still have it in my stomach. They were having a hard go. We knew they were wet, we knew they were cold, we knew they were in severe weather, and communications eventually degraded into nothing. I was telling the wives none of this." Doc began calling his friends in the military rescue service, just to keep in touch.

Bob Rice was not alarmed by the first reports of rain. This had been forecast. The balloon was flying so fast that the loss of ballast was not, in Rice's view, critical. Rich Schwoebel agreed. On September 11, he estimated that *Double Eagle* could stay aloft for five days, total.

At 1345 Zulu on September 10, Bedford had sent Ben and Max a message, giving wind speeds at selected altitudes (fifty to sixty miles an hour from 4,000 feet up to 10,000 feet, and right on track). "Estimate your position at east coast of Labrador north of Belle Isle at twenty-one hundred Zulu. Expect clouds and possible precipitation. Daytime altitudes below seven thousand feet are desirable. Altitudes of approximately seven thousand feet may be desirable in evening and we will advise."

Pat Abruzzo and Patty Anderson were busy in the control center, talking to reporters. Photogenic, blond, fluent, comfortable in the confident affections of their long marriages, they were splendid interviews. Jim Mitchell, quiet in the background, drafted press releases that gave the exact track of *Double Eagle*. To look at the chart with its red track running northward to its rendezvous with the high-pressure center over Labrador, it looked as though *Double Eagle* were flying a perfect mission. The chart did not show mountains and rain, or give off the smell of wet goose down.

Ben and Max had received this message from Bedford, relayed through Gander control: "It is a local weather phenomenon you are experiencing. Ignore local weather."

"Ignore local weather!" Ben expostulated. "We're flying blind in the middle of a goddamn cloudburst! How are we supposed to ignore local weather?"

Inside his soaked clothing, Ben was shuddering. The goose down had lost all its insulating qualities; it gave off an odor like that of a wet chicken. Max noticed the smell, but not Ben's distress. Max himself was warm; the thermometer stood just below fifty degrees Fahrenheit.

Ben had put on his foul-weather gear over his wet clothes. The rubberized jacket and trousers did not fit properly, and the rain seeped in around the neck and the waist. Inside the poreless material, Ben sweated, and his sweat turned as cold as the rainwater. Logic said that a man, heavily dressed and in good physical shape, could not be in danger under such conditions. Nevertheless, Ben Abruzzo was beginning to freeze to death.

Ben was in control of his thoughts and actions. He was a little irritable — "hot," as Ben would himself express it, but under the circumstances that was understandable.

The rain slackened as *Double Eagle* crossed Labrador. Max lifted the rain skirt and looked down. The landscape below was one of the most beautiful he had ever seen — green as a bowling lawn, dotted by sparkling glacial lakes and what seemed to Ben and Max to be hundreds of tumultuous rivers. "Every one of the rivers had a waterfall," says Ben, "and we could hear every one of them."

In addition to all this beauty, there were rocks, huge outcroppings, all over the terrain. Ben and Max had been talking about the possibility of making a landing, aborting the flight.

They were flying at sixty miles an hour at 3,600 feet through the last gray light of the day; it was about 2300 Zulu, and Ben and Max had been in the air for twenty-three hours.

Max said, "Ben, if we've got any second thoughts, we'd better have 'em right now."

Ben, looking down at the lakes, wondered if any of them was large enough to take the balloon. He did not think so.

Neither did Max. He studied the rocks, the great expanses of stunted pine trees, the roaring white rivers.

"I don't think we can land this thing on this kind of terrain, Ben," he said. "Our only option would be to put it down on the coast."

"In the open sea," Ben said.

"We might pass over Goose Bay itself. There's sheltered water there."

"That would mean a night landing in the water," Ben said.

They dropped the subject. Both men knew that the chances of putting *Double Eagle* down safely at night near the shore, with winds sixty miles an hour blowing on the surface, were nonexistent.

114

They had crossed the southern coast of Labrador at 1,000 feet, but warming air had gradually lifted the balloon to its present altitude. On the map, Max noted that a mountain 3,900 feet high lay dead ahead of them. They ballasted off frugally and rose to 4,000 feet. Max had thought again about the ballast situation; it no longer worried him. At their present speeds, he was sure they could make Europe. Ben had long before made the same calculation: he knew the weight of every item aboard, and he was ready to throw everything overboard — radios, batteries, C rations, instruments.

Max said, "There'll be no star sights tonight." They were in solid overcast — the zero-zero conditions forecast were closing down.

Max said, "Ben, I think I'll get a little sleep now. Call me after awhile and I'll take the helm."

It was then about 1030 Zulu, and *Double Eagle*, flying at sixty miles an hour on a course of 60 degrees, would cross the coast in about two hours.

Max lay down in his sleeping bag. The sleeves of his black ski suit had got wet while he was working on the rain skirt, but the rest of his body had been protected by his poncho. He thought, as he drifted off: It's very important not to get wet. I only have one other suit and my lightweight parka. Max fell almost at once into a deep sleep.

Ben was wide-awake and fully alert, but he was still very cold. He studied the chart of the Atlantic. Max had found it, with the other maps Doc Wiley had given him before takeoff, just before he went to sleep. While they were discussing the possibility of ditching, Ben had said, "Where's the map?"

"What map?"

"What map? Max, the map of the Atlantic Ocean!"

Max didn't know. Had it even been brought aboard? Ben felt gall squirting into his middle as Max spoke. Earlier, when they had been redeploying the homing beacon, Gander had asked them for the frequency on which the beacon broadcast. Max looked puzzled. Ben was working furiously — he was the one with the good hands — on the antenna.

"Where the hell would I find the damn thing, Ben?" Max asked, mildly, as if nothing mattered less in the world than their homing beacon.

"It's in your flight manual, Max! The frequency sheet! Don't let it get away from you."

Max found the manual after a long fumbling search through his flight bag. Into the radio, still calm, he said, "Gander, our beacon frequency is 1677."

"Turn it on!" said Ben. Max did so.

They had gone through the same routine with the Atlantic charts. How could they fly the Atlantic without charts? Their loss would be a disaster, Ben realized that; but Max was unperturbed. Finally they found them, jammed out of sight under the foredeck, behind the radios.

By now, Ben's irritation had subsided. It was raining hard, and water had poured into the gondola through the opening at the load ring. The rainwater gathered in the bottom of the gondola, on the undecked half. It occurred to Ben that, for all the discomfort the rain was causing, it was also a blessing. It could be used for ballast. A quart of water weighed two pounds, and from the look of the deck, there was at least one hundred pounds of water inside the craft. The envelope, instead of acting as an umbrella, acted as a great funnel, with the rainwater running down its sides and swirling into the opening around the load ring. It splashed over Ben's clothes and soaked through them. By the time he put on his slicker, he was wet to the skin. It was like sitting under a waterfall, he was to say later.

When Ben took the watch, *Double Eagle* was a hundred miles west of Goose Bay, at 5,400 feet, and she was climbing slowly despite the added weight of the accumulated rainwater. Ben used the radio — he had clear communications with Gander — and talked through the tower radio operator to Schwoebel and Rice. There was a solid cloud deck below the balloon at 5,000 feet and another above it at 8,000 feet. Visibility was good between decks, and Bedford advised Ben to fly between the layers. Rice had warned him that the freezing level, once over the Atlantic, could be as low as 5,000 feet. That concerned Ben. It had always concerned him. Ed Yost may have said that balloons will not ice, but Ben now believed that any aircraft would ice if it flew through icing conditions. He expected to cross the coast at midnight Zulu; Max would still be asleep at that hour.

At 0050 Zulu, in the black of night, *Double Eagle* crossed the coast of Labrador, just south of Goose Bay, and entered the Atlantic

Ocean. For the previous fifteen minutes, Ben had heard the waves crashing against the shore. They sounded to him like hundreds of locomotives, like the shriek of steel parts, as if the ocean were some great machine battering the land. The sound grew louder as the balloon flew on and when it was at its most intense, Ben had the feeling that the balloon must be much lower than the altimeter said, because it sounded as though the waves were inside the gondola with him. He lifted the rain skirt and looked down. Five thousand feet below, the coastline stretched away, a great soapy line of angry froth, with waves leaping into the air. The shore was phosphorescent, glowing; Ben remembered all the dreams he had had about the sea. Max was sleeping peacefully. Ben decided not to wake him; it was the greatest moment of the voyage, and would always remain so in Ben's mind. He let Max sleep.

Huddled inside his slicker, Ben sat down and spoke quietly into the tape recorder. After twenty-five hours aloft, there was deep fatigue in his voice; he was panting and snuffling.

"We've had a fearful night," he said, speaking as softly as he could so as not to disturb Max. "It's been raining for seven hours. I'm wearing my slicker, thermal boots, my down clothing. It's fifty degrees Fahrenheit. We're soaking wet.

"We made the decision three hours ago to go for it and now there's no turning back. The coast is behind us. Present altitude is fifty-three hundred feet — just a little higher than we wanted to be to stay out of the freezing level. We've let the water come in for later use as ballast. We've finally stabilized after a terrible series of ups and downs over the mainland.

"At Goose Bay it was very difficult not to try landing. There was a very large lake we could have made a letdown into. Our decision was made, however, to go on.

"Max is sound asleep and has been for an hour now. He's smart enough to know that we have to have our rest and he's able to go off to sleep quickly. I'm not so fortunate. My sleep has been fitful. First night, I slept well on the first watch but have had no sleep since.

"It's now 0100 Zulu. Starting to rain again. Temperature constant at fifty degrees. Altitude steady at fifty-two hundred. Level and finally smoothed out. No radio contact for two hours. Decided to conserve batteries and get some rest and peace, if possible."

Ten minutes later, Ben decided to look out and see what was going on. He gazed down at the raging sea, a mile below; rain froze to his face, stinging the skin.

He told the tape recorder, "It scared hell out of me."

Ben, though his mind was almost supernaturally clear and quick, and he was in complete command of the balloon, knew that he was approaching total exhaustion. As Max slept in his unstirring way, Ben could not even imagine himself asleep. He struggled to remember what it was like to fall asleep, as if this were a lost skill he must recover.

At 0200 Zulu, Ben awakened Max and asked him to take over the watch. He described the look of the coast as *Double Eagle* crossed it, and the roar of the surf. "I almost woke you, so you could see it," Ben said.

Max could hear the ocean below. "I'm glad you didn't," he said. He put his hand against the rain skirt. "We're in a full storm," he said. "I wonder if they realize we don't run off and leave these damn storms."

"I don't know," Ben said, and his voice was weary. "We'll see tomorrow."

Ben lay down in his wet clothes. Max sat in one of the lawn chairs Patty had borrowed at Marshfield, his head resting on the instrument panel. How pleasant this is, he thought, how really pleasant. He looked forward to daylight, so that he could see what was going on outside the balloon. After a time the rain abated, but he left the rain skirt down because it made the gondola warmer; Max supposed that was because some of the body heat radiated by him and by Ben was trapped inside. It was warmer now than it had been when Max went to sleep; he felt comfortable. It did not occur to him that Ben could be suffering: it was warm, the rain had stopped, they were flying on track. Max was very glad to be where he was.

First light came at 0430 Zulu. Max got out the stove and made some hot chocolate and fried some ham. Max ate an orange. Ben ate with an effort. Neither man wanted any of the fruit juices or water they carried. Max had not drunk a Dr Pepper for twenty-four hours, a personal record for a man who consumes a half-dozen large bottles of this soft drink daily.

Max enjoyed the pink glow cast by the feeble sun through the soaked rain skirt. At 0630 Zulu, Max lifted the rain skirt and looked out. The clouds were breaking. He thought, By golly, I guess Bob and Rich were right! The flight was in its thirty-first hour.

As soon as the sun touched the balloon, it started to climb. The rate of climb amazed Max. In no time *Double Eagle* rose from 5,000 feet to 8,500 feet. Max and Ben knew that if they kept climbing they would break through the long invisible slope of the high-pressure ridge and leave the storm below them. The right things, the predicted things, were happening at last. All during the climb, they could hear the sea below them. Ben remembered asking the TWA pilot, on his way back from the Mediterranean, what the sea looked like from the air; the pilot had replied that he was always too high to see anything but tiny whitecaps. If I ever talk to that guy, I'll tell him what it's like, Ben thought. It sounds like somebody has put all the hungry lions in the world into one big cage, and they're right below our tightrope. He hoped the TWA pilot would be in the air during the flight of *Double Eagle*, so that he could tell him that. They had talked to a number of airliners during the night and morning.

As they rose into the sunlight, they hung some of their clothes on the load ring, hoping that they would dry. As the balloon climbed, the temperature, of course, dropped. At 8,600 feet it was slightly below freezing. At about noon, Ben had to move his bowels; he had felt the need for some time, but had delayed the act because he did not want to remove his clothes. Now he could wait no longer.

Ben had to strip to the skin. Under his sopping down jacket and overalls, he wore a one-piece flight suit and long underwear. All this clothing was soaked, and all of it had to be removed completely. When he sat down on the teetering camp stool he was naked. The temperature was low enough, Max noticed, that he could see Ben's breath; his friend was panting and shuddering.

For the first time, Max realized that something was amiss with Ben. He looked at his clothing and saw how wet it was. He said, "Ben, maybe you ought to put on some different clothes."

Ben rummaged in his bag and found a towel — apart from one sleeping bag, the last dry item Ben had aboard. He scrubbed his damp gooseflesh with the rough towel, trying to bring some blood to the surface and warm himself. He clenched his jaws in an attempt to keep his teeth from chattering. The air, cold as it was, was a warmer garment than his soaked clothing. Ben had to dress himself again in the clothes he had just taken off. His skin felt clammy and raw, and the drenched synthetic fabric touching his body was as cold as marble in winter. Ben said nothing about his discomfort. He moved as briskly as he could, going about his tasks, keeping control. But he could not move very quickly. His water-soaked clothes were as heavy as diver's weights, and Ben would stumble because his mind flew ahead of him faster than his muscles could move.

The radio came to life. A U.S. Air Force C-141 was flying a practice mission on *Double Eagle:* Doc Wiley's work. A youthful tenor, dead serious after the relaxed mature voices from the overflying airliners, identified the military aircraft as "MAC Zero One Zero." He told Max that he was in contact with Gander, which had messages from Bedford.

Double Eagle's position, as reported by the Nimbus satellite, was latitude 56.2 degrees north, longitude 45.5 degrees west: immediately south of the tip of Greenland.

"We have you making forty-two knots [forty-eight miles an hour] over the ground, and you are on track."

Ben guffawed. Only an hour or so before, he had calculated their position, doing the math in his head, and come up with the same position.

"On track?" said Max to MAC Zero One Zero. "I didn't bring my polar-bear gun. We prefer this altitude. We want to know if we stay at this altitude can we reach Paris."

Ben, panting and gasping as he struggled back into his clothes, gave another laugh. "Not if we can *survive,* but can we reach Paris," he chortled.

It was raining again, torrents of rain beating on the envelope and the rain skirt, swirling into the gondola. There was no way to keep it out — far from being an "umbrella," the balloon was a sluiceway.

Max turned up the volume on the receiver. They could not, of course, see the Air Force plane; it was circling high above them, at 37,000 feet. The young radioman aboard MAC Zero One Zero did not for a moment lose the level military intonation he had been trained to employ; let Max make all the jests he wanted about polar bears on the Greenland ice pack. He talked to Gander; the man in the tower there had Bedford on the telephone.

The young airman said to *Double Eagle*, "Your headquarters recommends minimum ten thousand feet, higher if possible up to fifteen thousand. Expect slight deviation south. Weather approaching Europe excellent. Expect northeasterly flow."

Ben listened to that. "They want us to freeze to death," he said to Max. "Ask them this question — what do they want us to do about icing? Ask 'em if they have considered icing conditions."

To MAC Zero One Zero, Max said, "We're in continuous rain and expect icing at about eight thousand feet. What do they expect?"

While he waited for the reply, Max turned to Ben. "Get your dry clothes on?" he asked gently. "Down's not worth a shit."

The balloon was descending. *Double Eagle* had flown into a large storm cloud. Snow fell all around them, the sun could not penetrate the cloud, and the air was the color of milk.

"We're at fifty-six hundred," Max said to Ben. "I imagine if we pumped all the water out of this mother, we'd make five, six hundred feet, Ben."

Ben was loath to use ballast unless it was necessary. "We might get sun," he said. "It looks like it's trying."

They figured the local time. It was 8:20 A.M., and they had been flying for more than thirty-five hours. They decided to wait until ten o'clock to see if the sun would superheat the balloon.

MAC Zero One Zero came back on the air: "Your headquarters expects icing at nine thousand. Recommend ballast off to seven thousand, then go to ten thousand when clear of rain. Winds at seven thousand are two hundred eighty-five degrees by forty knots [forty-six miles an hour]. You are moving at forty-two knots at this time."

Ben immediately began pumping water from the gondola, and Max had to raise his voice as he spoke into the microphone above the squeak of the pump.

To MAC Zero One Zero, Max said, "If you stop in Paris on the way back, we'll buy you a little champagne."

In his toneless voice, the boy on the radio said,"Good luck," and MAC Zero One Zero flew away.

Max took over the pumping. "Give me two pumps," Ben would say, watching the altimeter. "That was *three*, dammit! When I say two, I mean two!"

Double Eagle flew on, still making phenomenal progress. They were five hundred miles off the Labrador coast, with fifteen hundred miles to go to the shores of Europe.

Max, as he pumped, kept looking at a big cloud ahead of the balloon. It was a tower of cumulus, reaching perhaps 16,000 feet high, and it looked to Max as if it were boiling. He thought, I believe we're closing on that cloud. He didn't say much about it to Ben — Ben could see it better than he could. Besides, he had noted already that flying in a balloon over the ocean deprives one of certain senses: there are no reference points, you are in a void; it's impossible to judge distances. The gondola revolves constantly, with what effect on the inner ear nobody knows.

But at last Max said, "Ben, I believe we're going to fly into that cloud."

Ben replied, looking up, "I think you're right." Until that moment he had not seen the cloud, or realized how fast they were approaching it.

Double Eagle pierced the cloud, and says Ben, "flew into the goddamndest snowstorm I ever saw."

Both Ben and Max were astonished. Snow cascaded into the gondola, through the load ring, coating Max's sheepskin cap with rime and sticking to Ben's eyebrows and the stubble on his unshaven chin. The balloon began to fall through the cloud and the snowstorm at a rate of 500, then 600, feet per minute. Max and Ben waited to ballast off, believing that the balloon would recover and rise on its own. It did not do so. Finally, with great caution, they ballasted and stopped the descent at 1,500 feet above the ocean. Slowly, *Double Eagle* rose to 2,000 feet and stopped.

The snow stopped as well. The air at 2,000 feet was seductively warm after the frigid temperatures at 8,600. Ben and Max floated for a while at that altitude.

It was about noon Zulu, or thirty-six hours into the flight. They received a transmission from an overflying airliner. The man on the radio spoke English with a heavy accent, and Max felt a sting of irritation with him. Why did he have to be so curt?

He said, "Five Zero Double Eagle balloon, we have a message from your base." Max and Ben strained to hear and understand; the man's accent was very thick, and he spoke with great rapidity. He

122

said, "Recommend two thousand feet, maximum five thousand feet, expect Europe tomorrow afternoon. Good luck."

Max asked him to give them a navigational fix but he was not able to; airliners had earlier mentioned that the balloon's beacon was a little weak on its signal.

Ben said, "That message makes no sense at all."

Max agreed. The last weather report they had had, from an overflying airliner, had told them that low-level winds off the southern tip of Greenland were blowing due north. If they stayed at their present altitude, they would be blown onto the ice cap. Into the mind of Max, the reader, sprang the phrase "Greenland's icy mountains." These were 10,000 feet high.

Max thought, They have all the facts at Bedford, and we don't. He feared that if they ballasted off and flew up through the cloud into the sunshine, they'd have to ballast again at sunset. It would be a waste of ballast — again, they would be throwing away time.

Ben said, "I think we're okay on ballast." He didn't say for certain, because he hadn't been able to keep accurate records. "You start to write something and the water would wash it away," he said, explaining. "Pretty soon you get mad and say, 'Oh, piss on it! Let it run down your leg!' "

Ben's memory of the moments that follow is that he pleaded with Max to ballast off, break up through the clouds. He thought the message from Bedford was crazy.

"Remember the last thing Bob Rice said to us," he argued. "Up is east and down is north! If we stay down, we're going to hit Greenland. We'll eat it, Max."

Ben examined Max's face. His friend wore a determined look, and Ben supposed that his own features were just as fixed. Max wanted to stay down; Ben wanted to go up — that, at least, was the way Ben perceived the situation.

Ben thought: I can ballast off and take us up. But what if Max starts valving to bring us back down? He decided to do nothing.

With frustration and anger boiling within him, Ben said to himself, "The flight is lost, right here and now, by this decision. Up is east. Down is north."

Max thought so, too. After the flight, he could not remember Ben's anger or the argument. After the flight, he could only remember his own puzzlement at the message from base. Whatever happened between Ben and Max off the tip of Greenland on September 11, they remained at 2,000 feet, in a driving rain.

They ate C rations and drank some fruit juice. Neither man felt hungry. They had been aloft thirty-six hours and Ben had slept for three. Max threw his empty C-ration can overside and felt an irrational flash of guilt for having littered the sea. He could hear it so plainly below them.

It was raining inside the gondola almost as hard as it was raining outside. Max thought, again with pleased surprise, that it was pleasantly warm.

"I was so damn cold I thought I was going to die," Ben said later. "Already I thought I was going to die."

 In the control center at Bedford, Bob Rice and Rich Schwoebel were devoutly hoping that the message to remain at 2,000 feet would never reach the crew of *Double Eagle*.

Both men regarded it as a blunder. Rice thought it was an error that might doom the flight because it was in direct contradiction of his theory. Schwoebel, with Luther-like hammer strokes, wrote on the margin of the outgoing message: "I question that this message should be sent."

According to Rice, it had been transmitted only after heated discussion with another meteorologist at Weather Services. On satellite photographs, thunderstorms had been spotted in the cold front trailing the balloon. "One of the opinions was that this storm that was showing up behind them would bleed off to the east of Greenland and at low level might have a little northwest wind in it," says Rice. "But I wanted to go back up badly because I was worried about the storm in back."

"There is a tendency sometimes to think of the things that could happen theoretically," says Rice. "In an operational forecast you can't take this gamble. I was hoping that the message never got there. We had a fail-safe agreement with Ben and Max that if there's any question, if you're in trouble, *go up*. I thought if they never heard from us they'd go to the fail-safe thing and say we're supposed to go up. And go up."

Had *Double Eagle* climbed, with a prodigal expenditure of ballast (a factor that worried Schwoebel on the ground as well as Max

125

in the air, because by falling through the cloud the balloon had gone through another false sunset), it would have gone north of its planned trajectory. But a storm was developing over Scandinavia. Rice believes that the flight would have come across Scotland, and by staying very high, would have turned south over Norway under the influence of this storm, and come straight across the North Sea into Germany.

But the balloon did not climb; it remained at 2,000 feet, right in the middle of the whirlpool of a developing storm, with winds whipping out of the Davis Strait and off the tip of Greenland.

Ben and Max think that the flight failed at the moment they received the message to remain at 2,000 feet and they decided to listen to Bedford instead of doing what their instinct and the fail-safe agreement told them to do: go up.

Was that the moment of failure?

"Yes," says Bob Rice. "It was. It was. I don't think there's any question about it. This really hurts me. They pay you to talk, Max and Ben, and they listen, and they get a message and they listen to it . . ."

Ben, for all his apprehension about remaining at 2,000 feet, knew what the risks were if they ballasted off drastically and tried to break through the cloud cover in a rush. They would have to go to 20,000 feet; they might go higher. The cold would be unimaginable at such an altitude. They had oxygen equipment, but as a result of still another neglected last-minute detail, they had never tested it.

But he was filled with foreboding. There were those thunderstorms, rushing up behind them. There were the mountains of Greenland, towering above them. He remembered a teenage boy, rescued on the Sandias. The boy seemed to be fine; he was talking one minute, even smiling, and the next minute he was dead. Hypothermia. Freezing to death. How could they survive, down on the ice pack or down in the howling seas?

He and Max, in any case, did what they could to keep more water from coming in on them. Rain had been pelting the radios for hours; they covered the electronic equipment with plastic garbage bags and spread the sail over the bow of the gondola as further protection. Near nightfall, Ben couldn't sleep, but he went off into a state that was half wakefulness, half delirium. He imagined that benevolent people came into the gondola and took him away and put

126

him in a warm shower, in a hotel room. Each time, in his waking dream, he would feel the warm water touch his chilled back, he would be wrenched out of the delusion by a pang of guilt: if he left the gondola even for a moment, this would put the record of the flight into question. That was the rule: you had to stay aboard the gondola all the way. He did not know whether he was in the hotel or in the gondola — which was the dream and which the reality. What Ben was beginning to experience, though his conscious mind did not grasp the fact, was that most dangerous stage of hypothermia, when the body stops feeling cold and the mind relaxes. Perhaps his fight against the dream of a warm shower was the struggle of his subconscious against death.

Shortly before 2330 Zulu, forty-seven hours into the flight, *Double Eagle* received its last transmission from base before the drowned radios quit altogether. An overflying airliner, homing on Syd Parks's unfailing beacon, radioed as follows:

"Imperative rise to five thousand feet, eight thousand to ten thousand if possible, thunderstorms closing from the southwest. Freezing level, six thousand feet."

Ben and Max ballasted and the balloon climbed to 5,000 and went through 5,000 to 5,500 feet before coming to rest. Here they had another discussion. Max, from his experience as an airplane pilot, believed that icing levels are almost never more than 2,000 feet thick. He thought they could punch through them — get above the weather and into winds that were blowing toward Europe at speeds up to eighty miles an hour. He also thought they could penetrate the icing level and reach altitude in four or five minutes. Flying at 5,000 feet, they would be right in the middle of the thunderstorms if these overtook them; higher, on the slope of the high-pressure ridge, they would be above and ahead of the thunder and lightning.

Ben listened, and disagreed. "Max, if we don't make it up through we'll ice up and we'll never be able to stop the balloon. We'll go into the ocean."

Max persisted. For once, Ben would not take the gamble. What if the icing layer was 4,000 feet thick instead of 2,000? (After the flight, on examining the data, Bob Rice concluded that Max had guessed right: the gamble would have been justified. The icing layer, given the temperatures and the amount of moisture known to be present, was probably no thicker than 2,000 feet. Whether Ben, or

127

even Max, could have survived the freezing temperatures at higher altitudes remains an open, and troubling, question in Rice's mind. "Among the more classic famous last words uttered in history," Rice said later, "may well have been Max's preflight comment, 'We don't mind getting a little wet.' We simply did not comprehend what 'wet' really meant.")

At length Ben and Max dropped the subject, and flew on at 5,500 feet.

"Fatigue," Ben was to say afterward, "does the most amazing things to your mind." As the night wore on, he became convinced that the balloon was flying in the wrong direction. He lined himself up with the compass — an almost impossible feat because the needle revolves with the balloon. After long minutes of concentration, he said to Max, "We're going northwest."

"That's not possible."

"I don't care," said Ben. "We're going northwest — back toward North America."

Max said, "Ben, why don't you try to get a little rest now?"

Ben, muttering that he knew they were flying the wrong way, crawled into his wet sleeping bag in his wet clothes.

Ben was right. *Double Eagle* had been caught in the teeth of a cyclonic local storm, and it was carrying them in a great circle into the Denmark Strait, off the east coast of Greenland. They had no idea where precisely they were.

"Ben," said Max, "is Greenland high?"

"High? Boy, is it *high*," said Ben. He knew as well as he knew his own name that they were headed right toward Greenland, an open jaw with jagged mountains within it.

Max, earlier, had stripped off his damp clothes. His ski suit, his boots, his sweater, were useless. From Patty's sealed plastic bags he removed a wool turtleneck, a cashmere sweater, and a set of quilted long underwear. He was already wearing two pairs of long underwear. After a moment's hesitation, he put on his last pair of dry socks. Over all this he put on his lightweight ski parka. Then he donned his rubber survival suit; it was clumsy, difficult to work in. But it would keep him dry and warm.

He looked down at Ben and thought, I oughtn't to let him do that, go to bed so wet. But Ben hadn't slept, and Max believed he needed the rest.

Ben was dreaming about eating a complete meal in a hotel: roast beef, vegetables, salad, beer sparkling in the glass; and, at the end, the waiters brought cognac, a great balloon of the delicious stuff. In his hallucination, it made a fiery path down his throat, and its heat moved through his veins and capillaries, warming his blood.

At midnight Zulu, as Sunday, September 11, changed into Monday, September 12, Max sat relaxed in his lawn chair; he was a tight fit for it, in his squeaky bulging survival suit. *Double Eagle* had been aloft for forty-eight hours. Ben had been asleep for about twenty minutes. Max kept his eyes fixed on *Double Eagle*'s wake, watching for thunderstorms. He had seen no lightning, heard no thunder; he concluded that the storms must still be behind them. The balloon was at 5,000 feet. Max began to relax. Then he noticed that the balloon cycled a couple of times — went down to 4,800 feet and back up to 5,200, and then returned to 5,000 feet. Max felt a slight trembling; he thought it was his own body, for the balloon never stirred.

Max thought, Gee, I'm getting tired. He got up and stretched, and picked up the box with the altimeter and the barometer sealed inside it, and moved farther back in the gondola, near the bilge pumps. The balloon sank and rose again, about 400 feet — just a nice little wave. Again Max felt a quivering, and he said aloud, "My damn knees are shaking."

Ten minutes passed. The balloon went down slightly. Max pumped out some water. He had to lean across Ben's supine body to do this and Ben woke with a start. Max told Ben what he was doing, and Ben went back to sleep. Max kept pumping until the bilges were nearly dry, holding the altimeter in his lap, and watching the needle as the balloon continued its cycle of descents and ascents.

Then, suddenly, the balloon shuddered. To Max it seemed that a giant hand had reached out of the darkness and seized *Double Eagle* and shaken it as a terrier shakes a rat. A moment later, the same thing happened again. Max went back and woke Ben.

"I think you'd better come forward, Ben," he said. "Something's not right."

They used tiny amounts of ballast to trim the balloon; at first, it was not falling fast. Then it started down and it accelerated. Ben and

Max looked at the altimeter needle in disbelief; they were going down at 1,300 feet a minute — perhaps faster, because that was the maximum the altimeter would register and the needle was on the peg. Ben and Max hit the side of the gondola at the same moment, and began ballasting with abandon.

At about 2,500 feet, the balloon stopped. Ben said, "I think we've overballasted," because the craft started up again immediately, and quickly. At 3,500 feet, though, it stopped and hung in the freezing rain. Moments later, it plunged toward the sea again. The rate of descent was faster than before, or so it seemed to them.

Max thought they were going to hit the water. He slashed loose the oxygen bottles hanging over the edge of the gondola. If we hit the water, he thought, those damn things will come into the gondola and bash us on the head.

Double Eagle stopped and rose again, back to 2,200 feet.

Max said, "What the hell do you make of this?"

"I don't know," said Ben. He broke out a powerful flashlight and played its beam over the balloon. There was something on the envelope — it looked to Ben like popcorn.

They had no time to think about it. *Double Eagle* fell again. Despite their fears that they might tangle in the radio antennas, they had cut loose the trail ropes — they did not know how far down they would go, but thought they would go into the water. They ballasted off everything but the precious bottled water and the sand and lead remaining to them — they would need those if ever they landed. They threw over cases of C rations and oxygen masks and batteries. They plunged downward, flying blind beneath the rain skirt, passing from regions of driving snow to regions of driving rain, and at last the balloon bottomed out. The altimeter read 390 feet. Both Ben and Max thought they must be lower; the waves were raging so that they expected a wall of water to crash over the side of the gondola at any moment.

"I lifted the rain skirt," says Ben, remembering. "We had just come out of the bottom of the clouds, and I was looking into a maelstrom. The wind was blowing at fifty knots, there was a circular area of white everywhere, and it wasn't whitecaps. I realized I was looking at small icebergs that had calved off the coast of Greenland, and the water was breaking over these little — little? *huge!* — chunks of ice. The tops of the waves were being broken, I mean like a knife was

130

cutting the water — and spray was flying in all directions. I couldn't believe what I was seeing and hearing."

Shouting to make himself heard to Max, who was standing six feet away in the stern, Ben said, "Jesus Christ, you won't believe what's out here. Max, come look."

Max, watching the altimeter, said, "No, thanks."

Double Eagle hung for a moment over the ice-filled seas, and then it began to rise. By this time, Ben and Max realized what had caused the downs: the "popcorn" Ben had seen when he shone his flashlight on the envelope was ice. As they fell toward the sea and the air warmed, the ice peeled off the balloon — little kernels of it at first — Ben's "popcorn" — then chunks, then great sheets of it, like guillotine blades.

Ben and Max had decorated the gondola with two *ristras,* long strings of the dried red chilis that are the popular symbol of New Mexico. Ben drew his knife and cut them loose, and watched them as they fell drunkenly through the eddying winds into the sea.

"Take that, you goddamn sharks!" he shouted through cupped hands.

Both he and Max collapsed in laughter. Max said, "Apologize, Ben. Those hungry bastards may have heard you."

Max had believed, as the balloon plunged out of control, that he and Ben were certainly going to die. All his life, he had wondered how he would feel in the presence of that knowledge. He had felt sad — sad that he would leave his wife, and his children before they were grown, sad for others. For himself, he felt nothing — no fear, no regrets. He had been standing outside of himself, watching Max Anderson die, and it had not frightened him.

He and Ben talked calmly, sitting in the chairs. Max asked Ben what he had felt. He knew that Ben had thought they were going to die, too.

"Sad," said Ben. "Sad — that's all."

Ben and Max, back in clouds, heard a voice on the VHF. It was the pilot of an Empress Airlines flight who had spoken to them two days before, at the beginning of their flight. Now he was on his way back to Canada.

Double Eagle's radios, drowned by the inpouring snow and rain, would not transmit. The Empress Airline pilot said that he could not read them; Ben was barking into the microphone.

"If you're all right, push your mike button once," said Empress Airlines.

Ben and Max did nothing.

"If you're all right, push your mike button *twice*," said the Empress pilot.

Again, Ben did not touch the microphone.

"Very good," said the Empress pilot. "I'll report to your base that everything's all right."

"Jesus, *he's* got a lotta smarts," said Ben. He flipped the switch of the emergency locater transmitter (ELT). From that moment, it would send out a continuous distress call, a peculiar, high-pitched electronic signal that could be picked up by all ships and aircraft within a radius of five hundred miles.

Double Eagle's own receivers picked up this signal and fed it back; its mocking tone, which sounded like the twanging of an enormous jew's harp, mingled with the tumult of the sea.

The sound made Max feel better. If we go in, he thought, leastwise they'll know where we went in.

Ben's quick thinking and quick action in switching on the ELT aroused Max's admiration. Only Ben, he thought, would have been smart enough to do such a thing. Max had not even thought of doing it.

The two men sat in silence. The balloon seemed to be in equilibrium again. Ben did not want to lie down; the activity, the pumping of adrenalin, had alerted him to the danger of falling asleep. He sat up and, from time to time, would lose consciousness for an instant. As soon as his body began to fall, he would wake.

Suddenly, he snapped wide-awake and fixed a burning stare on Max. Ben said, "I want to tell you something straight ahead, Maxie. One thing bothers me."

"What's that, Ben?" asked Max.

"You bought more of that insurance than I did. I don't like that."

Before takeoff, Max had purchased a $300,000 policy on his life from Lloyd's of London; Ben had only bought $100,000 worth.

Max did not have the energy to laugh, though he had never been more amused by anything Ben had ever said. He replied, "Yeah? Well, Ben, that may be the only bargain I had on this trip."

It was almost 0400 Zulu, fifty-two hours into the flight. Max said, "Ben, do you want to lie down for a while?"

Ben said no, he did not want to sleep. They were huddled under plastic sheets, and they were (so Bob Rice told them later) being rained on in a way no human beings had ever been rained on before. No one had ever lived through such a storm, or even been in such a storm, at those altitudes and those latitudes.

"I think I'll sleep for a while, then," said Max. "If you need me, just pull on my foot." He put his head down and went immediately to sleep.

Ben, his mind teeming with images of the icebergs and the sea and the wind and the whistling descent of the balloon toward what he had believed was almost certain death, stared at his friend in amazement.

He thought: He's gone to sleep! He's actually gone to sleep!

Rain poured into the gondola through the opening at the load ring. It froze as it fell, coating Ben's soaked clothing and his exposed face with a film of ice that crackled and shattered when he moved. He was able to move only with the greatest difficulty. Inside his sopping down clothes, his limbs moved like the arms and legs of a man in a dream.

Double Eagle was at 1,500 feet. The weight of the ice took it down again. Ben, painfully, ballasted sand and brought the balloon to equilibrium. It flew on at 1,000 feet. The rain continued to pour into the gondola. For Ben it was an icy shower bath he could not escape from.

Panting and shivering, he moved everything away from the forward part of the gondola, where he was sitting. He kept falling over, and he didn't want to strike his head on something hard or sharp and injure himself. He did not have to force himself to think of these things; he did what he did as a matter of instinct. The cruel weather, though it could punish his body almost beyond endurance, could not reach his intelligence. His mind was still in control of the situation.

A little later, Ben spoke into the tape recorder. "I've just experienced the worst situation of the entire journey from a personal viewpoint," he said. "I became completely soaked. By nightfall I decided to go to sleep in my sleeping bag. Delirium. Shaking. My mind kept wandering to the point where I was being taken out of this balloon."

Ben had put on his survival suit over his wet clothing and he felt slightly more comfortable. His voice was stronger, but he was coughing and shuddering. He thought, Keep it aloft and survive.

He did not know whether he could do this. He watched the instruments, ballasted carefully, kept in his mind a running total of the sand expended. The temperature was about thirty-five degrees Fahrenheit. Though he was wet, and though spasms of shivering and coughing wracked his body, he was not unbearably uncomfortable. He listened to the rain. Below the balloon, the sea snarled in its fury.

At 0620 Zulu, with the balloon at 5,300 feet, Ben spoke into the tape recorder again. "Although this journey would seem romantic, I wouldn't recommend the attempt to anyone, regardless of their experience or equipment."

Ben looked at the rising sun and at the whitecaps below, to tell the direction of the wind. They *were* flying the wrong way, toward the polar ice cap. The beacon sent out its piercing distress call. How could the pilot of the Empress Airlines liner not have heard it?

To hell with him, Ben muttered.

The rest of the radios were dead. Ben thought that he and Max would not live very much longer. I suspect, he told himself, that this is the end. Pat's face, her eyes filled with love, formed in his mind, and he saw his mother and his children in his memory. Ben felt no fear, only the sadness of leave-taking.

Max slept on. Ben thought of waking him. He thought, It's unfair: if we go into the sea while Max is asleep, he won't even know that he's died.

In Bedford, Doc Wiley said to Pat Abruzzo and Patty Anderson, "The guys are going like a speeding bullet for Europe. I think you ought to fly to London tonight; I wouldn't want you to miss the landing."

Patty Anderson had known Doc Wiley and his diplomatic ways for a long time. "I questioned him," she says. "I didn't think he was being truthful. I had a feeling that something was wrong. I *did* sense it — Doc may not have thought so."

"The only reason I'm staying behind," Doc told Pat Abruzzo, "is that I honestly think I can be more useful here." Pat, too, suspected that Doc was trying to protect her from worry. Later, like Patty Anderson, she worked hard not to resent a gesture Doc Wiley had meant as a kindness. "Worrying does no good, but praying does," says Pat. "I prayed anyway — don't misunderstand me — but not as hard as I would have if I had known Ben was out there and in trouble. It's something I should have shared with him."

Pat and Patty got aboard a flight at Logan at seven o'clock Sunday evening and left for London. Patty, unable to sleep, kept pushing the worry out of her mind. Pat had a silent talk with Jesus, something she does when she is troubled in her heart, and went to sleep. They flew through the night, and from the window Patty watched the cloud deck below them, touched by faint moonlight, and then, as the plane approached Europe, by the rising sun. It was full morning when the plane descended through the clouds over the green fields of England.

By the time Pat and Patty left Boston, the Bedford control center had had no word, direct or indirect, from *Double Eagle* for almost seven hours. "I didn't let the girls know there were any problems whatsoever," says Doc Wiley. "But I knew the flight was really in trouble."

The homing beacon was transmitting constantly. "We'd talk to airplanes and they'd say yes we have the beacon," Doc recalls. "We knew they were probably still in the air, because the beacon operates from a trailing antenna."

Neither Doc Wiley nor Rich Schwoebel nor anyone in the Bedford control center knew precisely where the balloon was. Because it was a weekend, and the Goddard Space Flight Center was operating with a minimum staff, no navigational fixes from the Nimbus satellite had been transmitted to Bedford. Wiley and Schwoebel had been unable to get in touch with supervisory personnel at Goddard who could speed the processing of data gathered by Nimbus from *Double Eagle*'s transmitter; the balloon flight was low on the Nimbus list of priorities — Nimbus was collecting all sorts of other information as it orbited the earth. Navigational fixes by overflying aircraft might be off by as much as two hundred miles; they were, for all practical purposes — such as directing a rescue craft to the scene of a crash — useless.

"We suddenly got a message that the emergency locator transmitter was on the air," says Doc. "It was the worst possible thing we could have heard. Aircraft off the coast of Greenland are picking up the emergency signal, the ELT, but they were calling the balloon on the emergency frequency. There was no answer."

This could mean that Ben and Max had crashed. It could mean that they were incapacitated or dead while the balloon was still flying. Sixteen hours were to go by with no communication from *Double Eagle*.

After the flight, Doc reconstructed what had happened. "Max and Ben thought the radio was dead," he explains. "They didn't understand. When they turned on the ELT, they blocked the frequency. They had to turn off the distress beacon in order to talk. They didn't understand this basic thing."

"It was agonizing," Rich Schwoebel recalls. He and Doc Wiley went upstairs into an empty office to talk. Doc made a baleful joke

136

1. Double Eagle *over Iceland. This is one of the few extant photographs of the first flight.*

2. Double Eagle II *undergoing an inflation test in the Hippodrome, St. Paul, Minnesota, July 26, 1978.*

3. Larry practices getting into his hang-glider from the red and yellow gondola of Double Eagle II.

4. Checking the gondola's seaworthiness on Cochiti Lake, near Albuquerque.

5. *The ground crew for the flight of* Double Eagle II (*left to right*): Pat Abruzzo, Doc Wiley, Rich Schwoebel, Jim Mitchell (seated), Patty Anderson. Absent: Bob Rice, Syd Parks, Pete Leavitt.

6. *Supplies for the flight laid out around the gondola.*

7. *The Abruzzo family in front of the gondola on the afternoon of the launch, at Spragueville, Maine.*

8. *The Anderson family.*

9. The eleven-story gas envelope being inflated.

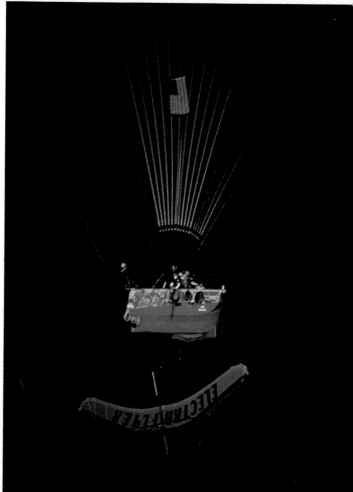

10. The balloon lifts off in the night, with Larry's hang-glider suspended beneath it.

11. *Larry using the facilities, off the coast of Newfoundland.*

12. *Larry feeds Ben a sardine on the first day of the flight.*

13. *Ben is cold, weary, thirsty, and chafed by his oxygen mask as the balloon reaches 25,000 feet three hundred miles west of Ireland.*

14. *Huddled under the yellow rain skirt, lowered for warmth, Ben works on his logs as the balloon approaches Ireland.*

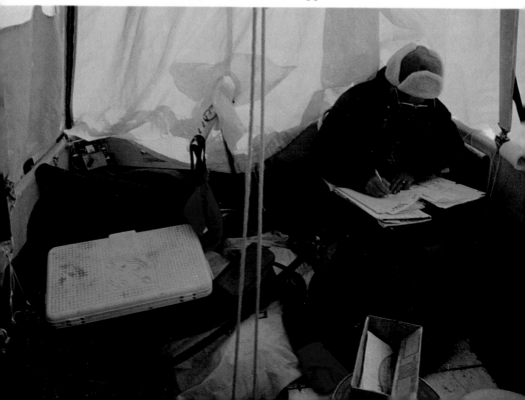

15. At a lower, warmer altitude of 14,000 feet Max takes a sightseeing break over Poole, England.

16. Overleaf: The balloon floats over France.

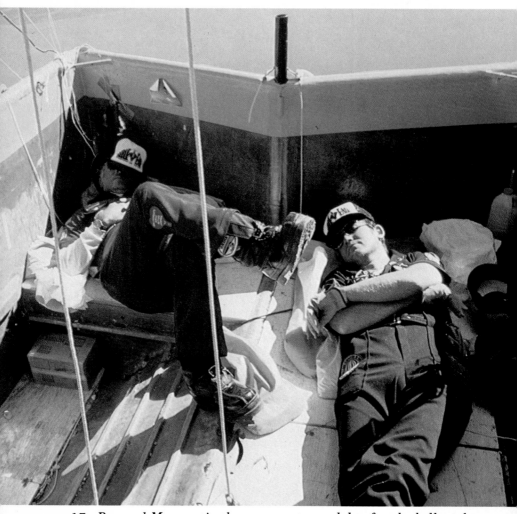

17. *Ben and Max nap in the near-empty gondola after the balloon has crossed the French coast.*

18. Double Eagle II *grazes a cornfield and sets down in a field of barley.*

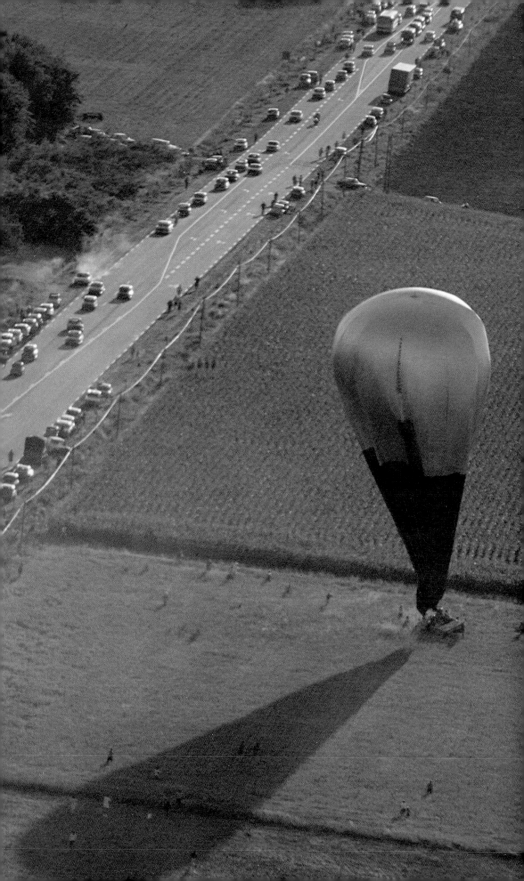

19. *The gondola rocks along the ground with Larry on the high side, Max and Ben on the low.*

20. *Pulling down the balloon.*

21. *The crowd swarms around the deflated balloon.*

22. *Max, Ben, and Larry in their moment of triumph.*

that Max would have appreciated. "Well, old buddy," he said to Rich, "I think it's possible we've got two frozen executive asses out there."

Schwoebel, too, believed that Ben and Max had frozen. He knew what the weather was off Greenland. So did Bob Rice, standing quietly by. He thought, Go ahead, guys — fly the Atlantic in a balloon, I just told you to.

Doc Wiley did not, at this time, believe that *Double Eagle* was still airborne. He thought it was down in the water or down on the ice cap. The antennas for the Nimbus and the VHF systems were rigid, mounted on the foredeck of the gondola. In a crash landing, Doc reasoned, the load ring could come down on impact and wipe out those antennas. The emergency beacon, after a crash, could be deployed with its trailing antenna from the small helium balloon Ben and Max had taken along for the purpose.

Then new data caused Doc to change his mind. "We got a lot of bearings from different airplanes," says Doc, "but they didn't compute. They weren't accurate. The reason they didn't compute, we finally figured, was because the balloon was still moving."

Schwoebel argued the worse case: Ben and Max were unconscious or dead in a moving, free balloon. Would it rise in the morning when superheated by the sun to an altitude at which oxygen was needed to keep human beings alive? If that happened, and the pilots were still clinging to life, they would suffocate, or freeze. If, by chance, they did not climb to a dangerous altitude, and survived, what would happen when the balloon cooled and started down at sunset? If the pilots could not ballast off to maintain altitude, *Double Eagle* would plunge into the sea, at night. "It's not a good alternative," said Schwoebel. Outlining these facts, Schwoebel felt curiously detached; it was a technical problem. He was surprised at himself, surprised at the emotional grip of all the men in the room. After all, Ben and Max were their friends; Schwoebel — everyone there — knew their families.

Doc Wiley kept the temperature of the discussion cool. It was obvious that if the pilots were alive but unable to help themselves, then somehow the balloon had to be landed safely and Ben and Max rescued.

All agreed that a night landing was unthinkable. "Rich was

worried about hypothermia," says Bob Rice. "I don't know if I thought they were dead. My overriding fear was the ocean. That's my job. I knew there was no way in the world they were going to survive in that gondola in those seas."

Doc Wiley, on the other hand, reasoned that Ben and Max had no chance to survive if they were freezing to death and remained in the balloon. Perhaps the chances of survival in a landing were slim, but slim was better than nonexistent. To Rich Schwoebel, he said, "Could we bring it down if we put some holes in the envelope?"

Schwoebel did not immediately understand what Doc was suggesting.

"My advice to air rescue would be," Doc said, "if when you reach the balloon on flyby and you see no people or eyeballs or waving hands over the side of the gondola, if it's a drifting derelict, then shoot a few holes in it. Then you could at least have a crack at picking up the residue."

Schwoebel saw the intelligence in this cold-blooded argument. He told Doc Wiley it might work if it were carefully done. They discussed the points, just below the equator, where the marksman should place his rounds.

Even earlier the media had begun to pick up the scent of a disaster. The telephones were ringing off the walls. Jim Mitchell, as calm as Doc Wiley, was dealing with the calls. He told the strict truth, but not all the truth. Finally he stopped taking calls. He did not intend to tell the press quite yet that he and almost everyone else thought that Ben Abruzzo and Max Anderson were very likely dead and adrift in an Atlantic storm, aloft or awash.

Mitchell knew he could not put the matter off forever. At about midnight, he and Doc Wiley sat down together and began to draft a press release announcing the loss of *Double Eagle* and its crew. They were in the depths of pessimism and sorrow and apprehension. Who would tell the families? What would be the effect of the loss of Max and Ben upon their businesses and the hundreds of people who depended on them for a livelihood, either as employees or investors? Neither Jim nor Doc had the heart to put a word on paper; they just drafted and redrafted the communiqué verbally.

At three o'clock in the morning, the Goddard Space Flight Center telephoned at last with a series of navigational fixes from the

Nimbus satellite. These proved that *Double Eagle* was still flying — flying in a circle 500 miles in circumference with its center about 180 miles east of the southern tip of Greenland. Ben and Max, if they were alive, were 450 miles west of Reykjavik, Iceland. That island was the mid-Atlantic base of the U.S. military rescue service.

As Bob Rice had feared, and as Ben and Max knew all too well, the balloon had been captured by the low-level storm blowing out of the Davis Strait, and was being spun in a great counterclockwise arc by its cyclonic winds.

Doc Wiley picked up the telephone and called the Air Force Rescue Center at Scott Air Force Base. "I tried to make arrangements for a search plane to go out and check 'em at first light," says Doc. "I had a big problem. I didn't know that the Air Force in Iceland is under the administrative control of the U.S. Navy." The Air Force itself could not order a rescue mission. Doc's request had to go through Navy channels.

Speaking to his Air Force friends, Doc said, "The ELT is on. I've got a real problem, and I want things moving before sunrise." He also sent a message to the Navy commander in Iceland. The Navy agreed that their air-rescue arm would put a search plane on the balloon at the break of day.

Jim Mitchell drafted a dry, factual press release, the first he had issued during the entire flight, giving the information received from the Nimbus satellite and summarizing weather conditions: "As a precaution, Double Eagle Tracking Center . . . has requested that aircraft be dispatched to the balloon's current position to determine if the balloon and its pilots are in distress." That was as much of an alarm as he felt justified in sounding; this was not a flight funded by the government — it was a private enterprise, and Ben and Max and their families and their investments had a right to privacy even with the eyes of the world upon them.

Doc Wiley figured that there would be an immediate ditching in the sea. Pat Abruzzo and Patty Anderson were asleep in the London Hilton. "I was trying to protect the wives until such point as I could call 'em and say, 'Hey, the guys are down, it's all over, they're okay,' " says Doc. In that, he would be unsuccessful.

Rich Schwoebel helped Bob Rice do all the necessary calculations so that Doc Wiley could give the Navy and the Air Force the fullest possible information. Then he went into a dark office by himself, and fell to his knees in prayer.

Max woke up at a little after 0700 Zulu. He had been sleeping in the chair. He felt refreshed. Ben was forward, with the tape recorder beside him.

Max called to him. "Ben, I wonder if you'd lie down and sleep."

"Okay," Ben said, and with no further exchange of words, he went aft and sat down in his survival suit with his back against the wall of the gondola. The night before, with much effort, he and Max had shifted the ballast and counted it, placing the lead shot around the keel to steady the gondola should it go into the sea, moving sandbags forward so that its prow would be lower than its stern. They thought that this would reduce the amount of rain that came inside.

Still, the deck was awash. As first light touched the balloon, it started to climb. The sky was filled with broken clouds and there was heavy haze around the sun. Ahead of *Double Eagle*, Max could see a storm, and there was another storm in the wake of the balloon. Max thought: We're between two storms. That's funny — maybe the storm that was following us passed us in the night because we were flying so low.

Only dimly aware of the squeal of the ELT over the loudspeaker — it was by now a homely sound, part of the atmosphere, like Muzak in an elevator — Max decided to try the radios. He put out several calls but received no response, even though he was transmitting, or so he thought, on 121.5 megahertz, the emergency frequency. He concluded that the rain had ruined the radios, that they were useless.

The balloon passed 6,000 feet, the icing level, and Max decided to pump out the bilges. He feared that the pumps might freeze and break, and they would then have no means of ejecting water from the gondola except by bailing. He wanted to avoid bailing. Ben seemed to be asleep. Ice on the envelope melted as Max pumped, and cascaded into the gondola.

Relieved of weight and warmed by the overcast sun, the balloon rose to 12,000 feet, the highest altitude of the voyage. Max was mildly pleased, reading this on the altimeter. He felt in perfect control, just as he did when driving a sports car and taking his eye off the road for the flicker of pleasure it gives to see the speedometer needle moving toward the peg.

140

The temperature fell to eight degrees Fahrenheit; everything that had been water was now ice, and Max congratulated himself on his foresight in emptying the bilge pumps. Ben, he noticed, was restless as he tried to sleep. He kept on jerking himself erect as he started to fall over from his sitting position. Each time he woke, he coughed.

Just before noon, to Max's surprise, a voice came over the speaker. It was calling the balloon: "Five Zero Double Eagle, this is P-3 Whiskey Hotel."

Ben woke up, coughing violently. Max didn't quite understand the transmission. He said, "Ben, what the hell is a P-3?"

"I don't know." Ben stared at the radio, which was once again emitting the high-pitched squeal caused by the ELT.

A full minute passed, perhaps longer. The call was repeated. Max picked up the microphone, but it just squealed.

"It's some kind of an aircraft," Max said.

The voice came back on. "Unable to read your transmitter. We're one hundred nautical miles from your position, homing on your beacon."

Max tried to say, "Roger," but his voice failed.

Another voice interrupted. "Navy, this is Icelandic Flight Two. We have *Double Eagle*'s beacon, bearing two twenty."

"It's a Navy plane," Max said.

"I know it is," Ben replied.

Max got out the damp chart and laid a line bearing 220 degrees from Reykjavik because the Icelandic airliner had said it had just left that airport, or was just approaching it. Max was not sure which. *Double Eagle* was somewhere on that line, which ran from Iceland to the shores of Greenland. The Navy radioman said that his aircraft would be alongside the balloon in twenty minutes. Max looked at his watch. The Bulova Company had given Ben and Max watches to wear on the flight; they had done the same for Lindbergh, and Max remembered that the man who made the presentation told him that the company had, as a result of Lindbergh's wearing their product, sold more watches in 1927 than ever before in the history of the company. They were good watches; his and Ben's had stayed precisely synchronized all the way on this flight.

Nineteen minutes later (Max checked his watch), a gray four-engined Navy plane appeared; it was an Orion submarine patrol bomber, the military version of the Lockheed Electra. Max wondered,

141

as the plane came out of the clouds, how it could possibly be at the same altitude as *Double Eagle:* their beacon would give their location but not their altitude. Then he realized, with a flush of embarrassment, that the Navy plane had radar on board, and he thought, The balloon is wet enough so that it must be giving a pretty good radar echo.

The Navy plane circled the balloon. Its radioman said, "Five Zero Double Eagle, we've had a lot of people inquiring about you."

Max thought, I'm glad. While waiting for the arrival of the Navy plane, Max had searched through the jumble of *Double Eagle*'s equipment and found the hand-held transceiver that Ben had borrowed from the New Mexico National Guard.

Max said into the walkie-talkie, "You guys look more like the cavalry than the Navy."

The Navy radioman hadn't expected a joke, and he asked Max to repeat his transmission. Max did so, with a croaking laugh.

"What are your intentions?" radioed Whiskey Hotel, the name by which Ben and Max would always afterward, with great affection, remember the Navy patrol bomber.

Max asked, "Where the hell are we?" He was embarrassed to ask. He said to Ben, "That's some question. We should know our position or stay home."

Whiskey Hotel told them they were at latitude 62.28 north, longitude 33.22 degrees west.

Ben had been looking at the map. "Right where we predicted," he said.

Whiskey Hotel told them that their track was 40 degrees true and their speed sixty knots. "Do you guys have an engine on that thing?" he asked.

"No, sir," said Max, "no engine."

Max took out his calipers, and after marking the course, measured distances with his trembling fingers. Meanwhile, Whiskey Hotel transmitted winds aloft, their speed and direction.

Max said, "Ben, the best I can tell, here, we can make Reykjavik if we go to fifteen thousand or we can make Norway about three o'clock tomorrow morning."

"A night landing?" said Ben.

Just before the arrival of the Navy plane, Ben had been feeling fine — drowsy, warm, peaceful. Now he was cold again. He knew

142

that his mind was not working as it should, nor was his body. Max, it seemed to him, was moving very slowly, speaking very slowly. The two of them were barely moving.

His mind grasped the situation. Max was suggesting that they go on — fly to Iceland, even to Norway.

Ben said, "I can hardly talk."

"He's going to give us a fix on Iceland pretty soon," Max replied.

"We've missed everything. We've missed Greenland too," said Ben. "That's too far to go."

He knew that if they went to 15,000 feet they would freeze. They had no oxygen equipment — they had jettisoned all of it, bottles and respirators and masks, during the terrible series of downs in the storm the night before. What if they overflew Norway? He looked at the track again — it would take them into the Soviet Union. What if the Russians shot them down? Ben voiced none of these thoughts, but Max may have divined some of them.

He said, "It's a hell of a problem."

Whiskey Hotel continued to circle *Double Eagle,* its four turboprop engines droning. Max switched on his transmitter; he turned it off between chats to conserve its one small battery.

"Are you guys in a hurry?" he asked.

Whiskey Hotel replied, "Take your time."

Ben looked at Max, as his friend examined the map, spreading it out on the foredeck, measuring, lifting his head to think.

Abruptly, Ben said, "Tell them to get a ship under us."

Max, startled, looked closely at Ben. His lips were blue. He was trembling and coughing, and his face, covered with stubble, looked like that of a man many years older than the one who had taken off from Marshfield only sixty hours before. Max saw, for the first time, that Ben was in serious trouble.

He said, "Ben, what's the matter?"

"I'm colder than hell. I can't warm up."

Max took off the heavy blue parka he had draped over his survival suit, and gave it to Ben. The parka was soaking wet. "I don't know how much good this'll do, but take it," Max said. "Put it on the outside of your survival suit."

Ben put on the parka, but made no reply.

Max asked for low-level winds and seas. Under them, the seas were Force 5 — waves eleven to thirteen feet high. Off Iceland, they were Force 8 — twenty to twenty-five feet.

To Ben, Max said, "Do you want a ship or a helicopter?"

"Leave the gondola?" Ben thought, and nodded. "That's all right." A helicopter was quicker. Let the gondola drift.

Max talked to Whiskey Hotel again. How long would it take for a helicopter to reach them? The Air Force had such a craft, the enormous HH-3 — "Jolly Greens." They could fly out to *Double Eagle* in about three hours, refueling from an HC-130 tanker en route.

From time to time, the Navy plane would fly out of earshot, and then Ben and Max could hear the creak of the balloon's rigging. Both realized that if they landed in the sea, they would have to release the envelope. It would go up like a rocket when cut loose from the gondola. They worried, wordlessly as usual, about its hitting the rescue helicopter if it happened to be overhead. Max warned Whiskey Hotel not to get below them — they might be ballasting.

Max checked the drift once again; Ben several times asked him to repeat it. They were tracking at 50 degrees. Max made a transmission: "What we'd like to do is attempt Iceland. Let us proceed until twelve o'clock and then we'll see what the prospects are. Then we can decide what to do."

It seemed possible to Max that they could land on Iceland. It still seemed possible to him that they could make Norway. They had the ballast, they had the winds aloft. They would be flirting with the polar ice cap, but it was still possible not to fail.

Ben said, "If we fool around waiting until three, four, this afternoon and the low overtakes us, then we'll eat it. The sea will come up. This ten-foot sea is no problem."

"Well," said Max, "why don't we go on for a bit and then do it? If we get higher, like I think we will . . ."

Max knew there was no point in landing the balloon. It would be hours before a rescue craft, helicopter or ship, could reach them, and they were better off flying than bobbing around in the water.

Ben realized that Max was still thinking of going on, of making Norway. He said, "Max, go ahead and make your best decision."

Max gave him a searching look. He saw again how distressed Ben was, how close to collapse. But he knew, *knew*, that there was no technical reason to accept rescue, to choose safety. They could fly all the way to Europe, just by ballasting off and going up.

Ben said, "Do what you want. I'm freezing to death. I won't make it either way. Go ahead and fly the sonofabitch."

Max looked at his friend. He believed that Ben was going to die. He called Whiskey Hotel. "Send out the helicopter," he said. "We'll put her down."

Whiskey Hotel, in a moment, radioed back, asking permission to make a photo pass.

"Come by and take our picture," said Max, "and we'll smile."

"You learn a lot of things, being educated in a military system," says Max Anderson. "But one thing you do not learn is compassion. It's a bad thing to be guided by in dangerous situations. Compassion can get you killed."

Over the Denmark Strait, with the Arctic Circle at his back, Max gave way to compassion. Almost immediately, he regretted it. Whiskey Hotel flew in a wide circle around *Double Eagle*. Ben, shuddering with cold, kept his eyes fastened upon the rescue plane. Perhaps the balloon *could* fly on, thought Max. Maybe if they overflew Iceland, Ben's spirits would be lifted. They could improvise something, get him warm again.

Max said, "We've still got the stove, Ben. What would you think about rigging up some kind of shelter aft, with the sleeping bags and the plastic sheets? We could put the stove inside. One of us could crawl in there and be warm and the other could stay on watch until he couldn't stand the cold any more. Then we'd swap and the other guy could get warm."

Ben's mind, always ready for an idea, grasped this one. "It might work," he said.

"We'd make Norway at three in the morning, but hell, that's way north, Ben. There'd be light, maybe." Max remembered, from his summer of uranium prospecting, how the midnight sun had wakened him in northern Canada. If they arrived a little earlier, they could valve and descend, perhaps pick up winds flowing south that would take them down the Scandinavian peninsula. They were carrying parachute flares; these would fall at the same rate as the balloon in a night landing, lighting the ground below with a shadowless phosphorus glare.

Ben was willing to accept the risk. He had already agreed to die. He knew that he was going to die if *Double Eagle* flew on; Max would land in some Norwegian fjord, or in some Russian marsh, with a corpse for cargo. But what about Max? Could he live through it? They would be flying over the polar ice cap; they might land above the Arctic Circle; they had no communications. These considerations kept marshaling themselves in Ben's mind.

Whiskey Hotel made its photo pass. Ben and Max could see the camera mounted on the wing, filming as the aircraft flashed by. There was some sort of strobe light shining from the camera.

"I don't know whether to smile or cry," said Ben. "Did he say it was three hundred miles to Iceland? We'll be making a night landing. We'll bust our ass."

"Ten hours," Max said. He meant: ten hours to Norway.

"That's a night landing." Ben wanted to be sure that Max understood that. "If he's right on his drift," Ben said, "we're going nowhere. In fact, we're going the other way. I don't give a shit about making Iceland. Not for a night landing."

Max had computed that they were little more than one hundred miles from Iceland; Ben was confusing Iceland and Norway. And their drift would be 60 to 70 degrees, at 15,000 feet, a good track. Max was willing to take the chance.

Ben said, "Get the chopper over us in good light. You've got to figure for a screw-up, the screw-up being that they miss us the first time. What are the seas? Give me the seas again."

"The seas are thirteen feet," Max replied. "That's about as good as you can expect for this part of the world. There're quite a few whitecaps, Ben, but certainly not that many."

"It's getting damn cold up here, you know that? We're down to thirty degrees. That water — it's ready to freeze . . . Helicopter got this sort of range? Ask him, Max — ask him what his capabilities are."

Max handed Ben the walkie-talkie. Ben fumbled with it in his gloved hands. Max had never before seen him do a clumsy thing. In a kind, quiet voice, Max said, "Put it on 243, push, and then talk, Ben."

To Whiskey Hotel, Ben said, "I'm concerned about waiting too long because the weather is deteriorating. How long does it take the helicopter to get here?"

The reply, again, was two or three hours, depending on head winds, launch time, refueling problems, the progress of the balloon. Whiskey Hotel would stay with them, though Max had told them they need not stick around, until the helicopter arrived.

"I know I'm freezing to death," Ben said. "I know that." He was gasping with the effort that speech cost him when he spoke to Max; but when he talked to the Navy men, his voice was perfectly controlled.

Max admired that. He admired everything about Ben. He looked off toward Norway. He wanted it; he knew he could have it. His will broke. He thought: Not that much; not that way, killing Ben.

Max called Whiskey Hotel and asked if the CBS camera crew was going to come out with the rescue helicopter. The Navy radioman said he thought so.

"Hell, Ben," Max said, "I think I'll just decorate this balloon." He got out all the little balloons they had carried and blew them up and festooned *Double Eagle* with them. He was glad the American flag was still flying. They would have no use now for the thirteen flags they carried, one for each of the countries in which they might have landed; they had no Icelandic flag. Max thought, and may even have said, "Hell, I always wanted to see Iceland."

Ben said, "They won't believe how we're dressed. We're not the best-dressed balloonists, huh?"

Max, stretching and yawning as he spoke, replied, "No — don't think we are."

Double Eagle was flying toward a cloud, and Ben, having had enough experience inside clouds, told Max that they had to valve and fly under it. Max had reservations — the balloon would cool once they were under the clouds, they would have to ballast off. Perhaps he was still, in some part of his mind, thinking that they would, somehow, fly on. He doesn't know.

Max had always feared the valve. How could they know it would reseat as it should? That thought had haunted him since the day the valve was tested. Up until now, they had never used the valve.

Ben pulled the cord, counting off the seconds, as Ed Yost had instructed him, "One thousand one, one thousand two . . ."

Water trapped on the concave top of the envelope rushed into the valve opening, and rattled inside the balloon like rain gusting against taut canvas. The sound startled Max. But the valve seated perfectly, just as Ben had always known it would.

The balloon dropped to 5,000 feet and the temperature rose immediately to forty degrees. The effect on Ben was immediate. He began arranging ballast. His speech, which had been slurred, became his old, clear, ringing voice again.

Max was seized with a sense of urgency. If they were going to abandon the gondola, then many valuable things aboard her ought to be saved. He found an Army-surplus duffel bag, heavy canvas with a shoulder strap, and began stuffing it with valuables. Inside, he put the boxes of special envelopes with first-day covers commemorating the flight. He crawled under the foredeck and found the barographs: these would verify their flight and certify any records for distance and longevity they may have set. He found the sextant, to his surprise: he had been certain that he had thrown it overboard during the downs in the storm off Greenland, and that had bothered him. How could he possibly replace it? Into the bag he stuffed clothes, boots, anything of value. He told himself not to forget the two borrowed walkie-talkies. In the military, you had to account for everything, and he did not want to repay the kindness of the National Guard quartermaster by saddling him with a lot of paperwork and a statement of charges.

Ben, watching Max work, was puzzled. What did all that stuff matter? "We might not be able to take anything with us," he said. "You know they pick you up in a sling."

"I'm going to take it right inside with me," said Max firmly.

Ben, with his sleeping bag draped over him, tried to get some sleep. He was not worried about the landing. He knew adrenalin would take over. But he had had less than three hours' sleep in the last sixty-five hours. He counted up Max's sleep period in his mind: Max must have slept eight or nine hours. No wonder he was so fresh.

Max, the duffel bag packed, took the watch. Since dropping below 5,000 feet they had been in voice contact with the rescue helicopter. Now, because he was conserving battery power, and because he was feeling melancholy, Max kept silent. He fought down his

149

annoyance with Ben. It was irrational. Ben had certainly been annoyed with him, Max, often enough. He owes me one or two on that score, Max thought. He remembered something: how, all the way across the ocean, and even before, he had held onto Ben and Ben had held onto him when one or the other had climbed on the stern to urinate overboard. To Max, the idea of Ben falling, and leaving him alone in the balloon, was unbearable. Ben must have felt the same.

Double Eagle was flying now at 2,000 feet and the air was even warmer. Ben and Max let down the trail ropes, tying two of them together to make one rope 220 feet long. The others were the normal 110 feet. The green military helicopter was in sight. Max kept asking for the distance to Iceland and finally the island came into sight ahead, wreathed in clouds, with sheer cliffs rising from the frothing seas.

Max said, "You know, if I could tell where we were, we might be able to stick this thing into one of those fjords. If they run in the same direction we're flying, we could fly right in. Iceland is considered Europe."

Neither Ben nor the commander of the rescue helicopter, Major Kenneth Key, made any reply to this suggestion. Soon Max himself saw that the idea was not good. *Double Eagle*, traveling at fifty-eight miles an hour or more, was paralleling the coast. It was almost 1700 Zulu, and the cloud level had fallen to 300 feet. Ben, agile and alert, was making everything ready for the landing. He was controlling the ropes. Max's job was to release the two straps that secured the bow to the load ring; Ben would release the stern. The stern went first, then the bow immediately afterward. To release the straps, after the safety locks were removed, required pulling a pin, a movement of only a quarter of an inch.

Max made a final transmission to the helicopter, hovering off their quarter. "Sir," said Max. "Now, as we are going to land, do not be directly over us. The balloon, when released, will accelerate vertically in a violent manner. We do not want to shoot you guys down now."

"Roger," replied the helicopter. "We will be in the three o'clock or nine o'clock position. If we are unable to get the probe into your gondola, we may have you go into the water and we'll drag it to you."

"Beautiful," said Ben.

Below the descending gondola, the seas were running at twenty-five feet. Ben, valving, had brought them down so that the trail ropes were in the water. The ropes transmitted the motion of the waves to the gondola. It, too, went up and down twenty-five feet each time the ropes dragged through one wave and into another. The balloon, of course, was moving faster than the seas, so the motion was exaggerated. Max thought it was exhilarating, like a bobsled ride. He put a sandbag on the side of the gondola so he could push it over if necessary, to take the balloon back up.

Ben was looking intently over the side at the water, one hand on the valve line, the other on the lanyard that would release the stern of the gondola. They were ready to release. Max thought they were within a few feet of the wave tops — it certainly seemed so, with the gondola mimicking every movement of the sea. With his back to the sea and his eye fixed on Ben, he could not see for himself. Ben's signal to release was a long time coming.

Max said, "Ben, what's the matter?"

The waves, green and opaque and veined with froth, looked like marble that had been granted the power of movement. The light seemed too feeble to have come from the sun. Ben heard the scream of a plane's engines. Max watched the Air Force tanker circling. The clouds were so low that one wing tip seemed to touch them while the other skimmed the surface of the heaving sea. Spindrift scudded like fog over the whole scene.

Ben shouted, *"Max, don't release!"*

Max snatched his hand away from the lanyard.

Ben said, "We're a hundred feet above the water."

The balloon had gone into a sudden climb, and it rose nearly 800 feet, until it was in the clouds. Ben valved off again, bringing *Double Eagle* down fast. Max read 500 feet per minute on the variometer and shouted a warning to Ben.

But Ben was flying with confidence. He watched the ropes as they floated on the water, and when the gondola was as close to the waves as Ben thought it would ever come — only a few feet of dry trail rope remained — he pulled his pin. Max, a split second later, pulled his.

The balloon, released, went over on its side for an instant, still in the grip of the wind, and then stood straight. Silver and black, a great cone, it shot straight up, accelerating rapidly, and in moments disappeared into the clouds. It was the only time during the entire flight that Ben and Max saw the balloon, all of it, and the sight lasted only for seconds. The feeling Max had as *Double Eagle* vanished was not so very different from the one he remembered from childhood, when he had let go the string of a bright toy balloon.

Ben did not take time to think about *Double Eagle*. He began throwing over sandbags, batteries, anything to lighten the gondola; it was riding too deep in the water. Max helped with that. Then Ben picked up the sea anchor and tried to deploy it overside. The wind blew it back in his face. He picked it up again — strength flowed through his body with the pumping of the adrenalin — and, cursing, threw the sea anchor into the waves, leaning far overboard to do so.

Ben cried, *"Ha!"* and fell backward into the gondola, striking his head on a metal ladder. Blood flowed from his ear. He pointed overboard.

Max followed Ben's pointing finger and saw, thrusting out of the water, the fin of a shark. The fin was as large as a big dining room table. The shark swam under the boat. That sucker is swimming at forty knots, Max thought. We've come all this way to be eaten by a shark. Then he looked more closely at it, remembered the pictures from the Air Force survival manual, and said, "Ben, it's a basking shark. They don't eat people."

Ben, holding his bleeding ear, replied, *"You* may know that. Does the *shark* know that?"

The gondola zoomed down one twenty-five-foot wave and up another. Neither man had ever sailed in such seas, and they looked upward in awe at the towering waves. Max struggled with the zipper of his survival suit — he couldn't close it. The basking shark, longer than the catamaran gondola, cruised by again. The boat was riding easily, but Max thought, If this thing rolls over I'm going to be back inside it so fast that shark won't have time to blink.

The helicopter had dropped three smoke flares, and now Major Key maneuvered the craft overhead. It was a marvelous piece of flying. Key held his machine stable above the gondola. A sergeant stood in the door, and lowered the probe in precise rhythm with the waves. It swung into the gondola and Ben and Max grabbed it.

Max slung the duffel bag over his shoulder. Ben adjusted the sling around Max's body, and Max went up first. As Max remembers it, he asked Ben to go first, taking the bag. Ben refused: "I'm not going to take that damn bag."

"Ben, we can't leave this bag in here. It's got all our valuables in it."

Ben doesn't remember that. He remembers thinking: Why is Max going up first? Who decided that?

As Max reached the door of the helicopter, the airmen waiting there pulled him inside. The youngster who took hold of Max's bag was very nearly pulled out the door by its weight, and instinctively Max grabbed him to keep him from falling, though he was secured to the aircraft by a safety harness. The bag weighed more than a hundred pounds.

With Max safely inside, the helicopter flew away, out of sight. Ben thought the pilot must have some reason for doing that. He was not alarmed. While the aircraft was gone, he cleared away the ladder, the tiller, the cables, the trail ropes. He did not want to catch an arm or a leg under one of these obstructions as he was winched out of the gondola and have his limb torn off.

The helicopter returned, and the probe was lowered again to Ben. It ricocheted all over the pitching gondola, and Ben, protecting his face with an uplifted arm, finally was able to control it. It was much more difficult to do this alone than it had been with two men, and Ben, with satisfaction, thought that Max probably could not have done it without help. He was so much less dexterous than Ben.

Ben adjusted the sling around his body, and an instant later he was in the air, free of the pitching gondola, twirling at the end of the cable.

Then another twenty-five-foot wave came, and Ben was in the water up to his neck. As the wave broke over him, he cried aloud, "My God, I'm still not going to get out of this!"

Ben had acted as he always did: to the last second, he had done everything that mind and muscle could do to control what was happening to him. He was ready to die but fighting to live. The helicopter plucked him out of the sea. Water streamed off his survival suit. His ears filled with the clatter of the helicopter engine, and looking upward, he saw anxious human faces in the door of the hovering machine.

The winch operator pulled him out of the water and into the helicopter. The airman apologized over and over to Ben for having dunked him. Ben put a fatherly hand on his shoulder and tried to smile reassuringly. Strong hands were holding him firmly, and he was glad of it. Until he went into the water, he had been feeling fine, adrenalin flowing. His exasperation over Max's love for the duffel bag had warmed him, too.

Within minutes after entering the helicopter, though, Ben was once again in desperate condition. He was cold and faint, and he sensed the return of his delirium. His color was ashen. Max spoke to him and he was coherent, but he was shuddering again. The Air Force physician aboard, Major Winston Bradley, and his medic helped Ben to the rear of the aircraft. There they stripped him and dressed him in dry clothes. He was not fully conscious, but he felt warm wool socks being pulled over his feet and gloves on his hands. The medics put him into a dry sleeping bag and laid another sleeping bag on top of him. The young medic put a compress on Ben's ear; when he got to Iceland, four stitches were required to close the cut. Ben, dry and beginning to feel warm, went to sleep.

It was 1730 Zulu when Ben came aboard. Major Key notified his headquarters, and someone there called Doc Wiley in Bedford.

Max found the helicopter almost unbearably noisy, and he realized that he had not heard a mechanical sound of any sort except the radios and the tiny noises he and Ben had made after leaving the land. They had been sixty-five hours and fourteen minutes in flight, forty of those hours in the rain. He would later learn that they had flown 2,440 miles to a point only three miles off the coast of Iceland. Only Ed Yost had flown longer and farther.

Max's mind was feverishly active. He went up to the cockpit and watched while the helicopter was refueled by the HC-130 tanker. He was amazed to find out that the tanker had come all the way from the Air Force base at Woodbridge, England. He learned that the Icelandic Coast Guard cutter *Oðinn* had been on a rescue track; had he thought to use the marine-band radio, he would have been able to talk to its captain, Commander S. Arnason. After the helicopter lifted away, the *Oðinn* arrived at the scene of the rescue and lifted the gondola of *Double Eagle* aboard, with all its equipment.

Max stopped thinking about the balloon, though his last glimpse of it, rocketing into the clouds, was still vivid in his mind's eye. A great sense of peace descended on him. At the time, he did not understand it. Later, he realized that he felt as he did because he knew

154

himself at last — knew the last and most important fact. He was not afraid to die.

He knew he could fly the Atlantic and that he had to fly the Atlantic. He said so to himself. To one of the Air Force officers, he said something about the danger of choosing safety. The man, who had just saved Max's life, looked puzzled.

Max was pleased to see Ben asleep and comfortable. He made repeated inquiries of the medical people about Ben's condition. All his anger at his friend vanished; he was glad Ben was all right. Max himself felt hungry for the first time in days, and he began to look forward to a good meal.

Much later, Max was asked this question: "If you had it to do again, would you fly on to Norway, even knowing that Ben would die?"

Max closed his eyes and thought about the question. "In time of war, yes," he replied. "But this wasn't war, and I didn't want it that way — not at the cost of Ben's life. I knew I had to do it, and I knew that Ben and I could do it. There'd be another time for both of us."

"It was an interesting trip," said Ben Abruzzo to the press that awaited him and Max Anderson when they landed in a driving rainstorm at the military airfield at Keflavik, Iceland, "but one that I will never make again."

Ben's words surprised Max. They astonished Pat Abruzzo when they were repeated to her in London. "No — my husband would never say such a thing," she said.

In Albuquerque, Ben's twelve-year-old daughter echoed her mother's words. "My daddy wouldn't say that!" Mary Pat protested.

Later, Pat would find it difficult to believe that Ben had been willing to die to save the flight. "I can hardly believe that Ben would give up his life without fighting," says Pat. "I mean fighting to the very end."

Pat Abruzzo and Patty Anderson had learned of their husbands' danger with the eyes of millions upon them. In London, a television man led them to the cameras without telling them, or even suggesting to them, that the flight was in trouble. While the wives spoke to Doc Wiley on the transatlantic telephone, and he told them at last that Max and Ben were going to ditch in the seas off Iceland, the cameras ran. Pat Abruzzo wept uncontrollably, with black mascara running down her cheeks, while Patty Anderson, crying as well, dried Pat's tears and her own. It was an unforgettable shot. Pat's tears were not for herself, nor did they owe anything to fear. Had she been able to see Ben's face and touch it, she could not have felt his disappointment more keenly. She cried out of the heartbreaking knowledge that Ben

156

and Max, after all their planning, all their work, all the risks they had taken, had been denied success.

Pat did not mind the cameras, but Patty Anderson has never entirely forgiven the callousness of the TV people. "They wanted that shot," said Patty afterward. "Our minds were on Max and Ben; we didn't know they were there with their lights and cameras and their cast of thousands. What right has anyone to expose you to strangers with your heart breaking?"

Because there was an air controllers' strike at Heathrow, Pat and Patty were unable to fly to Iceland. They spoke to Ben and Max by telephone, and it was decided that the men would fly to them in London. Promising exclusive interviews to the BBC, they used the network's influence to get seats for Max and Ben and Doc Wiley on an overbooked flight from Reykjavik. Doc was then on his way to Iceland from New York.

At the hotel in Reykjavik, Ben and Max found the best kind of welcome: a hot bath and a hot meal. They had not ordered the meal, the hotel had it sent to their rooms, and for Ben, the appearance of the food approached the mystical. It was precisely the meal he had hallucinated in the great storm off Greenland: roast beef medium rare, baked potatoes, green beans, salad — even the beer and the brandy. After supper, he settled into the tub, with water as hot as his skin could bear. He was in no doubt, as he had been during his delirium in the gondola, that this was reality.

Dozens of calls from the press flooded the hotel switchboard, and Ben dealt with most of them. The interest, amounting almost to hysteria, in the flight puzzled Ben. Why should newspapers and radio and television stations from all over the world be interested in an adventure that had failed to achieve its goal? The fact that he and Max had flown *Double Eagle* through worse conditions than those encountered by any balloonists in history, and survived, and made a controlled landing in impossible seas, did not seem heroic to Ben.

Pat Abruzzo thought otherwise. She told Ben to remember what he had survived, and what he had accomplished. "You should be *proud*," Pat insisted. Ben thinks his wife is the wisest person he has ever known. But he could not agree with her then, and he has never agreed with her since, about the meaning of the flight of *Double Eagle*. He did not do what he set out to do. In Ben's eyes, he and Max had failed.

Finally, Ben told the switchboard to stop putting through calls, and fell into bed.

Max, before he slept, talked on the telephone to Doc Wiley. He asked if Dewey Reinhard had taken off as yet in *Eagle*. Doc told him that Reinhard was still grounded, awaiting the right weather. Max had heard that Reinhard's partner, Charles Stephenson, might wish to withdraw from the flight if it were much longer delayed.

"Doc, what I want you to do," said Max, "is call Dewey and tell him I'm available to fly if he needs an experienced pilot."

"Maxie," Doc replied, "you don't know anything about Dewey's equipment. He's going to try to fly down on the water. You just got out of a rescue helicopter . . ."

"Call Dewey like I said," Max insisted, "and tell me what he says when you get here."

Doc, a wise colonel who knows when not to act on his general's whim, never called Reinhard. Instead, he went to sleep himself in a New York hotel for a few hours, and then flew to Reykjavik. He was astonished by the scene in the hotel room. Spread out on the floor were the dozens of items Max had rescued from the gondola. The remains of a meal, dirty plates and half-drunk glasses of beer and cognac, littered the coffee table. Ben and Max, unshaven, were in jubilant spirits. Ben was limping around, wearing only the pants of his quilted underwear.

Doc showed them the chart of their flight, and explained, in Bob Rice's words, what had happened to them. Looking at the chart, they knew for the first time that they had flown in a great cyclonic circle almost five hundred miles in circumference, off Greenland. Their actual distance flown, counting the circle, was 2,950 miles; for record purposes, however, only the straight-line distance from Marshfield to Iceland's coastal waters would count.

That night, Ben and Max threw a dinner party for the Navy and Air Force crews that had participated in their rescue. Ben was in splendid form, joking and making speeches.

During the evening his limp grew more pronounced. In bed after the party, he began to feel pain in his left foot. It was the same foot he had fouled in the anchor line aboard *Mariah*, and he thought it was acting up for some reason. The pain got worse, and when he could not sleep he took two aspirin. The right foot hurt, too, but not so badly.

158

At three or four in the morning, the pain in the left foot became unbearable. Ben, of course, had had all sorts of injuries and many bouts of surgery. Never had he felt such pain as this: daggers were being driven into his foot and he felt that the blood, somehow, was being blocked in the veins and capillaries. He called Doc Wiley and asked him to come down. "I've got more pain than I can accept," Ben told him; "I'm beyond myself."

Doc examined Ben's foot. It was swollen slightly and somewhat inflamed. Doc immediately suspected frostbite but said nothing to Ben. He gave him a sedative and sat with him, talking, until finally Ben was able to go to sleep.

The next morning, an Icelandic doctor confirmed that Ben had suffered severe frostbite in his left foot. There was no treatment except to stay off the foot and to avoid exposing it to cold. "You came as close as a man can come to losing toes, perhaps the whole foot," the physician told Ben. "You must be serious about this." It seemed unbelievable to Ben that there should be no treatment to correct his condition; the doctor gave him pain pills but no other medicine. "It will never improve," he told Ben in the solemn, assured manner of a man who has treated many such cases. Ben's blood, or that part of it which is water, had frozen, and this had destroyed tissue and small blood vessels; these would not repair themselves, and they could not be repaired by surgery.

At Heathrow, Pat Abruzzo and Patty Anderson waited in a bright pool of klieg lights for the arrival of their husbands.

Ben came into view first, haggard and limping. When he and Pat rushed into each other's arms, a silence fell over the onlookers. The Abruzzos, oblivious to the cameras and the strangers who surrounded them, embraced one another for long moments, with Pat's eyes gazing into Ben's. There was no need for words.

Max arrived in the glare of the television lights a few minutes later than Ben. By now, there was a baggage handlers' strike in Britain, and Max had helped to unload the plane. He had changed into his flight suit, and he looked dapper and rested. On the way into London, their friends Jack Hammack and Dave Slade mooned Ben and Max from the window of a taxicab. Max, who tends to underestimate the sense of fun possessed by the English, thought that this must be the first pair of bare bottoms ever seen on the Great West Road.

In addition to Jack and Shirley Hammack and Dave and Melody Slade, Bob Bowers had arrived, along with members of the ground staff. In his mind's eye, Ben had envisaged a grand party, a celebration, in London.

But the pain in his foot was still unbearable. Doc Wiley went with Ben to the American Embassy. The Navy doctor in the infirmary there told Ben that he must go into a hospital and remain off his foot for at least a week.

"I'm not buying that," said Ben, still wanting the party and the joyous reunion with Pat and their friends.

"Then you'll lose your foot," replied the doctor.

Pat Abruzzo and Jack Hammack took Ben to a hospital outside London. To Ben, the foreign hospital seemed strange, archaic. The food was healthful but tasteless; there was not even a mechanical bed operated by electricity, but the sort that is raised and lowered by handcranks. There was no telephone. During the night, as is usual in cases of severe frostbite, Ben had a series of high fevers, accompanied by chills and heavy sweats. When he complained of this condition, a nursing sister wheeled in a large electric fan and turned it on. Ben lay shivering in its wind.

"I'm going to die of exposure!" he told the nurse. "I'm not going to die of frostbite, but you're giving me pneumonia!"

"No, sir," said the cool British nurse. "You'll be perfectly all right. You must do the best you can, sir."

She gave Ben an extra blanket and he went to sleep. When he woke, another nurse stood by his bed.

Ben was very glad to see that the shifts had changed, and he had a new nurse. He said: "You won't believe what that other nurse did to me. She tried to kill me. Turned on that big fan. I'm soaked and I'm freezing."

"Well, sir," said the new nurse, "that's for your foot. I'm going to do it again."

She did so, and Ben, sweating and writhing on his soaked bed, protested that he had almost frozen to death. He still refused to worry about his foot. Pat knew how serious the injury was. She had been talking to the doctors, making friends with the nurses. Ben chafed at his confinement; Pat saw to it that he was well taken care of. The next morning he left the hospital. Neither Pat Abruzzo nor

Jack Hammack nor the entire staff of the hospital could convince him to stay. He went back to the hotel with Pat, and after two days of quiet talk and noisy parties, they all went back to America.

En route to Albuquerque, Ben and Pat and Max and Patty stopped in Bedford for a chat with Rice and his colleague at Weather Services, Peter Leavitt. Both balloonists had called Rice from Iceland soon after landing. "We think you did a great job for us," Ben reassured Rice. It was a compliment of such generosity, coming from a man who had nearly died in a storm at sea, that Rice found it difficult to reply. In Bedford, Ben sat in a wheelchair or hobbled around on crutches. It was evident to Rice that Ben was in severe pain, and he marveled at the way in which Ben put his suffering to one side and applied his intelligence to the analysis of the flight.

"The theme of the conversation," Rice recalls, "was how to avoid the same problems on the next flight. For Max and Ben alike, there was no 'if' about that next flight — only 'when.' "

Even before he returned to the United States, Ben had set the record straight on television. No longer was he saying that he would never make that interesting trip again.

In Albuquerque, Ben consulted a cardiovascular specialist. After tests, the specialist told him what all the other doctors had told him: that the foot would be no better, ever; that he must not injure it again. If he broke a toe he might lose it; break anything more major and the whole foot might be in peril. Ben had never heard worse news.

For a month he was confined to bed, unable to go to the office. He spent another month in a wheelchair, and two more on crutches. Only at the end of three months was he able to wear a shoe on his left foot again. He installed a whirlpool bath at his house and used that, and took pain pills. By midwinter, the pain had subsided. But the knowledge that he might lose his foot through some freakish accident, and the memory of the pain, never left Ben's mind.

He was overcome by remorse, sadness, confusion. He fell into a deep depression, so deep that he wondered, speaking of it to Pat, if he would ever come out of it again. Pat said, "As your feet get better, your thinking and your attitude will change."

But Ben's attitude never really changed. He believed that the decision to heed the message from Bedford and remain at 2,000 feet rather than climbing to a higher altitude had doomed the flight.

"Up is east and down is north," he would repeat to Pat. "If we had gone up, we would have made it!"

By the time the Sandia Peak skiing season opened in January, Ben was almost his old self. Still, he brooded. Rich Schwoebel told him it was a triumph merely to have survived the flight, and a miracle of skill to have flown through the Greenland storm.

Pat Abruzzo thought that both men felt a sense of horrible failure; this reaction irritated her, but it did not surprise her. "They knew what they'd been through," she says, "but that's of no value to men like Ben and Max. It would have to be appreciated by everyone. In Ben's case, it's like he has to have the bows and the applause and he has to have the audience to feel accomplishment. And not just within himself. It's not that I disapprove of that, but it's sad."

When Ben and Max returned to Albuquerque, they were met at the airport by a crowd of some four hundred persons. There had been a testimonial dinner at a local hotel, and many parties and warmhearted telephone calls. But their welcome home had not been a heroes' welcome.

Within two days of the rescue off Iceland, Max Anderson began making plans for a second flight. He had made the decision to go while he was still in the rescue helicopter. He knew, as Ben knew, the errors they had made and how to avoid them in the future. The balloon system had proved itself in the most extreme conditions. "If you just keep the balloon in the air," Max said to himself inside the clattering Jolly Green Giant, "you can make it."

Max believed that his own greatest error had been his insensitivity to Ben's physical condition. He had not noticed Ben's suffering until it was too late — in any future flight, the pilots must communicate with each other, watch each other. He and Ben had not done that.

The error, in turn, had forced him into what he regarded as the greatest mistake and the greatest lesson of his life: he had chosen safety when he should have chosen danger. He could not forgive himself this act of weakness. Even before the flight, he had sensed that men could defeat themselves in this way; despite this intuitive forewarning, he had done what others had done before him. He was

162

resolved never to let such a thing happen again. To test this resolve, he had to go again.

For six weeks Max could barely sleep. He paid the minimum of attention to business and personal matters. He would wake in the night, and lie in the dark, thinking about equipment — better ways to protect the pilots from the elements, better radio and navigational equipment. He carried a chart of the Atlantic in his mind, sleeping and waking, and in his imagination drew flight paths across it. "I was driven to do it, compelled to complete the task, almost beyond my will," says Max. "It was as if I didn't really have a choice, that my mind would not let me contemplate quitting. I was convinced that flying that ocean in a balloon could and should be done. It became almost an obsession, a driving force, a fixation."

After a month or so, he began discussing the possibility of a second flight with Ben. He detected little enthusiasm in his friend. Max did not want to fly with anyone else. He began to think about flying alone — Ed Yost had done it, sleeping for an hour at a time. Max wondered if he could train himself to sleep and wake in one-hour cycles; he knew that he functioned best on three hours' sleep. He hoped that Ben would change his mind. Max mentioned the possibility of flying alone to Jim Mitchell. "Apart from all the other obvious reasons not to do that," Mitchell told him, "you'll scare the hell out of your family." Max knew that was true. He knew, too, that if there was no other way to go, he would go alone.

Ben's mind was not, in this period, wholly engaged with the question of another flight. He was in the midst of a tough struggle for control of his group of companies, a $25 million enterprise. Maneuvering, negotiating, dealing, took up a lot of his time and intellectual and emotional energy. He could not fly away in a balloon, he told Max, unless the financial security of his family was assured. Max understood this. The two men have always been able to talk to each other more easily about business matters than about other questions — even such questions as entrusting each other with their lives.

In February, the Andersons and the Abruzzos shared a skiing weekend at Aspen. There, Ben and Max discussed the new flight. The decision to go had to be made soon if everything was to be ready for liftoff in late summer. Bob Rice had said that he believed late summer — August — was the best time to go. Rich Schwoebel

had some new ideas for modifying the design of the balloon. Schwoebel and Doc Wiley were working on ideas to provide the pilots with
better protection. Syd Parks could be brought in earlier, to help
design a more efficient communications package. Max thought the
flight would cost $150,000. Putting up half that sum did not trouble
him. Ben, who had need for all his assets because of the struggle for
control of his businesses, wondered if the investment was justified.

Ben was still having trouble with his frostbitten foot. He had
acquired a pair of heated ski boots, and he fussed with them, trying
to get them properly adjusted. Nearly every night, he took them to
the ski shop to have them modified. Skiing, which he loved so much,
caused him excruciating pain unless his foot was warm; he found
that if he lost feeling in his toes he was unable to control his skis.

In the ski lodge at Aspen, Ben asked Max a fundamental question. As Max recalls it, Ben fixed him with his familiar blue stare and
said, "Max, why should we do this?"

"To me," Max replied, "it's a way of entering history."

"You want to do that?"

"If I can do it by accomplishing something that has fired men's
imaginations because it seems impossible, yes," said Max. "I think
I can do it, Ben. I think you can, too."

Ben wondered if he and Max could do it without the help of
a third person. Another pilot would reduce the fatigue factor; he
ought to be chosen for skills that he and Max did not possess.

"There is no better team than the two of us," Max said. "We
don't need anyone else."

"I think we do," Ben insisted.

They made no final decision at Aspen. In the weeks that followed, they met for lunch or for skiing, and talked about the flight.
Gradually, it came to be understood that they would fly again that
summer. Once more, Ben and Max drifted into agreement on a
principle, without paying too much attention to specifics. Ben solved
his business problems. He discussed with Pat the expense involved;
there was little possibility of a return on the money. It was not an
investment, it was an indulgence.

Pat said, "You want to go? Go — and as far as the money is
concerned, don't even think about it as something you owe me or
your family. Think of what you owe yourself."

Ben wanted, somehow, to erase what he insisted on regarding

as a failure. The impulse came not only from within himself, but from others as well. As he went about on his crutches, he was asked, over and over, when he was going to go again. Gradually, he came to feel that he owed it to the public, to the world, to try once more. "You owe it to people you've never heard of, to go out and take that risk again," Ben explains. "They expect you to do it."

Partly because of the financial consideration, but mostly because he was convinced that a third pilot was necessary to the success of the flight, Ben kept pressing Max to consider taking on a third man. By early spring, CBS had aired its special program about the flight of *Double Eagle*, and that of Dewey Reinhard's *Eagle*. (Reinhard's theory about a low-level flight using water ballast scooped from the sea had not proved out: he landed off the Nova Scotia coast after flying only two hundred miles in forty-six hours.)

After viewing the film, Ben decided that he would go again. When he and Max appeared on television shortly thereafter and Ben, in his peppery way, announced the flight of *Double Eagle II*, nothing was said about carrying a third crew member. But by then, Ben had won his point. Max had agreed to take a third person.

Max had great respect for the flying abilities of a local physician, and the fact that this pilot was a doctor was, in his mind, an important additional qualification. Unfortunately, the doctor was a woman; Max, joking, told Ben that taking her along would require too much postflight debriefing by the wives of the two male balloonists. They never discussed the question with the physician.

Max saw that the question of a third crew member was important to Ben. He grasped the sense in some of Ben's arguments, but secretly he felt that taking along a third person would create more problems than it would solve. He and Ben had learned the lessons of the first flight and would apply them to the second. A new man would be just that. Ed Yost had been right — nobody could be taught by another human being the lessons the Atlantic would teach him. In the end, Max lost interest in the question of a third crew member, and left it to Ben to find the right man.

Weekend after weekend, the *Double Eagle II* team gathered around the swimming pool at Ben's house or Max's and played the game Rich Schwoebel had named "What-if?" What if the winds were slower or faster than anticipated? What if they installed a more reliable on-board navigational system? What sort of clothes would be best? What sort of shelter could be constructed in the gondola? How could protection from the rain and the snow be improved?

They played the game in the warm sun of New Mexico, but they all knew how cold reality had been, and would be soon again.

**14** On a Saturday morning in April 1974, an unemployed airplane pilot named Larry Newman knocked on the door of Ben Abruzzo's house. Newman, a Californian, was twenty-six years old. He had the looks and the manner of a much younger person, and Ben Abruzzo could not possibly have guessed, as Newman stood on his doorstep in faded blue jeans and a muscle shirt, that he had flown thousands of hours in all sorts of aircraft, including Lear jets, and that he was considered by the tiny group of enthusiasts who knew about such things to be among the half-dozen best hang-glider pilots in the world.

Larry Newman wanted to fly a hang-glider off Sandia Peak, and since the tram running to the peak was Ben's property, he had come to ask permission. Ben refused. Larry, undaunted by Ben's rejection of his plan, loaded his hang-glider onto his car and drove around to the back of Sandia Mountain and up a road that leads to Sandia Crest, which is 230 feet higher than the Peak. Larry flew his glider off the Crest — becoming the first person to do so — and landed it in Ben's front yard.

Ben himself had taken some hang-gliding lessons, and as he watched Larry's descent from the top of the 10,678-foot mountain, his exasperation gave way to admiration. The flight was a great act of daring, and Ben realized, as he watched the hang-glider soar and bank and climb, sensitive to Larry's every whim, that he was witnessing the work of a master pilot.

When Larry landed, Ben walked up to him and said, "Nice flight. I'd like to try that myself."

Very soon, after several lessons with Larry, he did fly off Sandia Peak. It was the first of many such flights, and the beginning of a friendship. For Larry, it was more than a friendship; he came to regard Ben as a second father and as a model for everything he himself wanted to become: a successful businessman, rich and respected, smart and free in his own life, wise and tolerant toward his friends and, especially, toward his children.

Larry's parents had divorced when he was about ten years old. His father, Herb Newman, called Speedy by his friends, is a man of great intelligence and verve. Born in New York, Herb Newman has been hustling all his life. After dropping out of high school in the Depression, he sold ice cream at Jones Beach, and at the 1939 World's Fair; as Crunchy-Wunchy Sam the Ice Cream Man, he sold ice cream in the snow on the ski slopes of Squaw Valley during the 1960 Olympics. When Larry was born, on September 28, 1947, Herb was selling ice cream in Los Angeles. Three years later he moved to Fresno with his wife and three children; Larry is the middle one. Herb had a brightly painted bus with a sign on the side: "Don't Be Needy, Work for Speedy!" In this bus, he would make the rounds of skid row each morning and collect stoop labor to pick the cotton, cantaloupes, peaches, grapes, and vegetables grown in the San Joaquin Valley.

In Fresno, between the ages of three and ten, Larry made the only friend he ever had until he met Ben. The friend's name was Baxter Richardson. He lived right across the street from the Newmans. "Baxter's parents always acted a little different," says Larry. "Baxter's father was a lawyer. He wasn't a labor contractor, like my father. I could tell his parents thought they were hot stuff. Once I threw a rock through their window because I didn't like them. Even though I was only six years old, I'd already learned from them what arrogance was. I could feel all that stuff."

After his parents separated, Larry returned to Los Angeles with his mother. He was an unhappy child, and his behavior did not please his teachers or his mother's family, who were devout Jews; Larry did not like school and he did not like Temple and *schul*. When preparing for his bar mitzvah, he felt like a parrot, learning Hebrew words whose meaning he never knew or cared about. He went through it for his mother's sake, but after being bar mitzvahed at thirteen, he never again set foot in a religious institution.

What he did like to do — to the exclusion of virtually everything else — was to fly in airplanes. His father had an airplane and from earliest childhood Larry had flown with him from farm to farm in the San Joaquin Valley. Between landings on dirt roads and plowed fields, Herb would let Larry sit on his lap and "fly" the plane. One day, when Larry was seven, Herb had been amusing him by flying loops on the way back to Fresno. Larry pulled back on the stick, put the plane into the loop, and at the top, turned out of it in a perfect Immelmann.

When Larry was twelve, Herb Newman was chatting with a farmer and the plane was parked nearby. Herb told Larry to take it up. Larry scrambled into the plane before his father could change his mind. "I took off, flew it around, landed on the little dirt runway, and took off and landed again," says Larry. " 'That's my kid, whaddya think of that?' my father is saying to the farmer. He wanted to impress him. It was like a monkey doing a trick, me flying that plane. I didn't really know what I was doing. But I have seldom been frightened of anything that has flown."

At fourteen, Larry went to live with his father in Fresno. Herb was living out of his office; he and Larry slept in a back room and Larry did the cooking and the housework. He went to school during the day and flew his father's airplane on weekends. He had seen a lot of the world. His father had taken him on trips all over Canada, following the royal train when Queen Elizabeth and Prince Philip visited there in 1959. Herb would fly ahead of the train, land in a field, and hustle the crowd on the station platform and along the parade route, selling photographs of the royal couple and flags and lapel buttons he had bought at rock-bottom prices from other hustlers who had no airplane and so could not keep up with the queen's progress. An equerry approached Herb at a railway station somewhere in Saskatchewan, and said, "His Royal Highness, Prince Philip, is rather curious about you. Wherever we go, there you are. How, His Royal Highness wishes me to ask, do you manage that?" Herb pointed to his battered Tripacer parked in a bumpy field.

Herb tried to teach Larry the tricks of working a crowd, of making a dollar, of talking faster than your ice cream will melt. Larry was not interested. He was interested in nothing but airplanes.

His teachers told him he was an underachiever. Larry had little respect for them, and a great deal of confidence in himself. "When you master an airplane, you either do it or you bust your ass," he says. "At sixteen, to be able to fly an airplane around is a unique mastery. And there I was, being told by my teachers what it was like to be in Canada. I'd already flown to all these places, and they'd never seen them." The girls he dated did not want to talk about airplanes; the boys he knew did not always believe that Larry could fly airplanes. After Baxter Richardson, he made no more close friends.

Larry graduated from the U.S. Grant High School in Los Angeles, near the bottom of his class, when he was seventeen. He went back to Fresno. Herb Newman, realizing where Larry's interests and talents lay, said something to him, in the thoughtless half-joking way fathers sometimes speak to their sons, which burned itself into Larry's mind.

He said, as Larry remembers it, "You're too dumb to be a businessman, so I'm going to help you go to a flying school. Maybe you can be an airline pilot."

Herb Newman's remark, which fourteen years later he only half remembered, ignited in his son fires of ambition and resentment. When Larry found Ben Abruzzo, the second true friend of his life, he would call him "the father I never had." If Herb couldn't be like Ben, Larry could be.

Larry went to a flying school called American Flyers, in Ardmore, Oklahoma. While he was there, a Lockheed Electra crashed into the side of a mountain. Eighty-nine people were killed. Larry went out with the rescue team, and nothing in the seventeen years of his life prepared him for what he found at the scene of the crash. "I'm tromping around in the woods, it's pouring down rain," Larry recalls, "and I'm picking up arms and legs and severed bodies and there were still some people that weren't dead yet and they were moaning and screaming. There were dead cows in the trees, blood everywhere. I decided right then I was going to be a safe pilot, not a chance-taker. I never, ever, wanted to be one of those people."

Licensed as a commercial pilot at eighteen, Larry flew as a company pilot and ferried airplanes from coast to coast. He went to Fresno City College for two years, part-time, hoping to improve his flying career, but once again the teachers seemed to him to be dullards and he quit. He flew cargo, including corpses. Flying over the Sierras, alone at night with his first corpse, he heard it moaning in the back of the light plane. Larry was terrified until he realized that the change in pressure as the aircraft reached altitude was permitting air to escape from the dead man's lungs and through his vocal apparatus.

By the time Larry was twenty-one, he had logged more than four thousand pilot hours. He took two years off from flying to manage a construction firm in Hawaii. Later, he worked with his father, who had in the meantime married again and moved to Albuquerque. He couldn't bear to be away from aircraft, and he went back to flying school; it took him just seven hours of flying time to qualify for his license as captain of a Lear jet. He got a job flying the U.S. Mail in Lears, and like Charles Lindbergh before him, he flew a great deal — six takeoffs and landings a day on a circuit from Grand Rapids to Chicago, Bloomington, St. Louis, Peoria, Chicago, and back to Grand Rapids.

The Lear excited him. It is a machine that normally flies above 40,000 feet. At sea level, on a cold morning with a minimum load, it will climb at a rate approaching 10,000 feet per minute — faster than many military aircraft. But finally the work bored him, packing the mail into the plane and taking it out six times a day. He got another job, flying automobile parts all over the United States. Sometimes he would fly for twelve hours, rest for one hour, and then fly for another thirteen hours. He flew through unbelievable weather, catnapping in the back of the aircraft among the crates of automobile parts while his copilot flew the plane, or flying while the other man slept. In one twelve-month period, he logged eighteen hundred hours; an average pilot-year is six hundred hours.

Larry is a natural athlete, and he became an expert skier and surfer and water-skier with as little effort as he had learned to fly airplanes. Flying remained his first love, and on February 19, 1974 — Larry has never forgotten the date — he and a girl named Mary Lou Long, while skiing in the Sierras, saw a hang-glider gliding along the face of the mountain. Larry knew at once that he was seeing the nearest thing to pure flight man had ever known, and the next day he took a lesson in Fresno. Flying off the velvety green hills there, he achieved heights of a hundred feet. The same day, he ordered a hang-glider and had it shipped to Hawaii; he followed it out.

On Oahu, he looked up an old surfing companion named John Hughes. To Hughes, Larry said, "Guess what? I can fly like a bird."

"So can I," replied Hughes. "I've been hang-gliding for six months."

"Oh? I've been flying for seven months," said Larry.

Hughes took him to a twelve-hundred-foot cliff and flew off. Larry followed him into the shadowy depths of the canyon. He had never had such a sensation. Now he really understood how a bird must feel on its first flight, once the anxiety of the first moments gives way to the instinctive confidence of a creature that has found its element. For the following month, Larry did nothing but fly his hang-glider off the most soarable ridges in the islands.

When he went back to the Mainland, he went to Albuquerque because he thought that Sandia Peak would be a good place to fly from. For a time, he ran a small hang-gliding school and gave instruction to Ben Abruzzo and his son Louis and some of Ben's employees at the tramway. His friendship with Ben ripened, and in a way that puzzled Larry, who was awestruck by Ben's easy cordiality. "Here I am, flat broke and seventeen years younger, and here he is, this mature, successful, well-recognized man-about-town," says Larry. "We were certainly a mismatch."

Since his return to Albuquerque, Larry had been selling hang-gliders, and when, in 1974, he decided to start his own manufacturing firm, Ben rented him space in one of his shopping centers. For the first year, Larry was unable to pay the rent; Ben carried him. Then Larry's firm, Electra Flyer, produced several revolutionary designs and began to prosper. By 1977, Electra Flyer was producing two thousand gliders and grossing over a million dollars a year, and few disputed Larry's claim that it was the biggest manufacturer of hang-gliders in the world.

Though he hadn't really flown an aircraft with an engine in it for three or four years, Larry in his new prosperity began to hanker after a Lear jet of his own. He and Ben formed a partnership, which eventually included several others, to buy a Lear. As Larry's business grew, he had often sought Ben's advice, and they saw each other fairly often for dinner at one of the little circle of restaurants in Albuquerque where the successful forgather.

To Larry, Maxie Anderson was little more than a name; he had met him three or four times, and the encounters had always been casual. Like everyone in Albuquerque, he knew about the flight of *Double Eagle*, and he had suffered with Ben through the long ordeal of the frostbitten foot.

Ben had been walking normally for some weeks when, in the early spring of 1978, he and Larry met for dinner at a restaurant called Liquid Assets. They were working on the details for the purchase of the Lear jet, for a sum that approached $1 million. Ben, sipping a Heineken's beer, his usual drink, told Larry that he and Max were thinking about flying the Atlantic in a new balloon.

"Again?" said Larry. "You gotta be crazy."

By that time, Ben and Max had already sent Ed Yost a check for $20,000 as a down payment on *Double Eagle II*, but they had not yet made a public announcement of the second flight. Once again, Max and Ben had made their decision on the telephone. After a brief conversation, each had put $10,000 into the kitty, and on April 12, Ben mailed the check.

Larry knew little about the first flight; Ben had never talked about it much. He did know that Max and Ben had undergone hardships, that they had nearly died. He had concluded that there had been a lack of proper planning and preparation. People who did not prepare and plan did not last long as pilots: they flew airplanes into mountainsides and killed eighty-nine people.

"What you need," said Larry in an outburst of brashness, "is somebody to keep you in order, somebody who's got his flying shit together — like me."

He was joking. Ben gave him a piercing look but made no reply. Larry thought nothing more about the matter; he was running this business and buying the Lear.

A week or so later, as Larry remembers it, Ben telephoned him. He told Larry that he and Max had made a final decision to go.

Larry said, still half in jest, "If you go, I'll go."

"Would you really like to go?" Ben said.

"Sure, I'll go." Larry thought that Ben might be inviting him to ride, free, as a passenger.

Ben said no more about it, and a few days later Larry spoke to him again. He had decided that he really did want to go — he loved being with Ben, it would be a lot of fun, a new way to fly. He had only recently decided to get married. A Lear jet, a bride, a balloon flight — it was a season for new experiences.

Ben said, "You realize it's going to cost you some money — thirty to forty-five thousand dollars."

That caused Larry a moment's thought. But as a picture of the great balloon formed in his imagination, he said to himself, "I want to go; I've got to go."

He said to Ben, "I've got the money."

"I'll talk to Max," Ben replied, and hung up.

Although Max had agreed to take along the third man, he had not conquered his reservations about the idea. Among the things that worried him was the image the new partner might project. Less than ever, in the restless months following the landing off Iceland, could Max abide any lapse of good manners. Even a badly set table at a dinner party upset him. His own behavior was more controlled than ever; it was as though his determination to control the circumstances of the second flight had reached out to grasp every other detail of his life.

Max felt, too, that he and Ben had been drawn closer together by their ordeal. Their natural competitiveness, their whimsical rivalries, had vanished at the crucial moment, and they had, each of them, submerged their rambunctious egos into the common good. Who could be sure that a third person, intruding into the finely tuned relationship between him and Ben, would behave as Max would behave, or as he knew Ben would behave? Six days in a gondola with a man who did not know the rules could be, for Max, an eternity.

There was a good case for Larry. He had great manual dexterity and mechanical ability. He knew about radios. He had intelligence and nerve and stamina. As an airplane pilot, he was extraordinary: after a four-year layoff, he had requalified as a Lear captain after a check ride of only one and a half hours. Most pilots would have required perhaps twenty-five hours of retraining to accomplish this. He could rebuild the gondola in his hang-glider shop; he had some ideas already about improvements. And, he was willing to pay a third of the costs of the expedition. Ben did not plead for Larry; he presented him as a candidate.

He was, of course, the only candidate. No balloonist had volunteered to go with Ben and Max, and it was unlikely that any would do so at this advanced date. Max knew of Ben's friendship with Larry, and that counted — if Ben liked and trusted him, Max was obliged to respect Ben's judgment.

Larry was not a balloon pilot. He knew nothing about flying a balloon. Both Max and Ben took it for granted that they could teach him, or any man with so extensive a background in aviation, all he needed to know before liftoff.

Ben called Larry back. "Maxie says okay," he said.

"I'm in," Larry replied.

To Ben's astonishment, Larry refused to learn to fly a balloon.

"You and Max are capable of flying the balloon," said Larry. "Right now I don't want to take the time and I'm not really interested. I'll learn on the flight."

Ben, in discussing the matter with Max, suggested that, in public references to the flight, the two of them should be described as pilots, with Larry listed in some other way — as radio operator, perhaps. Max said no. Larry was taking equal risks and making an equal investment of time and money; he should have equal billing.

Larry was not planning on coming to earth with Ben and Max in any case. Almost as soon as he joined the crew of *Double Eagle II*, he proposed a bizarre variation on the flight. He would suspend one of his hang-gliders beneath the gondola, and when the balloon approached its destination, he would fly the glider to earth in a spectacular grand finale.

This idea terrified Rich Schwoebel. Larry's plan involved lowering him in a harness some twenty feet; he would then have to mount the hang-glider, release it, and fly it through the swarm of aircraft that would certainly surround any successful transatlantic balloon as soon as it crossed a coastline. "I'll wear a parachute," shrugged Larry. His confidence in himself and in his glider — a craft that *really* flew — was supreme. Ben raised no objection to the scheme; if Larry was not going to learn how to fly the balloon, he would be of no use at the landing anyway; let him have a separate welcome wherever he came to earth. Max, with *Double Eagle II* floating in

176

his imagination over the hedgerows of Normandy, considered the hang-glider irrelevant.

Secretly, Larry believed that he would know as much about flying a helium balloon as Ben and Maxie after a couple of days in the air. He had learned by watching many times before. If he could make a perfect Immelmann turn at age seven, qualify in Lears in a matter of hours, and fly a hang-glider off a twelve-hundred-foot cliff after one day's practice, why should *Double Eagle II* defeat him?

Later in the summer, Ben rigged the gondola of *Double Eagle II* to one of the cars on his tramway, suspended the hang-glider below that, and helped Larry practice his climb down into it. The exertion left Larry sweating and panting.

"It'll be better," said Larry, "when we actually do it. This thing goes around and around."

"So does the gondola, all during the flight," Ben replied. "It rotates all the time."

"*All the time?* Why didn't you tell me this?"

"You're the guy who didn't want to learn," said Ben.

Larry did make one flight with Ben and Ben's son Louis in *Mariah Tambien*, and he lost himself in the experience. As the balloon was swept by the winds along the rocky face of the Sandia escarpment, deer leaped from the sparse desert covert and ran before it. Ben pursued them, burners whooshing. Larry could not take his eyes off the lovely animals. Then Ben announced that they were running out of fuel. "I knew we were in trouble," recalls Larry. "But what did it matter? Beautiful things were happening. Besides, Ben had the balloon under control." They landed safely on the mountainside.

Later, Larry dropped in his Olympus 160 hang-glider from *Mariah Tambien*, with Ben and Max flying the balloon. The glider fell, nose down, then pulled out after achieving the necessary airspeed, and flew beautifully. Larry circled the balloon all the way down to the desert floor, 4,000 feet below, landed thirty feet from the balloon, unharnessed himself from the glider, and jumped into the gondola to assist in the landing. It was a new experience for Larry, but Ben had previously dropped his son and other hang-glider pilots from *Mariah Tambien* — and may, he believes, have been the first balloonist to perform this feat.

The target date for the launch of *Double Eagle II* was August 10, 1978. The date was chosen on April 1, during a planning session around Ben Abruzzo's swimming pool, and although there was no realistic expectation that the launch would actually take place on the chosen day, Max spoke of going no later than August 15; he dreaded the dawdling wait for the right weather, and the dulling of the edge that would result.

In June, Ben and Max and Larry flew to Maine to choose a launch site. It was their first flight in their new Lear jet, and the precision with which Larry flew impressed Max. Their search was unsuccessful, but later Max returned and found what Larry described as "the perfect place." It was a clover field, sloping and sheltered, on Merle Sprague's farm in Spragueville, a hamlet lying along a brook about ten miles west of the border with New Brunswick. Near here, just before the first dawn of the flight of *Double Eagle*, Max had mistaken the Aroostook River for the St. John and wondered if he and Ben had crossed into Canada. By launching from this position in northernmost Maine, just above the 46th parallel, they would save a whole night of flying. With any sort of windfield at the planned altitude, the balloon would cross the coast and enter the Atlantic around first light the next day, after a post-sunset launch.

Double Eagle II would be a larger version of *Double Eagle*, and it would display the same registration number: N 50 DE. In photographs, it is difficult to tell the two craft apart. The new balloon was designed to carry 160,000 cubic feet of helium, 59,000 more than *Double Eagle*. The additional gas would give it greater lifting power, needed because it was carrying three men instead of two, and a heavier load of equipment. Inflated, the envelope would be sixty-five feet in diameter and ninety-seven feet high. Fully inflated, with its rigging and gondola, it would be as tall as an eleven-story building. It was designed for a flight lasting seven days, with a payload at takeoff of 10,500 pounds.

Rich Schwoebel made a small but sophisticated modification in the design. On the duct, he placed two small triangular rip panels, one above the other. By opening these holes late in the flight, when the volume of helium had been reduced by normal venting, the ceiling of *Double Eagle II* could be reduced by as much as 10,000 feet by spilling controlled amounts of gas. No such device had ever been

178

used on a manned balloon, and Schwoebel and the balloonists believed that this refinement, which they kept secret, would conserve ballast and prolong the flight.

An unusually large area of the sphere was coated with silver paint, to reflect the midday sun more effectively and prevent excessive heating and expansion of the helium. This modification, designed to prevent *Double Eagle II* from rising to undesirably high ceilings, was to have unexpected and puzzling results during the flight.

They planned for a flight of four and a half days, at maximum altitudes of 26,000 feet. With a full load of helium, the flight should take no longer than six days. The seventh day of duration was a safety factor.

Bob Rice told them that they could expect a slower flight this time; wind speeds over the Atlantic in August are at their lowest average of the year. But, if they climbed onto the right high-pressure ridge, they would have a drier flight, in fair weather. Max (sometimes accompanied by Ben) made a number of trips to Boston, to confer with Rice. Max's preoccupation with thunderstorms remained: the idea of being blown up the "chimney" to an altitude that would cause abortion of the flight haunted him. He was determined this time to find the right weather, insert the balloon into it at the right moment, and fly a preplanned profile.

The planners were preoccupied with safety factors, with backup systems. Schwoebel insisted that the pilots be better protected: the rain skirt had to be redesigned, and there must be some sort of shelter, equipped with a heater. Doc Wiley's plea for seafarers' clothing fell, this time, on receptive ears. They would wear layers of wool and waterproofs. Fiber-filled parkas and sleeping bags, which retain their insulating characteristics even when soaked, would be substituted for the goose-down bags and garments of the first flight.

Syd Parks designed an improved communications system. Rich Schwoebel, like Parks a dedicated "ham," made the fateful decision that an amateur-band ("ham") radio would be added to the package. The balloonists decided to carry an Omega navigational device with which they would be able to read, on a digital display, the exact latitude and longitude of the balloon by receiving signals from three radio beams triangulating upon an antenna fixed to the gondola. Doc thought they ought to have two Nimbus satellite transmitters aboard. As a final navigational backup, Max added a hand-held computer to the sextant as a quicker and more reliable way of deducing the balloon's position from star sights.

They decided to divide the voyage into three-hour watch periods: one man on watch, one man resting, one man asleep. Ben and Max would be the pilots, with Ben being responsible for ballast and Max for celestial navigation. Larry would handle photography and communications, including the Omega navigational device.

Ben studied every detail of the balloon's design. He mastered not merely the technique, but the theory, of gas ballooning, and Rich Schwoebel came to believe that Ben understood these matters as well as any balloonist past or present.

Rich Schwoebel designed a flight manual that covered every contingency — daily altitudes, ballasting schedules, helium lifting capacity on a day-by-day basis, radio frequencies and procedures. He devised a simple letter-and-number code to transmit wind direction and velocity at given altitudes. This would avoid the garbled messages that had plagued the first flight.

Larry met Rich Schwoebel half a dozen times before he ever saw his eyes. Schwoebel always wore dark sunglasses at the poolside meetings, and at first Larry formed the opinion that Schwoebel was an aloof, cold intellectual. Gradually he realized that Schwoebel, though he would remain on the ground, would, in a sense, be flying with them in *Double Eagle II*.

"He knew more about it than anybody in the world," Larry says. "Even I saw that in no time. Rich is quiet — I'd never run into such a quiet guy. Nobody had to tell me what a genius he was. If Rich said it was so, we believed him. He wrote it down, and we did it."

Max returned persistently to his favorite theme: human error must be avoided, and the only way to avoid it was to anticipate it. He played "What-if?" until the game fatigued Ben and bored Larry. Max wanted to set up a more systematic schedule of physical and mental conditioning; Ben found it difficult to understand Max's preoccupation with such matters. When Max's questions probed areas that Ben regarded as his responsibility, Ben's fatigue turned to exasperation. He wanted to ask, "What if you drop the sextant? What if you can't find the chart of the Atlantic again?" But he kept his peace.

Max consulted Dr. Ulrich C. Luft, a specialist in the use of oxygen at high altitudes. All three balloonists went through a brief training session at Dr. Luft's laboratory at the Lovelace Medical Center in Albuquerque, which possesses a chamber that simulates high-altitude conditions. Dr. Luft, a transplanted German who began his research as a young man with the Luftwaffe, was asked by Schwoebel whether it would be a good idea for the pilots to breathe pure oxygen just before making crucial decisions — Max had wondered about that. "It will not," said Dr. Luft in his German accent, "make them smarter."

By the end of June, the planning sessions came to an end. With some help from Doc Wiley, Ben had procured most of the equipment, including electric socks. The radio system was nearly ready for installation, and Syd Parks was searching for opportunities to familiarize Larry with the gear. Larry completed the redesign of the gondola, and the improvements were major. He and his men at Electra Flyer had devised a new yellow rain cover, fitted with plastic windows, that would be completely watertight and much simpler to rig. The whole gondola had been floored, and storage space cleverly redesigned. A weatherproof compartment for the radio equipment had been added and — most important — a shelter for the member of the crew who would be sleeping. The sleeping box, and the gondola itself when the rain cover was fitted, could be heated with a propane radiant heater.

The financial situation had eased somewhat. A group of backers purchased a twenty-five percent share of the flight as an investment against any profits it might return, and ABC signed the balloonists to a contract for exclusive on-board coverage. There would be television cameras aboard the gondola. This was not a prospect that pleased Max: television was a nonessential.

Ben did not see it that way. "Max," he asked, "have you forgotten that we signed a contract to do this? That we accepted a $50,000 fee from ABC? That all of us, including you, were delighted to have that money to help offset our expenses? And, furthermore, that this film will be a record of this flight not just for us but for everyone?"

Max had not forgotten. But it rankled that the contract called for a much smaller payment if the flight did not succeed, and the thought of carrying the extra weight represented by cameras and all the baffling gear they required was not a happy thought. "The only thing that pays off," said Max, "is getting across the Atlantic. TV won't be worth a penny if we don't do that." This was a difference that would flare up time and again between Ben and Max and Larry.

In July, Max took time off to fly across the Continental Divide at Grizzly Peak, Colorado, in a helium balloon called *Columbine II*. He and his companions, Chauncey Dunn and Fred Hyde, all members of the Rocky Mountain Gas Balloon Society, were the first men to traverse the Rockies in a gas balloon.

Larry had married on March 24 and spent a brief honeymoon in Hawaii. His decision to fly in *Double Eagle II* put strain on the marriage from the start. Larry was investing a great deal of money for a thirty-year-old who had not been able to pay the rent only four years before. There was, besides, the odor of machismo upon this adventure, in which he and Ben and Max were risking their lives for some atavistic reason involving male pride, and his bride, Sandra, belonged to a generation that did not value such gestures.

Patty Anderson had no reservations. "I knew they'd make it," she recalls. "One of the greatest things that gave me comfort was that Max would not take off this time unless all the conditions were right. That gave me a confident feeling. I felt if they had lived through all they lived through on the first flight, they could live through anything."

Larry had met Patty only twice. She and Max seemed formal to him. He was struck by the grandness of their house, by their whole style of life, in which no single aspect seemed to have escaped the decorator's hand. Max was polite, but he was all business. There was no socializing. Max talked softly, suggested. If his suggestion was not adopted, he made it again, in a different way, until he had people agreeing to do what he wanted. Larry, himself so recently a self-made man, could never concede that Max was one too: Carl Anderson had been very rich before Max got rich.

When word of Max's plan to fly the Atlantic the first time reached his father, Carl Anderson offered his son a million dollars not to go.

"I don't need a million dollars," Max had replied.

Larry liked that retort, but from the start, he had not known how to deal with Max. "I always felt that Maxie somehow thought of me

182

as not being an adult, and certainly not as his equal," Larry said later. "I rush so fast with people that I often seem abrasive. I *am* abrasive — I don't just seem that way." In fact, Larry's personality, crackling though it was with energy and intelligence, did seem rough-hewn to Max. Larry said whatever came into his head, almost as soon as it came into his head; sometimes the things he said in his candor were very rude indeed.

"Having known Ben and respected him and had confidence in him, I knew that whatever he did would be quite acceptable to me," Max told his tape recorder. "I had considerable reservations about a third person going on the flight. I was concerned about the image that third person would project. My reservation hasn't changed. I am ill at ease."

"From the day we started planning this flight," says Larry, "there was no question in my mind that the actual author, the real planner, and the real captain was Ben Abruzzo. I still believe it. From the moment we started our initial preparations until our landing, I always deferred to Ben's judgment. That was a little bit unfair to Maxie."

Such an opinion would have startled Max Anderson. Certainly the first flight was his conception, and he began planning the second one long before Ben. This point is conceded by Ben. But Max, as Ben once told him, did not have to live with Ben's frostbitten foot for all those months; Max did not have to bear the searing pain and the thought of being crippled. And, in deciding to go for the second time, Max did not have to face the risk that Ben faced: if his foot were frozen again, he could lose it.

In his own mind, Ben regarded himself as the front-line pilot of *Double Eagle II*. Despite his desperate physical condition, he had done his full part in the landing off Iceland, and by quick thinking had averted a disaster when they had nearly dropped the gondola into the sea from a height of a hundred feet. He assumed that he would command the landing in France. Max was willing to share command with Ben, but he would not accept Ben or anyone else as a commander. In his long career in the rough-and-tumble business of mining, Max had never reported to a superior: he had always been in charge. "I hadn't conceived this venture, refused a million dollars to abandon it, and rounded up a crew to execute it in order to find myself with a boss for the first time in my life," he said later. "It never occurred to me to discuss the matter with Ben, let alone Larry." How could one of them be the captain when they were equals? Though they never spoke of it, this issue hung between them. It was a curious reversal of psychological roles: Ben, the individualist, worrying about establishing a figure of authority aboard the balloon system, and Max, with his military education and his martial imagery, attaching no importance to the question.

Hidden though it might have been, the emotional tension continued through the summer. Ben believed that he had made the final decision to go in April — in fact, had prodded Max into making the final commitment — when he sent their check to Ed Yost. Money binds; talk does not. But Ben's foot still throbbed in his memory. As he was to say, it wasn't the sea, or the killing cold, or the storms, or the plunge toward death off Greenland that he remembered and dreamed about, it was his foot. Though he had ceased mentioning it to anyone but Pat, the foot still bothered him: if he stumbled playing tennis, he would limp for days.

As late as June, Ben confided to Larry that he might yet change his mind about going.

"Ben had decided that maybe he wasn't going to go," recalls Larry. "This was only two months before the flight or a month and a half. He thought about not going. And had he not gone I wouldn't have gone — which would have left Maxie to go all by himself, I guess."

Larry was fascinated by the interplay between the two older men. He pressed Ben for details of the first flight. Nothing he heard frightened him; a great many things Ben did not tell him. He did mention Max's incredible decision to go to sleep after the downs off Greenland when *Double Eagle* iced up. Ben never understood that, either when he was alone and awake above the spuming seas with their herds of icebergs, or months later, when he was awake in the night and reliving the voyage.

Ben and Max continued to play their games of chicken with each other. They decided again not to take parachutes. Larry refused to part with his — he would need it on the hang-glider, and he might need it before that.

Max saw that Ben's injury, and financial considerations, and his business situation were tugging at him. "I felt like Ben had a sea

184

anchor on him," recalls Max. "He was still making progress forward, but it was holding him back a bit."

Max struggled to understand Ben's reluctance, or what he thought was Ben's reluctance. A friend of Ben's spoke to him about it.

"If you go," said the friend, "Ben has to go."

Max replied, "I think I know that; I don't want him to go under those circumstances, but I don't know quite how to free Ben."

In July, they met at Larry's factory for a television session. Ben invited Max into Larry's office for a chat. They went inside, the two of them alone, and closed the door. They sat down on a sofa together and Ben said, with his customary directness: "Max, I'm not sure that I'm going to go."

Max, of course, was not startled. He decided to offer Ben a way out: "Would you like for me to go on TV and say the doctors asked you not to go — your heart, blood pressure, or just medical reasons? You don't have to explain anything to anybody."

They sat in silence for a moment or two. Larry's office is small, hardly more than a cubicle, and its walls are hung with color photographs of his hang-gliders. He had added a picture of *Double Eagle II*, a painting of how it would look in flight.

"No," Ben replied at last.

"It's going to be awfully hard to quit now, but our lives don't depend on this."

"I know."

There was another silence. Finally Max decided that Ben was not going to say more. He said, "Ben you'll have to do what you need to do. And if you need not to go, then the only thing I ask is that you be there when I take off and land."

"Fine," said Ben.

They went out together and faced the cameras. Ben was in the forefront as usual, with his quick tongue and his flashing vitality.

Max and Ben never discussed the question again. But Max decided that if Ben decided not to come with him in *Double Eagle II*, he would go alone. He thought about asking Doc Wiley to go with him, but he was not sure that Doc wanted to go and he feared that Doc, as his employee, might interpret an invitation as an instruction. He was certain that Larry would not wish to accompany him. In truth, Max had no wish to fly with anyone except Ben Abruzzo.

185

Max began to think again about the problems of a solo flight. He had no time to train himself to sleep and wake at one-hour intervals, as he had earlier thought to do. He asked Doc Wiley to look into the possibility of rigging some sort of alarm that would sound if the balloon fell below a designated altitude. Ed Yost had carried such a device, actuated by a barometer, in *Silver Fox*.

By July, the crew of *Double Eagle II* was once again being chased by unseen ghosts. Two British balloonists — Don Cameron, a celebrated designer and manufacturer of balloons, and Major Christopher Davey of the Royal Tank Corps — were planning a launch from St. John's Newfoundland. Their balloon, *Zanussi*, was a hybrid system — a helium envelope surrounded by a hot-air balloon. The theory (a safe variation on the idea that had sent Jean-François Pilâtre de Rozier down in flames in 1785) was that the hot air would control the temperature of the helium, thereby providing controlled lift without waste of ballast. *Zanussi* was a sophisticated system, and Don Cameron, whom Max and Ben had met at ballooning events in Albuquerque, was a highly skilled pilot.

As *Double Eagle II* would not be ready for delivery until July 15, it was a certainty that *Zanussi* would launch first. Meanwhile, Ben and Max learned that a second transatlantic balloon was abuilding for an American team, and would be delivered only ten days after *Double Eagle II*. The pilots would be Joe Kittinger, of Skylab fame, and a man named Douglas Palermo. The latter telephoned Ben and suggested that *Double Eagle II* might wish to make a race of it across the Atlantic. Ben's reply was short and to the point: "No."

Ben called Ed Yost to inquire about the flight of Kittinger and Palermo. He discovered that Yost was building the balloon.

There was no hope of beating *Zanussi* into the air. Having spurned the challenge from Kittinger and Palermo, Ben and Max and Larry decided to challenge Cameron and Davey to a race across the Atlantic. On June 15, in Boston, just back from their search for a launch site in Maine, the Americans threw down the gauntlet. A flight from Newfoundland, a mere twenty-two hundred miles to the British Isles, was "hardly more than a warm-up," Max told the press. The launch should be from the United States, and as *Double Eagle II* could not be ready until August, or perhaps early September, "we hope the English chaps will reconsider and turn their trip into something besides a short outing."

Whatever Cameron and Davey, busily preparing for the launch of their $285,000 balloon, may have thought of this exercise in gamesmanship, they made no response to the challenge. On Wednesday, July 26, they launched from St. John's.

Bob Rice, in Bedford, followed the fortunes of *Zanussi* on his weather maps, forecasting the flight as a sort of rehearsal for *Double Eagle II*. As the days passed, he became convinced that Cameron and Davey, not Abruzzo and Anderson and Newman, were going to be the first to conquer the Atlantic.

"I'm sorry for your sake," Rice told Ben and Max over the telephone, "but the *Zanussi* is home free as long as it maintains altitudes above 12,000 feet for the remainder of the flight."

This conversation took place on a Friday night. On Saturday, *Zanussi*, to Rice's astonishment, went down at sea. A rip had developed in the helium envelope over the Atlantic, and after ninety-six hours and twenty-four minutes aloft, Cameron and Davey landed 110 miles off the French coast. They had come closer to success than anyone before them.

Max and Ben, knowing what a landing in the Atlantic meant, had never wished the Englishmen the slightest misfortune, and neither had Larry. But it was with a mighty sense of relief that they sent Cameron and Davey a comradely telegram:

CONGRATULATIONS ON YOUR HEROIC FLIGHT. WHETHER OUR FLIGHT SUCCEEDS OR NOT WE WILL FIND IT DIFFICULT TO EQUAL YOUR EXAMPLE OF COURAGE AND DETERMINATION. SEE YOU IN AUGUST AT THE SAVOY. DINNER IS ON US.

On August 10, *Double Eagle II* and its gondola were in place at the launch site. "And, as before," recalls Doc Wiley, "it developed into a last-minute panic because they had the weather they wanted and the equipment wasn't ready."

16

On Monday, August 7, the Abruzzos and the Andersons and all their children, accompanied by the flight crew and friends and a detachment of media people, descended on Presque Isle, Maine, the town nearest their launch site. The party numbered over a hundred, and the local motels and restaurants were filled to overflowing.

It was a festive atmosphere, with Max and Patty and their family and friends going in one direction for dinner, and Ben and Pat going in another with theirs. No local eating place was large enough to accommodate both pilots with their retinues. Larry and Sandra Newman had stopped over in New York, where Larry was to be interviewed on ABC's "Good Morning, America," as part of the network's coverage of the flight. While there, Larry visited all the international airlines and distributed flyers listing the radio frequencies *Double Eagle II* would be using, so that these could be distributed to the pilots of airliners overflying the Atlantic.

Larry's interview was scheduled for Wednesday morning. On Tuesday, he received a message from Maine: forget the interview, come at once. *Double Eagle II* would be launched on Friday.

A weather window had opened. Bob Rice told Max that a high-pressure ridge was moving slowly eastward from the Great Lakes, and would pass over the coast on Friday night. In order to mount the ridge, *Double Eagle II* would have to launch immediately after sunset. The second necessary control feature, a slow-moving, low-pressure system in the mid-Atlantic, was developing. This feature would anchor the storm system ahead of the high-pressure ridge, and provide a windflow toward northern Scotland after the balloon left the ridge, somewhere between Iceland and Ireland.

Rice warned that any delay past 6 P.M. EDT (2100 Zulu) would be risky. The flight plan called for the balloon to rise immediately to 5,000 feet, and after six o'clock those winds would diminish in velocity. At the chosen launch time, the winds would be sweeping east toward the coast at about twenty-eight miles an hour.

The gondola and all the equipment were already in Presque Isle. Peter Briggs, owner of the flying service at the local airport, had put a hangar at their disposal. Doc Wiley and Syd Parks had flown the radio equipment to Presque Isle in the Ranchers company plane, and since their arrival Syd had been busy installing the radio equipment and the electronic navigational devices.

Once more George Fischbeck, the Los Angeles broadcaster, was at Max's side. Fischbeck is an intellectual magpie, with a nest filled with anecdotes and jokes and shiny fragments of arcane knowledge. He also understands the weather from a scientist's point of view, and he was there to give counsel as well as good company. While Bob Rice remained in Bedford, a vice-president of Weather Services, Peter Leavitt, had flown to Maine to witness the launch and provide on-site weather briefing.

The advice from all three meteorologists was that another launch window might not open for a month. It was a matter of making another helter-skelter departure or submitting for long weeks to the mood of the weather. Neither Max nor Ben wanted to wait. As for Larry, he was the least patient of the three. There was no choice but to go.

Larry arrived on Wednesday morning and immediately went to Peter Briggs's hangar. It was a scene of feverish activity. The gondola had been completely refitted in Larry's factory. Larry's men had painted the gondola's new fiber-glass skin in brilliant hues of yellow and red; the craft glowed in the filtering sunlight and, later, under the work lamps as the crew worked through the night to make everything ready.

The vital element was communications. Syd Parks, this time, had installed a system that inspired confidence. Parks is a perfectionist. He knew that the flight could succeed only if there were a very good mission control and a very good meteorologist on the ground who had the capability of talking to the pilots in the air. As Rice had said, most weather forecasts tend to break down in less time than it takes any balloon to fly the Atlantic.

"What you want to do," says Syd, "is pick up a phone and dial them. That's what you can do if you go with satellite communications. But the problem with satellite communications is you've got to have a parabolic antenna and this has to be stabilized so it's always pointed toward the satellite."

That makes for a nice technical problem in a rotating balloon, but not an insoluble one; less easy to solve is the weight problem — a satellite communications system would weigh, with batteries, something like twelve hundred pounds. *Double Eagle II* could not accept such a weight penalty. Syd had, therefore, done all that human ingenuity could do on a limited budget, and with limited time, to make it possible for the crew of the balloon to "talk on the telephone" to Bob Rice and Rich Schwoebel. *Double Eagle II* carried four systems: VHF radios with which to talk and listen to overflying aircraft and airport control towers; a high-frequency (HF) single-side-band radio for speaking to the ground stations of Air, Incorporated, a North Atlantic network that monitors the HF frequencies (between 5 and 8 megahertz); a marine-band radio, as before; and last, an amateur or "ham" transceiver, intended only for emergency use. It had about ten times the power of the HF radio.

Double Eagle II would carry the same faithful homing beacon used on the first flight. The beacon had been recovered by the Icelandic coast guard, and though it had been soaked by seawater, it worked perfectly when Syd plugged it in to test it in his home workshop in Albuquerque where he had made the device.

Larry, designated the radio operator, had been using VHF radios on airplanes since childhood. He was familiar, too, with the other radios, and with the Omega navigational receiver. It would pick up three stations — one in the United States, one in the Caribbean, and one in Norway. Its computer would process the signals from these stations and flash the balloon's latitude and longitude on a digital display.

"They showed us how to tune the radios in one time," recalls Larry. "The only radio I didn't understand was the amateur band. All the other radios were simple."

They were not quite so simple as Larry thought, and he had spent only one hour with Rich Schwoebel, learning to use the ham radio. Watching and listening as Schwoebel worked the equipment with calm skill, he concluded that there was not much to learn. A human voice, speaking into a microphone on another continent, would be heard as the faraway buzzing of a fly or as the metallic twang of a banjo string. Schwoebel, turning a dial, would bring that voice into the room loud and clear. For Larry, this one lesson from an expert seemed enough. He did not have time to spare from his business for more lessons; besides, it wasn't expected that the ham radio would ever be used.

It takes a normal person at least six months to master one — its face is a forest of knobs and switches, and each one has a specific purpose. There are thousands of people talking on the ham frequencies all the time. "You've got to winkle out these various stations," Syd Parks explains. "It's like being in a great big room with eighteen thousand people talking all around you, and you're trying to hear a conversation in the far corner." That process takes skills Larry did not possess as he approached takeoff; this did not worry him or Max or Ben, but it was a matter of concern to Syd and to Rich Schwoebel; both are hams, as is Doc Wiley, and they knew what was involved.

Ben was supervising the loading of the equipment. Ninety water bottles had to be filled; Sandra Newman and Jennie Schwoebel did that, adding the purifier to each bottle with an eyedropper. Sandra worried about Larry's clothing, and with Jennie helping her, sprayed his garments with a waterproofing solution. Pat and Patty did the same for Ben and Maxie.

Ben's sisters, Terry Mathiesen and Marie Turiciano, helped Pat and Patty with the grocery shopping. C rations this time would be carried as emergency supplies only — the pilots chose their own food, the things they liked at home, and stowed it in the same big coolers Ben and Max had carried on *Double Eagle*. Ben had weighed and listed every item to go aboard. He knew the ballast available to him to the last ounce. In the last-minute rush in Albuquerque, he had neglected to have a checklist drawn up, so he loaded the gondola from memory. His mind whirred, grasping a detail, labeling it, packing it away. His friends were around him, Jack Hammack and Bob Wolfe and Jack Dailey and George Koury. And Pat, of course. Ben felt busy and full of purpose and happy. Each time he remembered a forgotten item — pocketknives, leather gloves for the launch crew, flashlights — someone would respond and fetch it. He decided he needed an extra sea anchor. None could be found — a fact that Ben could not understand; after all, they were in Maine — but Peter

Briggs saved the day, as he had done several times earlier. He turned up with an enormous burlap sack, used on the farms of the region in sorting potatoes. Grommets were sewn into its mouth, a nylon line threaded through, and Ben had his spare sea anchor.

Max was also involved in this activity, but he spent much time at his primary task — checking the weather. Larry bombarded Peter Leavitt with questions; both he and Ben, as veteran pilots, understood the weather, its jargon and its perils. On maps provided by Leavitt, all three balloonists charted the progress of the high-pressure ridge and its accompanying storm systems.

Bob Rice, on the telephone, assured Max that the high-pressure ridge was continuing to approach at a steady pace out of the west, that the Atlantic systems were good, that Max need not be more than routinely concerned about his old lurking enemy, the thunderstorm, though this was the peak season in the Atlantic for tropical storms. There was good separation between the ridge and the upstream storm system. If they got off on time and climbed to their planned altitude, they would have a high, dry, slow ride to Europe. George Fischbeck, listening with his trained ear, agreed with Rice's conclusions.

There was no reason, this time, why everything should not go as planned. All the games of "What-if?" were paying off; the errors were canceling out. Things were under control, as Max liked to have them.

Ed Yost arrived in Presque Isle during the afternoon on Thursday. By that time the gondola and the envelope of *Double Eagle II*, still in its packing case, had been moved to the launch site. Merle Sprague and his neighbors had shown some Yankee enterprise; the freshly mown launch site was roped off. Foodstands selling hot dogs and soft drinks and other snacks had been set up. Hand-lettered signs reading PARKING $1 had been tacked to the fence posts and the trees. This was quiet country, filled with quiet people. The Downeasters in their taciturnity reminded Patty Anderson of the phlegmatic Norwegians she had grown up among in Minnesota.

Ed Yost did not turn up at the launch site on Thursday. Ben was, by midafternoon, somewhat concerned about Yost. Had he got lost?

At about three in the afternoon, Dave Slade told Ben that Yost was in Presque Isle, having a beer.

Ben laughed. "That explains it," he said. His friend asked if he should go and fetch Yost. "No, tomorrow will be soon enough," said Ben; he knew that Yost would be there when he was needed, and that he was not a man to be fetched.

A few weeks before, Ben and Larry had met Yost in St. Paul, Minnesota. There, in the Hippodrome at the state fairgrounds, the only available building large enough to contain *Double Eagle II*, they had inflated the envelope with air. Ben and Larry had crawled inside the inflated bag to inspect it for holes. Even a pinhole appears, to the human eye inside the pitch-dark nylon bag, as a starburst. There had been one such hole — only one — in *Double Eagle II* when it was inspected. After the hole was patched, all had been blackness. *Double Eagle II*, like *Double Eagle*, was the usual Ed Yost product — a perfect balloon. Ben had known that it would be.

At day's end, Ben went into town, and the first thing he did was go to the bar. "There was old Ed Yost, sitting there nice and calm, just peaceably drinking the beer," Ben recalls. Ben sat down on the next stool.

"We plan to launch tomorrow," he said.

"Yeah. I heard."

"The helium trailer is in place. We've got our gear mostly stowed. We've got the balloon on the truck and you can put it wherever you want it. As far as I know, everything is ready."

"Fine."

"Do you want to have a drink?"

"Sure."

Ben, chuckling inwardly at this remarkable fellow, finished his beer. "See you in the morning, then."

"Fine," said Ed Yost.

That night, Joe Kittinger's partner Doug Palermo telephoned Ben and asked again if he and Max and Larry would consider delaying the launch of *Double Eagle II* in order to make a race of it with the second balloon.

"We would not," said Ben, "delay one second."

Friday was a beautiful day, sunny and mild and filled with the scent of clover. The balloonists and their launch crew were at the site soon after sunup.

Ben, with his crew of scurrying helpers, went on with the loading of the gondola. Max kept in touch with Bob Rice by telephone. The message was always the same: the ridge will pass the launch site by early evening; lift off as soon as possible after sunset. There seemed to be no reason why that should not be possible.

At midday, someone went into town and returned with a load of pizzas, and Ben and Max, munching the fragrant wedges, had their first meal in the gondola. They had planned to sleep in it at least one night before departing, and go through dry runs with the equipment, but there had never been time for that. Ben's plan to test all the radio equipment by suspending the gondola from the tramway and reeling out the hanging antennas had also gone by the board. The radios, with all their complicated wiring, looked beautifully reliable to Ben.

Max was edgy. Technicians from ABC scrambled in and out of the gondola, installing their own equipment — a camera on a boom, lenses, cartridges of film. He had read the memoirs of a balloonist who would never carry a camera because it was not essential to the flight and was too valuable to be used as ballast. The television camera, all the photographic equipment, annoyed him. It had no purpose. Besides, he disliked being photographed. Posing for the cameras once the balloon was under way would be stagy, a stunt.

Larry ate no lunch, and he had slept little the night before. He and Sandra had had words about the voyage. He had begun to see it as a great adventure, filled with risk, an honorable act. He now felt very alone. He watched Pat Abruzzo and Patty Anderson helping with the launch and performing kindness after small kindness for their husbands, and melancholy took hold of him. He walked away from the balloon some little distance and lay down in the grass on a hillside. "I realized that this whole marriage thing of mine was becoming a joke," Larry recalls. People tried to talk to him — his father was there to see him off — but Larry told those who tried to join him on his hillside that he had to be by himself.

The Abruzzo and Anderson sons and some of their friends helped Ed Yost to unfold the envelope. Yost fitted the valve to the top, and, with the help of the volunteer crew, attached the load straps to the load ring and, finally, the gondola to the ring by its four straps.

By midafternoon, when the inflation process began, a crowd of many hundreds of people had assembled. The launch site was roped off, so there was no repetition of the confusion of the first launch.

A tanker truck filled with helium had been brought from New Jersey. Max had long before ordered delivery of the helium, and Larry only days earlier had reconfirmed the order for 175,000 cubic feet of the gas. Although the balloon could contain only 160,000 cubic feet, the extra gas was needed to maintain pressure in the tanks so that the helium would flow through the hose at a satisfactory rate. The technicians from New Jersey inserted their hose into the duct of *Double Eagle II*, and gradually the great envelope began to stir and swell; at last it rose from the grass and stood erect, with the mild New England sun reflecting from its silver top and the American flag hanging limp from its equator.

It was virtually windless in the shelter of the hill where Larry lay. Ben and Max released some small helium balloons and watched them float over the trees at the top of the knoll. There seemed to be no rotor problem; Ben judged that the trees would break up any windflow over the ridgeline, preventing the cascading effect that had caused them so much trouble the year before over the Gaspé Peninsula. Just beyond the ridge were some power lines; the balloon should clear those easily.

Max and Ben synchronized their watches, then did it again for the news photographers. Inflation was progressing very slowly. Ben asked about that, and the supervisor told him that his men were filling the envelope with care, so as not to risk damaging it.

Jack Hammack, mothering Ben, asked him if he was hungry. Ben told him he had a longing for crab. "You've got it!" said Hammack, and he and Pat Abruzzo raced into Presque Isle, returning with a complete crab dinner. Ben ate it with relish, but he did not like the feeling that was beginning to come over him. Everything was going too slowly. Something was wrong. He felt it. Max had fallen into one of his silences, so he must feel it too. Patty had got him a basket of fried chicken, and he stood with her, munching on a drumstick.

Ben had carried a lawn chair inside the roped enclosure for his mother. Mary Abruzzo watched the proceedings with composure; she had smiles and words of encouragement for Ben's children and for Pat, and for Ben's sisters Terry and Marie. The Rockford relatives were here in great numbers again, and a lively family reunion was going on. From time to time, Ben left the gondola and sat down on the grass beside his mother's chair. They chatted quietly. Mary Abruzzo never let her son see any sign of her worry or anxiety; Ben was grateful again for her strength.

It was now two hours before launch, and things began to unravel. Rich Schwoebel talked to the Norwegian station that was to beam a signal to the Omega navigational device, and learned that it was going off the air for repairs the following day. It would be silent for an indefinite period. Without the signal from Norway, the Omega would not work. This news was irritating, but not disastrous. They still had the sextant and the computer, and the Nimbus satellite. These systems were less convenient than the Omega, but they would serve the purpose.

Ben grew more and more impatient with the slowness of the inflation. Max fidgeted about the loss of time. The high-pressure ridge was now only a few miles to the west.

Ben asked the technicians how much helium they had in their tanks. They replied that they had 162,000 cubic feet. Ben exploded. Why had they not brought the amount ordered, 175,000 cubic feet?

They explained that while the truck was being loaded, a state inspector had dropped by to make a routine spot check. The maximum legal load in New Jersey was 162,000 cubic feet. That was what they had brought.

"Why didn't you call?" Ben demanded. "We would have told you to bring *two* trucks — to bring two hundred thousand cubic feet of helium!"

The technicians replied that the cost of hauling the gas was more than a dollar a mile, plus the high cost of the helium itself, and they were trying to save Ben and Max and Larry money.

"Terrific!" said Ben.

It was evident to him and evident to Max that there wouldn't be enough pressure to fill the balloon.

"Shut her down and give us a reading," Ben told one of the technicians. The meter showed that the balloon contained 134,000 cubic feet of helium.

"Can you fill the balloon?"

"Yes."

"I don't believe you can," said Ben.

196

He and Max and Larry talked to Rich Schwoebel and Ed Yost. They were already more than two hours behind schedule because of the slow rate of inflation. The great balloon rose above them in the dusk, its black cone as slack as a shirt drying on a line. Dew was beginning to fall, and moisture sparkled in the lights of the television cameras.

What if they took off slack, with less than a full load of helium? The prospect infuriated Ben and it filled Max with apprehension. In Larry, anger mixed with the sadness that had filled his afternoon. To have planned so carefully, to have gone to the expense of building the bigger balloon, to have lived night and day with the problem for months — and now to have it thrown away by human error. All the contingency planning, all of Schwoebel's brilliant innovations were wasted.

"I say go with what we've got," Ben said. He had already calculated in his head that the loss in flight duration would be a day or a day and a half.

Peter Leavitt told them again that their flight would be a long, slow one — the ridge was moving at low speed, and when they departed from the ridge they would probably enter a windfield that would carry them toward Europe at a somewhat higher, but still quite moderate, speed. The flight would last five days, possibly six.

Rich Schwoebel did some calculations. "The penalty is roughly a day," he said. That meant that *Double Eagle II* would be able to fly only six days. They had lost their margin for error.

There was another problem. Taking off with a slack balloon meant that it might go through its planned ceiling and rise to a higher altitude than desired on the first night. Yost did not know from personal experience what exactly would happen; he had always lifted off in a balloon filled to capacity.

"We've got to decide, and we've got to decide right now," said Ben. "I'm all for going."

"Let's go," said Max. "Larry?"

Larry looked to Rich Schwoebel. The fact that he was not horrified reassured him. Larry nodded.

Ben climbed back into the gondola. The decision was made, and he felt the elation of command mingling with his anger.

"Shut her down," he said to the technicians. "We're going just the way we are."

197

There were still things to do. The duct had to be trimmed off to the exact length of the balloon and tied off. Ballast had to be recalculated — more would have to be left behind in order for the balloon, with a smaller load of helium, to rise.

Larry checked his hang-glider for the last time; he worried that one of the newsmen or crew members who were scurrying around the gondola in the half-dark might run into the fragile craft. Larry caught a glimpse of Sandra and her parents, and he saw with a pang of jealousy that being with her parents had made her carelessly happy.

There were thousands of people standing by. It seemed to Larry that hundreds of them were members of the press. They kept talking to him, asking him questions. He could not trust himself to be civil, he was so upset; he walked away from the gondola, where television crews were shining lights on Ben and Maxie and recording Ben's every terse word. He found Sandra and she walked with him. The cameras followed them: the youngest balloonist and his blond young wife in blue jeans, two slim figures.

Earlier, Pat and Patty had gone into town to buy last-minute supplies for Ben and Max. They asked Larry if he would like anything. As a joke, he asked for bagels and they brought him some. "They were the wrong kind of bagels — the gentile kind," Larry said after the journey, "but I guess Sandra wouldn't have known the right kind, either."

It was a short leave-taking. Patty Anderson knew that *Double Eagle II* would be in the air within minutes. There was no music. She remembered how much difference the music had made at the first launch, and she ran from Max's side to a truck parked nearby that had a public address system. Jennie Schwoebel is a professional singer, and Patty took her to the microphone. "You've got to sing 'The Star Spangled Banner,' Jennie! They can't leave without that."

Patty asked George Fischbeck to say a prayer, but even his rich, clear voice could not be heard over the defective loudspeakers. Jennie did not sing. Someone called the local radio station, and the announcer asked the people watching from their cars to open their windows and turn their radios to full volume: the station would play the national anthem and perhaps the chorus of radios would be loud enough to be heard by the balloonists as they ascended.

It was dark. At the gondola, George Fischbeck opened a bottle of champagne and proposed a toast. Max could not taste the wine in his mouth. They were almost three hours late. He had talked to Bob Rice, and he knew that the surface high-pressure system had already passed the launch site; they could still catch the ridgeline if they ascended to their planned altitude of 5,000 feet.

Bob Rice, ordinarily the calmest of men, had a frantic note in his voice. Wind speeds, he said, were diminishing at all altitudes, but would fall off in a particularly dramatic way up to 5,000 feet.

"If you don't launch at once, errors will begin to cascade," Rice had said. "Go *now*."

Human error breeds human error — and they were starting out on a resounding note of error.

Rich Schwoebel and Ed Yost began to cut loose sandbags. *Double Eagle II* carried eighty-four of these, beautifully sewn in Larry's hang-glider shop. Schwoebel, judging the level of gas in the envelope by eye, and knowing the weight of the system, calculated that sixteen hundred pounds of ballast had to be left behind in order for the balloon to achieve equilibrium and rise into the night sky.

No one had explained that to Larry. He watched Ed Yost cutting sandbags loose, running around the gondola, slashing with his knife. Schwoebel was counting the bags as they dropped, realizing that Yost knew precisely what he was doing. Larry, watching Yost, turned to Ben. "Jesus, the bags are dropping everywhere," he said. "Is it supposed to be like that?" Ben looked over the side and saw a mountain of sand; he understood what was happening and why, but the sand was time, trickling into the grass. "No," he said.

Ben and Max had embraced their wives and children a moment before that, and Larry, conscious of the cameras on them, had kissed Sandra goodbye. He felt a strangeness. Did she think husbands flew the Atlantic in balloons every day — that this was an ordinary leave-taking? I may never see her again, he thought. I'm going on a balloon flight and if I don't come back, that's it.

The balloon came to equilibrium: it was no longer touching the ground, but it was not yet flying. Ben cut two additional sandbags loose and laid them on the deck: the weight of the hang-glider. Larry clipped the hang-glider load line to the load ring and *Double Eagle II* began to move. Ben and Max poured sand from the two bags over the side. Max, watching the instruments, listened for the strains of "The Star Spangled Banner," but he could hear nothing but the hiss of hundreds of photographers' strobe lights. The crowd sent up a murmur of cheers — nothing like the roar at Marshfield. It was 8:42 P.M. eastern daylight time, on August 11, 1978 — 0042 hours, August 12, Zulu time.

Larry was blinded by the flashbulbs. To his surprise, the balloon as it rose began to move horizontally over the grass. He had thought that *Double Eagle II* would just float away, like a soap bubble, and nobody had told him otherwise. The balloon was rushing over the ground, leaving the little island of light behind and below.

Patty Anderson, watching them go, wondered with a leap of the heart if the gondola and the hang-glider would clear the power lines to the north of the launch site.

Pat Abruzzo could see Ben's face clearly, and she knew from the look in his eyes that he could see her, too. She sent him a silent message: *This time you'll make it!* Pat believed that he understood.

She was concerned about the other two wives. Patty Anderson's face, usually so controlled, was the picture of anxiety; Patty had told her that she was more worried about this flight than the first one. The two old friends clung to each other. Then Pat noticed that Sandra Newman was sobbing. She seemed young and vulnerable and alone. Jennie Schwoebel was standing near her, her own eyes filled with sympathy for Larry's wife. Pat went to Sandra and embraced her; Sandra put her face against Pat's, and Pat felt the warmth of the other woman's tears on her own cheek.

Larry, looking down into that blackness, thought that the hang-glider had missed the high-tension wires by no more than ten feet.

Then he heard Ben and Max shouting: "Down twenty-five, down fifty, down a hundred!"

"Ballast off!"

They were in a rotor at the hilltop. Ben saw people running beneath the balloon. He had an open clasp knife in his hand and he cut open a bag of sand. The balloon was only 150 feet in the air and it was falling at a rate of 200 feet per minute. That meant that they would hit the earth in forty-five seconds.

Then the hang-glider struck the ground, and relieved of its weight, the balloon went into a slight climb. The wing of the hang-glider, bounding off the spongy turf, came right by Ben's face.

Larry heard the hang-glider hit the gondola, and he heard it bouncing along the ground, making a fearful noise. He unclipped the load line and threw it overboard. He cursed: that was the end of the hang-glider. But he had forgotten that it was attached by a second rope, and it continued to drag along the ground.

In the dark Larry saw a neighboring field, covered with tan stubble that stood out in the darkness, coming up at him. He was hypnotized by the sight, and he was sickened by the sounds made by the hang-glider, as translucent as a moth, as it dragged over the earth.

Ben saw that there were no people beneath the balloon. He cut loose a bag full of sand and heard it strike the earth. Max ballasted off more sand. Ben cut loose yet another bag.

Double Eagle II escaped from the rotor and began to climb. It rose very rapidly, carried by a wind to the north, and finally reached a ceiling of 5,700 feet and stayed there. Before liftoff, Rich Schwoebel had told Ben and Max that he estimated they would rise to 5,300 feet.

Even as he cut loose the extra bags of sand, Ben had calculated in his mind what it was costing them: perhaps twelve hours of flying. They were only two minutes into the flight, and already he was adding up the penalties. He thought: I'll chop off the bow and stern of the gondola if I have to — we're going as far as this thing will fly; we'll land in our skivvies, ride in on the load ring.

Ben and Max did not speak about the rotor, they just went about their routine tasks. That seemed odd to Larry, but his own mind was elsewhere: with Sandra, with the ruined hang-glider, dangling out of sight below them, with the mistake with the helium.

For a few moments he was listless. Then he switched on the Omega. It worked fine — but Norway was already off the air. Larry turned to his next assigned task: he switched on the VHF transmitter and tried to contact the Loring Air Force Base control.

Loring control reported that Larry's transmission was faint. After two or three minutes of conversation, Loring told him he was totally unreadable.

Then the controller asked Larry to turn on the transponder, an automatic device that sends a signal to radar stations on the ground, permitting those stations to track an airborne object.

"As soon as I turned on the transponder," says Larry, "the radios made this *doyingggg brrrrrrr* sound. I couldn't believe it. We couldn't operate the radios and the transponder at the same time."

After he and Ben maneuvered *Double Eagle II* out of the rotor over Merle Sprague's woods, and the balloon climbed into the night, Max waited for the emotions of the first flight to return to him. But they did not come back. He felt no elation, no thrill of adventure, no arc of affection and comradeship between himself and Ben.

From the moment they hit the rotor, Max was seized by the suspicion that there was something wrong with the balloon. He believed there was a leak in the envelope. He did not understand why he felt as he did. Objectively, he knew that if *Double Eagle II* flew for two hours as she was flying now, they would have a good balloon. His intuition told him otherwise, and he could not, for once, subdue his emotions with the power of reason.

When the radios failed, Max took that as another omen. The balloon had barely reached altitude when Doc Wiley's voice came over the loudspeakers. He was aloft in the company plane; *Double Eagle II* could not talk back to him. Max peered into the night, the sky was as dark as pitchblende, but he saw no winking aircraft lights. In the distance he saw the lights of Presque Isle. Bearings and speeds came over the loudspeaker, transmitted by Loring radar. They were moving very slowly. In the first hour of the flight they traveled fewer than fifteen miles: another sign. A curious sense of peace welled up in Max; he had done all he could, and so had everyone connected with the flight; he would accept what came.

For the first three-hour period, Larry had the watch, Ben the rest period, and Max the sleep period. Max took off his boots and crawled into the sleeping box. He concentrated, cleared his mind, and went to sleep.

Larry had never been in such a quiet place as the gondola. He noticed, as Ben and Max had done in *Double Eagle*, how clearly one could hear sounds on the ground thousands of feet below. The slowness of the flight bothered him. The failure of the radios infuriated him. What was wrong? How to fix them? To Ben he said, "I can't stand ambiguity. I can't stand imperfection, and, man, are we off to a great start!"

On the voltage meters Syd Parks had wired to the communications systems, Larry noted an alarming rate of drainage on the batteries. Each time he tried to transmit, or turned on the Omega, the needle would jerk to the left. The radios were designed to operate on twelve-volt batteries, and merely *using* them pulled the voltage below twelve volts. Therefore, there was not enough power to transmit. Ben was not communicative, though Larry wanted to talk to him. They decided to try to repair the radios in the morning. Larry was sure he could rig something.

On the ground, Rich Schwoebel, at the Presque Isle airport, was seated in a parked Cessna, attempting to raise the balloon on its radio. He was unsuccessful, but he spoke to Loring control and determined that the tower had contact. He was pleased with the altitude reports. Radar showed the balloon at 5,500 feet, rather than the 5,700 Ben had read on the altimeter. Loring radar was having some trouble with the balloon's transponder, but was able to adjust. After two or three hours of listening to tracking reports, which showed the balloon on course to the northeast, Schwoebel and Doc Wiley, carrying Pat Abruzzo and Patty Anderson with them in Max's airplane, flew to Bedford.

"Doc thought maybe one of the antennas had broken off," Patty says. "The balloon couldn't transmit. They were heading out over the Atlantic for the second time with no radios. We couldn't believe that such a thing was possible."

To Larry, it seemed that at least two hours passed before the lights of Presque Isle vanished over the horizon. The slowness of the flight bothered him at first, but then he was overcome by the beauty of the experience. The silence, the feel of the air (damp on his skin like breath on a glass), the vastness of the sky and the earth, filled him with excitement. He forgot the overwhelming sadness he had felt only a few hours before, saying goodbye to Sandra.

Four or five hours into the flight, sometime between 0400 and 0500 Zulu, or around midnight local time, Larry looked to the north and saw something that took his breath away. The aurora borealis suddenly appeared. "God almighty, Ben, this is unbeliev-able!" he cried. "Look!" Ben roused himself and gazed at the sky. Larry did not understand how Ben could not be visibly moved. While flying Lear jets out of Michigan and New England, Larry had many times seen the northern lights, but he had never seen such a display as this. "The phenomenon was so intense I almost didn't believe that it was what it was, and I knew what it was," he recalled. Huge rays of light pierced the darkness. Holes would open and new rays, enormous and brilliant, would spring to life within the holes.

"Then, all of a sudden," says Larry, "here comes a meteor shower and I'm watching the aurora borealis and its rays of light, these fingers of light are coming out at us, and then, across the whole horizon is this comet, or shooting star, but not like the kind you see where they just go whoosh and they're gone. This display lit up the whole northern horizon."

The show went on until dawn. Larry could not take his eyes off it. He felt that he was in a space movie. His excitement mounted. Max replaced Larry on watch, and Ben went into the sleeping box. It seemed to Larry that Max was less interested, even, than Ben had been in this amazing light show. Larry, who was supposed to be resting, stood or paced the gondola the whole night, watching. He did not want to miss anything. The gondola, laden with eighty-eight hundred pounds of ballast and equipment, was as stable as a concrete floor beneath his feet, and yet he knew himself to be hanging more than 5,000 feet above the surface of the earth, suspended from a balloon by four taut nylon straps that felt, when he seized them, almost as rigid as steel.

Ben had brought his sleeping pills with him, and he slept when it was his turn to do so. Larry did not sleep at all, and as soon as the light was strong enough in the morning, he leaned over the side of the gondola to check on the condition of his hang-glider. It was undamaged. A clump of sod, with green grass on it, was wedged in its nose, but the wings were intact and the aluminum frame was unbent. Ben and Larry worked for a long time, fishing for the revolving glider with a makeshift lasso. Finally they snagged it and made it fast to its safety cable.

The rescue of the hang-glider cheered Larry, and as *Double Eagle II* approached the Gulf of St. Lawrence, he was hopping with excitement and very talkative. Ben and Larry deployed the trailing antennas for the homing beacon and the high-frequency radios. Neither worked.

"Oh, boy, this is ridiculous," said Larry. "Damn radios! Shit! What are we going to do?"

Max and Ben, or so it seemed to Larry, were unconcerned. "We had this problem last year," said Max. "It's just one more thing to cope with."

"I'll get it fixed, we'll have radios sooner or later," Larry said.

He removed the lid from one of the boxes. Inside, like spaghetti covered with lumpy sauce, were the myriad wires and transistors. In disgust, Larry screwed the lid back on the box.

A few hours later, Larry heard his father's unmistakable barking voice on the loudspeaker, sounding even louder and cheerier in the hush of the gondola than it had sounded on all those Canadian railway platforms along the queen's route. Herb Newman, in his twin-engine Beechcraft Baron, was flying around *Double Eagle II*. With him, at Rich Schwoebel's request, was Syd Parks. By the time they arrived, Larry had figured out why the high-frequency radios had not been working: Syd had not told him to press the talk button on the microphone when he tuned the antenna. The problem with the homing beacon remained; its signal was very weak. After going through the checklist, with Syd circling the balloon in Herb Newman's airplane, Larry found that one of the connectors had been ripped loose. They reattached it, but even with the connector back on, the beacon's signal was breaking up. Syd concluded that the cable had been damaged — possibly by one of the television technicians who had been stumbling around in the gondola installing the on-board camera equipment. Larry, throughout the flight, was convinced that the homing beacon could not be heard more than five or ten miles away. In fact, aircraft were able to pick up its signal from distances up to three hundred miles, its designed range. Because it used so much power, the beacon was switched on and off at predetermined times, at the suggestion of Schwoebel.

The VHF radio was now working normally, and Larry contacted the French weather ship *Romeo* on the marine-band as they passed over the Gulf of St. Lawrence. Like Ben the year before, Larry expected the Atlantic to be teeming with ships he could talk to, but after the balloon left the Gulf of St. Lawrence they never saw another oceangoing vessel until they reached the coastal waters of England.

The high-frequency radios never worked properly. As it was the long-range equipment with which the balloon was supposed to be able to talk directly to Bedford, this failure was, to Larry, a maddening imperfection. The high-frequency equipment simply drained its alkaline batteries faster than the batteries could supply power to the equipment. "As soon as you key the mike, that's it," Larry told the others. "It will put out enough power to broadcast for twenty miles instead of the thousand it's supposed to." A Canadian Coast Guard plane had circled them before the arrival of Syd Parks and Herb Newman. "You could yell at them with a megaphone just as well," said Larry, and slapped down the microphone in disgust.

Double Eagle II had been averaging less than twenty miles an hour; unless the winds picked up, the flight would last longer than the ballast. Larry, chattering, joked about feeling wind shears. He would look down at the water and cry, "Look at the waves! I can see we're going faster." Ben and Max made few replies. Larry thought they weren't being very sociable, and he talked all the more, trying to stimulate them into the kind of companionship he craved. Sandra had been aboard his father's airplane and they had exchanged a few words, but her voice had lacked the tone he wanted to hear.

As soon as the balloon started across the waters of the Gulf of St. Lawrence, it began to lose altitude. In theory, with the midmorning to midafternoon sun shining strongly upon it, the helium should have superheated and lifted the system to its planned altitude of 10,000 feet. In fact its altitude was 6,500 feet, as it flew between Prince Edward Island and Grindstone Island. Only by ballasting sixty-five pounds per hour were Ben and Max able to prevent a precipitous descent. Rich Schwoebel, in Bedford, wondered about a leak; he did not communicate his fears to the balloonists. *Double Eagle II* was approaching Newfoundland, and even with a leaking system the pilots would be able to get through the night and land. Besides, it was his policy not to send alarming messages to three men in a balloon.

There was no need for Rich to sound an alarm. It was ringing persistently in Max's consciousness, and it soon began to sound in Larry's as well. Max, watching the balloon's inexplicable descent, was more convinced than ever that there was a hole in it.

Max said, "Ben, I wonder if maybe we've got a leak."

"A *leak?*" said Larry. "In the balloon?"

"There is no leak in the balloon," Ben said.

Max was convinced there was. Ben reminded him that the balloon had been perfect when he inspected it in St. Paul. The balloon had flown steadily through the night; a leaking balloon causes a slow, continuous descent, not a sudden plunge followed by a recovery: *Double Eagle II* was already beginning to climb again.

Max and Larry were not convinced.

"Okay," said Ben, with exasperation. "I'll stick my head in the envelope and *inspect* it."

He climbed on Max's shoulders and thrust his head into the appendix. He wondered if he would be able to breathe: if he found himself in an atmosphere of pure helium, instead of a mixture of helium and air, he would have to get out quickly or suffocate. With his head inside, he found that he could breathe easily. Some light was entering from the appendix, so he asked Larry to tighten the fabric around his neck until the darkness was total.

Ben could see about half the balloon. The sun was bright, and he knew that any hole in the fabric would show up as a burst of light in the blackness. Max rotated Ben's body a full 360 degrees. Ben dropped back into the gondola.

"There is no leak," he said. "No leak."

Maybe not, thought Max. But we can't see inside the duct.

The three men, sailing along in seventy-degree temperatures, took off their shirts and sunbathed. Larry was aware, for the first time, of the rotation of the gondola; he felt that he was on a great skewer, turning in the sun. He thought, I'll have the best tan in history if this keeps up. He stopped looking over the side. *Double Eagle II* was not an aircraft in which the pilot was encapsulated; it was an open boat without lifelines, and Larry, for the first time in all his experience in the air, felt uneasy about looking down from a great height. He wondered how he could feel such a sensation, having spent most of his golden moments in the skies. He had been higher than this in a hang-glider.

At 1750 Zulu, about three in the afternoon local time, *Double Eagle II* climbed to 10,000 feet, but it was still difficult to maintain altitude. The flight was almost eighteen hours old. Schwoebel, relaying messages through the control tower at Moncton, New Brunswick, and through the Lear jet, which was parked at St. John's after flying past the balloon during the morning, advised Ben to ballast off immediately at sunset and maintain the balloon at 10,000 feet. VHF communications, though indirect, were adequate.

Ben noticed, during the day, that the rip line for the main rip panel had been rigged too tautly. Fearing that it might accidentally open the panel as the balloon stretched out with the contraction of the helium, he pushed several feet of slack up inside the envelope through the appendix as a preventive measure. Ed Yost, worried about the same problem, had called directions to Rich Schwoebel earlier in the day, but by the time the message reached the balloon the pilots had already taken action.

Max cooked hot dogs for supper. Already he and Ben were experiencing the loss of appetite they had noticed on their last flight. Larry, munching his frankfurter, descried a glorious sunset in their wake. He could not arouse the others to its beauty, but he gazed on it until it faded and the darkness came on them. All day, as Ben computed ballast schedules and Max worked on navigation and pondered in silence, Larry had been fooling with the radios, trying to diagnose the problem, and taking photographs. He had bought a camera just before takeoff, and having never used color film, he wondered aloud how the pictures would come out. Ben was trying to teach him how to fly the balloon, and Larry, watching everything that Ben did, was beginning to master the tricks involved, just as he had done more than twenty years before in his father's Tripacer — sitting on two telephone books in the copilot's seat.

That night Larry took a sleeping pill for the first time in his life and slept for almost four hours. When he woke, he stripped off his trousers and unselfconsciously relieved himself. The older men turned modestly away, and Larry was amused by their embarrassment. Since takeoff, Ben had been breaking wind, and Larry cracked a joke or two about the extra gas he was supplying. Throughout the voyage, Larry stuck to his lifelong, regular toilet routine, and by the time the balloon approached the shores of Europe, Ben and Max understood that they were traveling with a man who was not embarrassed by body functions.

Before daybreak, *Double Eagle II* crossed the coast of Newfoundland, having overflown Fortune Bay during the night. Once more, Larry's eyes fell upon marvels. Below him were the sparkling inlets of Placentia Bay, and the wild forests of the empty northern land. He took a great many photographs, jabbering all the while. He could see St. John's in the distance, perhaps fifty miles away. At their sluggish pace, it took a long time to get there, and the prospect of overflying the place from which Alcock and Brown had taken off, from which Guglielmo Marconi had received the first transatlantic radio message, the place that had been Lindbergh's last landmark in the New World, gave him much to talk about. Too much, from Ben's point of view. "Larry," he snapped, "you're a goddamn babbling brook. Either talk less or say what you have to say in fewer words."

But nothing calmed Larry. As they approached St. John's, the signal cannon on Signal Hill fired a salute. A helicopter containing an ABC film crew flew up to meet them. Larry, in a spirit of bravado, put a lawn chair on the tiny foredeck, a place that made him exceedingly nervous, and posed for the cameras while nonchalantly reading a hang-glider magazine. The deck was less than three feet wide, and Larry's legs dangled overboard. He took the precaution of tying a rope around his waist and securing it to the mast step, but the cameras could not see that.

As they passed over the launch site of *Zanussi*, Ben cut three red chilis off the *ristra* hanging from the bow, and dropped them overboard for the cameras. He had climbed onto the foredeck without the aid of a safety line, and he gave Larry a look full of mockery. Larry missed it: he had spotted their Lear jet, parked below them on the airport runway, and he was gazing at it through binoculars.

"It's our Lear! Look — that's fantastic!"

It was a crystalline day, warm and sunny, and the ground looked inviting to Larry. Beyond them — he could see it, limitless and treacherous — lay the Atlantic. He thought, Nothing but ocean from here on out.

Max had hardly spoken to Larry so far in the flight, but he had noticed his agitation. He knew, too, that the ballast situation might become critical. Larry weighed 170 pounds, his hang-glider about sixty. Max, half wondering if Larry might like to get off while he could, and half hoping to calm the younger man's antic nerves, made a suggestion. He did it with his saturnine smile.

"If you've got any second thoughts, Larry," Max said, "you can fly down here or bail out, and there'll be no hard feelings." Had Larry left, Max would not have been disappointed.

One of Larry's hang-gliding friends had made the same suggestion to him before the flight. Larry had not taken that suggestion seriously. He knew that Max was serious enough, but he stayed where he was. Days later, over the ocean, he thought back to that moment and wondered what had made him stay aboard. It would have been such a beautiful flight down.

Max's words, Ben thought, did have a calming effect on Larry. But he still talked too much. Ben's spirit, as *Double Eagle II* passed over the Newfoundland coast, was deeply at peace. His mind went back to the year before when, all alone and in misery, with his soaked goose-down garments slowing his movements and reactions until he felt like a man in a diving suit, he had looked down at the surf raging against the rocks of Labrador. Today, in the full light of morning, he stood in his shirt sleeves with the taste of doughnuts and hot chocolate he had had for breakfast still on his tongue, and looked down 9,000 feet upon a milder coast. The sight filled him with elation. He had talked to the ABC interviewer, Bob Beattie, with élan, and now he said a word or two to Larry — nothing important — just helping Max to steady the youngster. There were no doubts in Ben's mind, no apprehensions.

When they crossed the coast, at 1457 Zulu, Ben's optimism rose within him like mercury in the midday sun. Looking at the endless expanse of open sea before him, he was filled with confidence. The flight was going to succeed. After thirty-eight hours aloft, he knew that as well as he knew anything.

Max shivered as he had shivered on the first takeoff, and in his mind he lined up, like lead soldiers on a rug, all the things he knew could happen to cause another failure.

He was more certain than ever that *Double Eagle II* was not flying right. Ben was keeping the ballast log, and his transmissions to Schwoebel at Bedford tallied with Schwoebel's estimates of the situation. But the balloon was flying low, and it was descending when it should be climbing.

In Max's mind, as he sorted out all the possible reasons for this erratic performance, one answer kept burning more brightly than the rest: there was a leak.

Max's obsession took hold of him again in all its overwhelming strength. Nothing mattered but this flight — and his entry into history. He wondered at himself. I regard myself as a rational being, he thought; but this seems to me irrational, to be driven the way I am.

As *Double Eagle II* moved out to sea with the ABC helicopter still chattering beside it, Larry took one last photograph of St. John's. Then the helicopter flew away, and Larry realized that they would see no more aircraft until they reached Ireland. A phrase formed on his lips: "Nothing but ocean." He watched as St. John's became smaller and smaller in the distance, and finally disappeared. With his keen eyes, he was able to see it long after it became invisible to Ben and Max.

The Omega navigational device emitted a high-pitched squeal and ceased functioning. Though Ben and Max and Larry did not know it, the balloon would receive no position reports from the Nimbus satellite for many hours to come. In Bedford, Rich Schwoebel had got word from Goddard that a computer had broken down, and until it was repaired, incoming data from Nimbus was being processed on a priority basis. A Venus probe had been launched, and *Double Eagle II* ranked well below the rocket on the priority list. Schwoebel telephoned a NASA supervisor at home at two o'clock in the morning, to remind him that there were human beings aboard the transatlantic balloon.

Both Max and Larry thought that the balloon had accelerated as it crossed the coast. The VHF radios crackled; *Double Eagle II*'s only contact with home, now, was by way of messages relayed through overflying airliners.

An hour out of St. John's, an airliner called the balloon. "We've got a fellow named John Motica aboard," said the voice from the loudspeaker, "and he'd like to talk to Maxie Anderson." Motica, a warm friend of Max's, is a vice-president of Ranchers. Max could hardly believe his ears. He grasped the microphone and called, "Hey, John!" When Motica's voice came back, Max felt tears welling up, and he bit his lip. He was taken unawares by his own emotion, and for some time afterward, remembering that transmission, he would feel himself on the edge of tears as the sound of John Motica's voice returned to him.

Minutes later, an overflying Pan Am flight reported that Ben's friend Dave Slade, the mooner of the Great West Road, was aboard. The clipper had the balloon in sight; Slade, shouting and pointing out the window, brought all the passengers scrambling to one side of the plane, and the great jet actually tipped with the sudden shift in weight.

At midday, after the land had been left behind, the balloon was flying under high cirrus, with the sun directly overhead. Despite this thin veil of clouds drawn across the sun, *Double Eagle II*, according to all theories applying to helium balloons, should have been climbing as the noonday sun caused the gas to expand.

Instead, the system went into a down. Ben and Max ballasted carefully, in considerable puzzlement, but without panic. Before they achieved control, *Double Eagle II* had fallen from 10,000 feet to 6,500, a loss of 3,500 feet — more than one third of its altitude.

Ben was reminded of the downs over the Gulf of St. Lawrence on the first flight. He thought: Maybe there's something wrong with this part of the Atlantic; maybe this is some freak of nature we're dealing with; maybe rotors are going to plague us all the way across the ocean again this time. He could not understand what was happening. He assumed that this event must have something to do with the atmosphere because he had absolute faith in the balloon.

Max, however, was still certain that there was a leak. If not in the envelope, then it must be in the duct. He said nothing to Ben or Larry about his new suspicion. He didn't want to alarm them. Schwoebel, in a message relayed by an airliner, had recommended that they remain at 14,000 feet that day and avoid dropping much below that level at sunset. Schwoebel reminded them to test the oxygen equipment, as they would rise the following day to altitudes where its use would be essential. The balloon was traveling almost due east, still at speeds below twenty miles an hour, along the 47th parallel.

Larry woke on the morning of the third day with a splitting headache. He knew the cause: altitude. They were flying for the first time in thin air. He checked his fingernails to see if they were blue, and checked his mood to see if he felt euphoric — both classic signs of hypoxia, or oxygen deficiency. He seemed to be all right.

After breakfast — hot tea and the last of the doughnuts — Larry began to set up the ABC television camera and do some filming. Max, who had the watch, paid as little attention as possible to this activity. He pictured himself on the first flight, throwing the CBS cameras overboard in one of the frantic ballasting sequences, and being glad to see the frivolous things go. He was in no mood this morning to be on television. ABC technicians at the launch site had loaded two cameras, a tape recorder, film magazines, and finally a heavy metal suitcase filled with film and tape aboard the gondola. None of this equipment had been weighed, and as each item came aboard, Max's irritation increased. Now, in the first tense hours of the flight, his anger was ready to spill over.

Larry made ready to climb on the perilous foredeck in order to mount the camera on the boom. He asked Max to hold the camera for a moment.

"Get that goddamn camera away from me, son," Max said. "I don't have time for this nonsense."

Larry recoiled. "All I asked you to do was hold it," he said. Max was glaring at him. In Max's look and tone, Larry thought he detected hostility, and something more than that. "He called me *son*," Larry said afterward when reliving what he had felt at the time. "Like I was his subordinate — I mean, his subordinate as a human being, like he thought maybe I was some punk kid. From that moment on, I was always on my guard with Maxie. Always."

Ben helped Larry set up the cameras, and they had a filming session. Max submitted in silence — the only way he could step out of the frame was to leap out of the gondola.

The balloon, rising with superheat, was flying at 15,000 feet along the 49th parallel, some four hundred miles off the coast.

Larry thought out the problem of the radios and attacked it.

After five hours of plugging and unplugging batteries, checking voltages, rewiring connections, and testing antennas, Larry rigged the ham radio to an antenna system that gave maximum power output. The needle on the gauge leaped when he made the right connection at last.

"Chooch!" cried Larry.

Ben and Max, who had watched stoically while Larry clipped wires and fussed with the equipment, made no response. Larry turned the volume up, and he heard voices, dozens of human voices, coming over the loudspeaker of the ham radio. He had been working for five hours on this stubborn problem, and he had solved it. He shot a prideful look at Ben and Max. "I was beating on my own chest," Larry recalled. "Were *they* excited? No. I was the radioman — I guess I was supposed to perform miracles."

Larry, tuning the set delicately, brought in a ham station in Georgia. The voice was faint but understandable. Larry called him, using the *Double Eagle II* amateur call sign, and the man in Georgia responded.

"We are a transatlantic balloon over the middle of the Atlantic Ocean," said Larry. "We'd like you to make a telephone call for us."

"Do you have any other form of communications?"

Larry thought he would impress the ham in Georgia. He responded, "Yes, sir, we have two VHF radios, a transponder, a homing beacon, and a VLF Omega."

"Well, sir," replied the man in Georgia, "it is illegal for me to make any commercial phone calls if you have alternative communications."

"Sir, this is an emergency."

"Oh. Okay — what would you like?"

Larry gave him the number of the Bedford operations center and asked him to call collect and get Rich Schwoebel on the line. To Max and Ben he said, after unkeying the microphone, "Real technical SOB, ain't he?"

Five minutes passed. It was bitter cold in the gondola, and Larry fidgeted. Then the man from Georgia came back on and said, "I'm sorry. I can't reach an operator."

Max, stirred at last, said, "Of all the damn things not to be able to do!" Max suspected that the man in Georgia thought Larry's broadcast a hoax; Larry did not know the ham lingo. He had agreed to get his license before liftoff, but had never done so. Max believed it was because Larry did not want to learn the Morse code.

Larry kept tuning. It was a job requiring skill: signals would fade as the gondola rotated, and Larry, in effect, had to keep up with the fugitive beams by making delicate adjustments in frequency.

"All of a sudden," Larry recalls, "a guy with this very nice fatherly English voice came on. It sounded like the telephone, it was so clear. It was like finding your mother in a big crowd."

Tears nearly came to his eyes as he spoke of it. The voice belonged to an English ham named Art Davies. In minutes, Davies contacted an American ham, who telephoned Rich Schwoebel. It was 0910 Zulu on the third day of the flight, and as *Double Eagle II* entered the fifty-eighth hour of its flight, its crew was doing just what Syd Parks had planned for them to do — they were talking to their technical director and their meteorologist on the telephone.

Schwoebel had good news for them. Goddard, that morning, had reported five satellite sightings of the balloon, and he was able to give them their position and speed. The balloon was just about on the high-pressure ridgeline, but well separated from the storms behind the ridge. Speed was slow, but the balloon was moving at the same speed as the weather system, on a steady northeasterly track.

However, Bob Rice was beginning to worry, at this point, about a storm that was developing over Newfoundland. He believed that this storm would move more rapidly than forecast in the direction of the balloon. *Double Eagle II*, if it lost its position and fell behind the high-pressure ridge, might have heavy weather. The three-hour delay in launch was, as Rice and everyone else had anticipated, proving to be costly. Had the balloon lifted off on time, it would have been as much as ninety miles farther into the Atlantic — ahead of the ridgeline, and in a much safer position.

Rice and Schwoebel did not pass on this information to the pilots: the storm might not develop after all, and there was no need to cause needless anxiety aboard the balloon. Schwoebel was unable to offer an explanation for the down *Double Eagle II* had experienced, though in his own mind he speculated that it may have had something to do with a cooling effect caused by the cirrus. The report of Larry's headaches disturbed him, and he diagnosed these as possible altitude sickness, brought on by a mixture of fatigue and apprehension — in Schwoebel's opinion a devastating combination.

Both Ben and Max talked to Schwoebel. Larry, watching and listening, saw some reason for Ben's conversation — after all, he and Rich had to compare notes on ballast. Rich seemed pleased with Ben's work in this regard; their calculations tallied almost exactly, and Schwoebel was very complimentary. Larry saw no reason why Max should have to talk. He had told both Ben and Max that the batteries were draining at an alarming rate. It was necessary to save power. It seemed to Larry that both older men were inept. They could not tune the radios properly; Ben did not use regulation radio terminology. Besides, it was Larry who was the radioman. He had got the ham radio working. The radios were his. He did not much like Ben and Max fooling around with them.

In Bedford, two hours after talking to the crew, Rich Schwoebel received a Nimbus fix that showed *Double Eagle II* south of the tip of Greenland. Its course was breaking eastward under the influence of a low-pressure system off Iceland. But the balloon seemed, also, to be turning toward the north. Everyone in the control center remembered what had happened the year before when Ben and Max, in *Double Eagle,* had turned north at Greenland.

The information from Nimbus was already more than two hours old — it took that long for the satellite to disgorge its data into the antennas at Goddard, and for the computers there to process the telemetry.

It was evident to Bob Rice that the balloon had, by 1200 Zulu, lost the ridge position, and in fact had fallen some sixty miles behind the high-pressure ridge. It was caught in sluggish but inexorable southwesterly winds. Behind the balloon, the storm was building. The flight was in its sixtieth hour.

At 1420 Zulu, Schwoebel received a report from *Double Eagle II,* relayed by a passing airliner, that reported the craft's altitude at 13,500 to 14,000 feet. The pilots were flying at least 5,000 feet lower than they should be, and they had expended 470 pounds of ballast — more than should have been required. In his log, Schwoebel put a row of red question marks after this information. Were they under clouds? Had they gone through a false partial sunset?

Schwoebel sent a message through the airlines: climb. Half an hour later, TWA Flight 877 reported a contact. At 1500 Zulu, in the sixty-third hour of the flight, *Double Eagle II* was at 14,000 feet and rising slowly. Ben added this message: "We will go in naked."

Schwoebel chuckled — nothing daunted Ben and Max and Larry. Schwoebel, plotting inaccurate navigational fixes from airplanes, longed for an accurate and current position report. The balloon was tracking too far to the north.

There was some talk around the control center that the balloon might be drawn into a circular course over the Arctic. Certainly that possibility haunted Rich Schwoebel, though he did not give voice to it.

Pat Abruzzo worried that *Double Eagle II* might even be hurled back toward North America and be forced to land — the worst thing that could happen to them, she thought. "I would rather have seen them go down at sea," she said afterward. "I just ached in my heart, because what an impossible thing it would have been for two men like them to accept."

Pat did not know Larry well enough to guess how he might feel. She hid her feelings from Sandra, whom she had taken under her wing. As Pat tried to make Sandra feel at home, Patty Anderson watched her in admiration.

Patty did not force her own company on Sandra. Her mind was elsewhere. Her last words to Max before she kissed him goodbye had been, "Honey, if you don't make it this time, I want you to know that it's all right with me if you try a third time."

Aboard *Double Eagle II*, it was bitter cold. Larry had the watch and Max the rest period. The balloon was at 13,700 feet, having descended from its daylight peak of 16,000 feet. They were lower than Schwoebel wanted them to be. Max was attempting to take a star shot with the sextant. Larry watched him idly. The moon was bright, and it was difficult to identify the fixed stars. But Max persisted, squinting through the sextant. Larry noticed the trembling of Max's hands. He did not think that he himself would have been able to hold a sextant in position for such a long time. I give him credit, he thought. His arms must feel like they're falling off. Boy, he really trembles when he's tired. Larry had noticed that Max's tremor disappeared when he signed his autograph. Then, he wrote with a steady hand — a beautiful signature. Larry's mind played with the meaning of that.

Larry and Ben had rigged the rain cover and lighted the butane heater. The rain skirt made a difference in temperature of about ten degrees. The heater, going full blast, would warm a man sitting directly in front of it. If he were five feet away, he got little or no benefit from it.

Ever since the cold set in, Ben had been worried about his feet. He wore heated socks, and spent much time changing the batteries and inspecting the socks to be sure that they worked perfectly. To Larry, Ben's anxiety was touching, and he asked him several times a day how his feet were feeling. Ben would smile or glower, depending on how often Larry had spoken to him in recent moments, and grunt an answer. Max never inquired. Larry thought that Max's behavior toward Ben in this regard was callous.

Larry, a fastidious man, was beginning to feel the effects of several days without bathing. No member of the crew had shaved or brushed his teeth since takeoff. Changing his clothes, Larry had stripped to the skin, once again causing Ben and Max to shake their heads in feigned shock and embarrassment, and thrown his dirty underwear overboard. The stained shorts and T-shirt floated down, wheeling and flapping like gulls. There was a thin layer of sand on everything: it rasped beneath the soles of the men's boots as they moved about the gondola, and filtered into their clothes and their food and the wrinkles and folds in their skin. They had forgot to bring a broom, or even a brush, so there was no way to clean it up.

Larry amused himself by watching the older men. Ben, when Larry failed to wash his hands after making water, cried, in mock disgust, "Larry, you dirty savage!" Ben, ostentatiously washed his own hands, then handled the empty sandbags hanging over the side of the gondola. On these same sandbags, all three men urinated daily. Larry, grinning with secret delight, watched Ben at his ablutions and never said a word.

Max had brought a book with him, *The Great Atlantic Air Race*, and in idle moments he would start to read, then gaze off into the sky. Larry himself was mesmerized by the clouds, the play of the light, the absolute absence of reference points. The gondola turned constantly. Apart from their own voices and the constant muttering of the sea, there was nothing to hear, or to see or smell: their food had no particular taste, nor were they hungry. They drank a great deal of water. Max had peeled and fried some Maine potatoes for their supper that night. He remarked, as they ate the fries, that the military was right as usual: a hot meal did wonders for morale. There had been specks of Maine dirt stuck to the unwashed potatoes. Someone at Presque Isle had given two bags of them as a farewell present, and they hung from the gondola. Ben calculated them into his meticulous daily ballast log.

Sandra kept coming into Larry's thoughts, and he fantasized scenes with her in Paris after he landed in triumph. Emotion raged within him. Then he would look upward at the balloon, thinking he had spent ten minutes in a thorough inspection of the envelope. Glancing at his watch, he would find that he had in fact passed a full hour. He had taped the main rip line to the envelope with a gob of silver tape. The rip line, which would spill all the gas from the balloon, looked just like the valve line. "It would be easy, I mean *easy*, to pull the wrong line," he explained to Ben and Max.

They only grunted in reply. Larry decided it was no use trying to be sociable, those two just did not want to talk. They were always concentrating on something. To Larry, who did things so quickly, their glum, methodical manner was comical.

They were wearing oxygen masks all the time now. Doc Wiley had equipped each pilot with a demand system, so that he had to inhale strongly in order to pull oxygen out of the tank. They sounded like three fat men walking up a steep hill. Larry believed that his mask was not a good one. It was an effort for him to breathe, and oxygen flowed sluggishly into his mouth, like soda through a pinched straw. Max, who did not seem to require as much oxygen as the others, often went without his mask.

When Ben was asleep, Larry would listen intently, to make sure he was still breathing. He also watched the indicator on the tank — an iris that winked like a robot's eye each time a breath was taken. This night, Ben stopped breathing. Larry pounded on the sleeping box.

"Ben, Ben!"

"What?"

"Are you alive?"

"How the hell could I talk with you if I was dead?" Ben demanded.

"You stopped breathing."

"I took off my mask to scratch my goddamn beard."

Larry went back on watch, staring at the altimeter and variometer. His feelings were hurt — he had thought he was saving Ben's life, and Ben had cursed at him.

Later, after the watch had changed, Max was roused from sleep by a noise he could not identify. It sounded like pounding, but who could be pounding? At first he thought the noise might be the lingering echo of a dream, and he tried to remember what he had been dreaming. Then he realized that Ben, who had the watch, was hammering on something. Max assumed that Ben was dealing with some problem — he has a saying about Ben: "He'll do something quick as a wink, even if he doesn't know what to do" — and he went back to sleep. It was too warm for Max in the insulated sleeping box; he pulled down the zipper of his sleeping bag to let in some air around his sweating body.

Larry, asleep on his rest period outside, was feeling the cold, though he was warmly dressed and zipped up in his sleeping bag, with an insulated jacket draped over it for extra warmth. Ben's hammering kept rousing him. The noise neither irritated him nor interested him; he was very tired, and he kept trying to swim down into deep sleep again.

The time was about midnight Zulu. Shortly after taking the watch from Max an hour earlier, as the third full day of the flight approached its end, Ben had noticed that the balloon was descending gently, at about fifty feet per minute. He opened his big clasp knife and stabbed a sandbag. The blade slithered off as if the bag were made of ice. Ben stabbed it again, and again. The results were the same. The sand inside was frozen. Ben had noticed, at the launch site, that the sand had been delivered wet. Because they were running out of time, he had said nothing, but he had thought: Wet sand is a no-no. You go with very dry ballast so it doesn't freeze.

This sand was frozen as solid as a rock. Ben kept chopping away with his knife. It slipped and nicked his trousers, and he decided he had better use some less dangerous implement. From the tool kit he took a hammer and began smashing the sandbags with that.

Double Eagle II continued to descend. Ben ballasted off thirty pounds of sand in an hour. He kept track of the amount, but his mind was dull with fatigue and when, in the next hour, he jettisoned another thirty pounds, and then another thirty, he did not stop to analyze what was happening. To ballast off thirty pounds an hour over a three-hour period is to give up a great deal more than the normal amount of sand. Ben realized that truth in a sudden flash of comprehension, as though a particle of electricity had flown from one part of his brain to another. To himself, but aloud, he muttered, "What the devil's going on?"

Above the balloon hung gossamer clouds. The moon, shining through these, had lovely rings around it. Ben reasoned, very ponderously fitting one bit of knowledge to another, that such thin clouds could not produce enough moisture to form ice. Only heavy clouds could do that, and if the clouds were heavy, the moon would be dim and diffuse, like a car headlight in a fog.

Perhaps ice was forming inside the balloon as a result of condensation. When that happens, one can hear a patter inside the envelope, like rain. He and Max had heard that on the first flight. He listened intently in the deep silence, broken only by the click and gasp of the respirators. He heard no sound within the envelope. Ben examined the outside of the envelope with a flashlight. He saw no sign of ice as he had known it on the first flight — no "popcorn," no nodules of it along the equator. He noticed that the duct had collapsed, as it does when the balloon is below its ceiling.

Then, Ben shone his light on the duct and saw little pieces of white material. He did not consider the possibility that it was ice. It looked to him like that white Styrofoam packing material, shaped like peanuts, which is used to pack fragile objects. Or perhaps like talcum powder. He thought it must be some substance Ed Yost had used to pack the balloon. Ed had always insisted that a balloon would not ice, and despite Ben's own experience off Greenland the year before, and despite the fact that he knew that there is no law of thermodynamics which states that ice will not form on nylon in the presence of moisture and subfreezing temperatures, Ed Yost's dictum was still lodged in Ben's mind.

Ben decided to forget about the problem, though he kept ballasting off to maintain altitude. It was a night of great beauty and peacefulness, with the white moon shedding a pure, almost bridal, light on the cloud deck far below. Not for the first time Ben considered the possibility of stepping out of the gondola. It was so calm in the sky, so quiet, so welcoming. During the first flight, when

Double Eagle was flying through solid cloud, Ben had had the illusion that he could get out and walk on the stuff. It seemed solid, like a field of snow. This sky was different — Ben felt that he could join with it, become part of it, float within it like a particle of the atmosphere itself, if only he leaped over the side. The urge was strong, but his rational mind and his sense of humor were stronger. He was toying with an idea, not fighting a temptation.

Ben's heart swelled with happiness. He was absolutely certain that this was the most glorious moment of his life, and he wished that Pat and his children, all his friends — everyone on earth — could be in the gondola, so that they might feel what he was feeling now.

He shook the duct to see if anything would fall off. Whatever had been there had disappeared.

At about 0230 Zulu, Ben was overpowered by fatigue. He knocked on the sleeping box and woke Max. He told him what had been happening.

"Thirty pounds an *hour?*" Max exclaimed. He could not understand Ben's calm acceptance of what seemed to him a potentially disastrous situation. His first thought, again, was that the balloon was leaking. He asked Ben to describe the descent. It had been a slow, gradual loss of altitude; the duct had collapsed. The clues fitted together.

Ben went inside the sleeping box and composed himself. Just as he had said nothing to Max then, or ever, about his compulsion to jump overboard, Max said nothing to him about the suspicion — flashing like a heliograph in his innermost mind — that the valve must be leaking. He thought of pulling the line to test it, but he feared that it might not reseat properly.

"It's hard, for me, and maybe for all men, to discuss inner emotions and inner thoughts," Max explained after the flight. "You don't know if you ought to be ashamed of them. They're a sign of weakness. If you don't talk about them they aren't there. Then they turn into reality. I guess that's where reality starts."

Max examined the envelope with great care. He, too, saw the particles of white material forming along the duct. And he, too — strangely, for Ben had said nothing about Styrofoam — thought for a moment that it was packing material that had somehow adhered to the balloon.

Max continued to ballast off at a rate of about forty pounds an hour to keep the balloon level. Larry, sprawled on the deck behind him, kept hearing the hammer in his half-sleep. He was wet as well as cold now; a cold mist covered him. Larry, trying to dream so that he could go to sleep, fantasized a boxing match: he was boxing, and each time Max's hammer struck a sandbag, Larry's fist, in the dream, landed with a thud on his imaginary opponent's body.

Inside the sleeping box, Ben woke with a start from a deep sleep. As soon as his conscious mind had got a little rest, it realized what was happening and woke him up. He knocked on the side of the box, pulled off his oxygen mask, and shouted to Max: "Max, Max, I know what's pushing us down. It's ice — it's the same ice as before. Look at it. It's that damn popcorn again."

Satisfied that he had solved the problem, Ben went back to sleep. Max kept the watch for three hours, and then he handed it over to Larry, explaining the situation as Ben saw it. He said nothing about a leak.

Before Max went to sleep he tried to make another star shot, but the moon was even brighter than it had been before, and he was unable to work out their position. He lay down on the deck, leaving Ben in the sleeping compartment. Ben had fussed with his electric socks before he retired, even though he was nearly toppling over from fatigue, and Max knew that he would be more comfortable where he was. Besides, Max wanted to be on deck with Larry at the controls. Ben, in little ways, had established a commander-subordinate relationship with Larry, or so Max thought. Ben liked to give orders and Larry responded because he knew that it made Ben happy. Max thought Ben was playing captain; let him stay in the sleeping box.

The balloon was stable at 14,800 feet. As Max settled into his sleeping bag, Larry thought, "Well, I guess I'm the captain now."

It was the first time he had had the watch in a difficult situation. He watched the instruments and ballasted with finesse; he threw over only ten cups of sand, about twenty-one pounds, all during his time on duty. He hesitated to pound on the sandbags. He feared that Ben and Max might wake if he made too much noise, decide that the situation was critical, and take over. He did not want them to do that. He wanted to fly the balloon.

Larry let the balloon drop to 13,500 feet. It stabilized at that altitude and flew steadily. Larry was pleased with himself — he had solved a problem the others had not been able to solve without squandering ballast.

At first light, all three men were up. Max still could not see any ice on the balloon; neither could Ben. They heated their breakfast water and made tea and coffee and hot chocolate. Ben made toast. Their bread, perhaps because of the condensation within the ice chests, remained fresh all the way across the ocean, as did their lettuce. Pat and Patty had washed all their fruit and vegetables, and had packed the stuff in plastic sacks. Ben, whose turn it was to cook, fried ham. He would have fried eggs, but they had forgotten to bring any. He had little appetite, but he could have eaten an egg. He felt a flash of irritation that such an obvious thing should have been left behind. No eggs and wet sand. Beautiful, he thought.

"Look!" exclaimed Larry.

It was a perfectly clear, cloudless morning, with a sky as blue as pottery. The rising sun warmed the balloon, and as it did, flakes of snow began to fall all around the gondola, straight down, unlike any snowfall any of the balloonists had ever seen before. Ben thought, It's our own private snowstorm. The flakes grew larger, and then, as the sunlight grew more intense, the moisture — formed, of course, from the thin film of ice that had coated the balloon — turned to rain and then to mist.

They saw, as they gazed toward the sun through this sheet of mist, all the colors of the spectrum, bars of vibrant light shimmering against the morning.

 In Bedford, meanwhile, Bob Rice was living through the longest day of his life. The storm trailing *Double Eagle II* was growing in intensity. If the balloon was flying at an altitude of less than 12,000 feet at any time between midnight and 1800 Zulu on Tuesday, August 15, it would almost surely be drawn into the storm. The result would be another ride in a cyclonic weather system, another great circle — and, almost certainly, another failure. *Double Eagle II* would pass the halfway point in its flight toward the coast of Ireland on that day if it continued to move eastward. But the balloon was running out of ballast, and therefore it was running out of time.

Rice and Rich Schwoebel did not know with any precision where the balloon was. The Nimbus satellite was devoting most of its capabilities to tracking the Venus probe. Its reports, the only reliable ones, came in at intervals of twelve hours; sometimes thirty-six hours would pass with no word from Goddard. Then a whole series of fixes would come in, and Schwoebel and Doc Wiley would plot the course on the wall map. Nimbus fixes showed *Double Eagle II* moving inexorably toward the northeast. By noon Zulu (8 A.M. in Bedford), Rice estimated that the trailing storm was no more than eight hundred miles south-southwest of the balloon. It could overtake *Double Eagle II* in a matter of hours.

During the sleepless nights, stubble grew on Rice's cheeks, but his graying blond hair remained neatly combed throughout the ordeal, and neither he nor Rich Schwoebel, as they discussed the possible development of a disaster, showed any outward sign of the tensions within them. Jim Mitchell, watching them, quietly took photographs of the scene with his Nikkormat. Doc Wiley, in a room where the press could not overhear him, began quietly telephoning the military rescue services, to let them know where *Double Eagle II* was heading. He and Rich Schwoebel discussed the possibility of asking the Air Force to fly a practice mission on the balloon from England. Doc, once more, was keeping the worst news from Pat Abruzzo and Patty Anderson. But he and Rice and Schwoebel and Jim Mitchell were downhearted. Schwoebel, in his cool rationality, believed that their mood might be affecting their judgment; he knew the mood would pass. He had noted that he and the others in the control team passed through cycles of elation and depression, with the responses interchanging almost exactly every six hours. The emotional atmosphere could have been plotted on a graph.

Aboard *Double Eagle II*, Ben and Max and Larry had no notion of the danger they were in. When, during the melting of the ice, the rainbow appeared, Larry, wildly excited by the colors, seized a camera and tried to photograph the phenomenon. The camera was frozen.

Freed of its burden of ice, the balloon began to climb under the influence of the morning sun. It was a gradual, classic ascent. Ben watched the altimeter with a mixture of satisfaction and irritation. Lightened by the ballast expended to offset the weight of the ice, *Double Eagle II* would climb to a higher ceiling than they desired; that would mean the expenditure of still more ballast in order to restore the flight profile at sunset.

Ben, speaking through his mask, said to Max, "You know what we were last night? A big snowflake. Snowflakes form around a nucleus of dirt. All this balloon is is a great big particle of dirt. We turned into a snowflake!"

It grew colder as the balloon climbed. Ben changed the batteries in his socks once again, and even Max put on a heavier coat. Each man wore two pairs of woolen underwear, heavy wool melton trousers, felt boots over two or three pairs of woolen socks, two thick Norwegian seaman's sweaters with the lanolin left in the fiber, wool watch caps, and the warmest fiber-filled parkas obtainable. Max wore the great shaggy sheepskin hat that had kept him warm and dry off

Greenland in 1977. It had taken them months to collect these clothes.

Ben and Max fiddled with the radios. Larry had rigged the VHF transmitters in such a way that three battery cables had to be plugged in and three switches thrown in a certain sequence. He could do it with his eyes closed; Ben and Max could never master it. He watched them, sometimes, talking for five minutes into a dead radio. It gave him something to smile at. From the beginning of the flight, he had carried an icy lump of anxiety in his stomach. He got used to it, as one gets used to a stiff neck, and went on with his job. But the feeling was always there, and almost every day something would happen to make him remember it.

Now Max looked back toward America and saw the storm. It was a towering system, and long fingers of cloud reached out of it, as if an enormous hand were groping for *Double Eagle II*. Max tried to estimate the storm's distance from the balloon. It seemed to Larry, the eyes of the expedition, that it was no more than seventy miles away. *Double Eagle II* was flying at twenty miles an hour or less. Unless the storm turned away, or the balloon climbed fast enough to overtake the ridge and get above the weather, the consequences were obvious. That storm was filled with whirlwinds and rain and snow — and possibly with Max's old bogey, thunder and lightning.

It looked to Larry as though they were going to fly right into the clouds. The rain cover was rolled back and they stood in the open; little puddles of rainwater, the residue of the melted ice, sparkled on the deck. Larry's eye fell on the Omega navigational device, which had been so useless to them. Even now they did not know where they were. He kicked the Omega, breaking the glass on its instrument display. He wanted to throw the machine over the side. "You can throw it over at sunset," Ben told him.

Heated by the sun, the balloon climbed rapidly, and finally reached 20,000 feet. Larry climbed onto the foredeck to adjust one of the antennas. He had given up wearing the safety harness, and he felt his old kinship with the sky as he worked. His oxygen mask, its hose running back into the gondola, pulled away from his face. He was short of breath and nauseated, and the space before his eyes filled suddenly with spinning white spots. Then his sight and hearing fled, and with a last effort of his conscious mind, he stepped toward the safety of the gondola.

Inside, he fell down on the deck, unconscious. Ben and Max

rushed to his prostrate form, and switched his regulator to pure oxygen. In seconds, Larry revived. He remembered precisely what had happened to him, and he had known what was happening as it occurred. He wasted no time talking about it, but immediately began to tune the ham radio. It was time for the scheduled contact with Bedford.

Larry, searching for Rich Schwoebel on the ham radio, found him at 0915 Zulu. Schwoebel's calm tones, relayed through a ham station in Grand Rapids, Michigan, warned them about the storm they had seen. The tops of the towering cumulus clouds would reach 18,000 feet. *Double Eagle II* was safely above the thunderheads.

"Maintain twenty thousand feet," Rich said. "Stay below the high cirrus."

The pilots intended to do precisely that, to avoid false sunset and sunrise. Inside their oxygen masks, they grinned: Schwoebel's thoughts were so in tune with theirs that he might have been in the gondola with them.

Ben told Rich that they had expended 3,720 pounds of ballast, and had 2,450 pounds remaining. "I figure we can go in with [at a net weight of] three thousand," Ben said. The total weight of the balloon, including pilots and gear, was fifty-one hundred pounds.

"Conserve ballast this evening," Rich replied. "It will take only a small amount to start the balloon up. All we need are two more nights — two more nights, Ben."

Schwoebel gave them six Nimbus fixes, and Max plotted these on his chart while Ben and Rich talked about the ballast. He saw for the first time how far north their track was taking them. Schwoebel, concluding on a note of optimism, predicted landfall in northern Scotland late Wednesday, the following day, and Belgium early on Thursday.

As the radio fell silent, Max worked for a few moments with his charts. Rich had given them the speed and direction of winds aloft, and if the data held up, their track would take them over the Shetland Islands. Max was concerned about the ballast situation. He had begun to mistrust Ben's calculations. That morning, they had assembled five hundred pounds of ballast for the sunset; Schwoebel had predicted they would use more than seven hundred pounds. In fact they had used that much, so Ben had been wrong. (He later recomputed the ballast and came up with a figure that matched

Schwoebel's.) Instead of using junk — dead batteries and useless equipment such as the television cameras — they had squandered precious sand. Max did not think that the ballast had been properly inventoried. While Ben slept, he had tried to estimate its weight. Not everything had been marked, and they had brought no scale — a fundamental oversight. Max thought they had enough ballast for about twenty hours of flight — at their present speed, barely enough to get them to Scotland.

An idea struck him. He showed Ben and Larry the chart with their projected course marked on it.

"We're going to go right over the Shetland Islands," he said. "If we could get rid of a lot of weight there, we could fly on over Scotland and maybe hit the Continent in the morning."

One of Max's alternative plans, held secret, was to fly on, if Paris was denied them, and land in Lake Geneva, or some other large body of water in Germany or Switzerland. Nobody had ever landed a transatlantic balloon on dry earth; Max was not sure if a safe landing could be made on land when all the ballast was gone, especially if ground winds were high. He and Ben *knew* how to make a water landing. (Ben had announced, in his more impulsive way, that they might fly over the Alps to Italy, in honor of his origins; the Italian flag flew among the others from the gondola of *Double Eagle II*.)

"Larry," said Max after a silence, "how would you feel about flying your hang-glider down when we go over the Shetland Islands? That would give us a hell of a lift, losing your weight and the glider's. Ben and I could make it for sure then."

Larry looked to Ben for a signal. Should he listen to Maxie? His friend was nodding, with his piercing blue eyes above the black oxygen mask fixed pitilessly on Larry. "It's an idea," said Ben.

Larry turned away from the two older men and gazed into the vast sky. He knew what the dangers were: if the winds off the island were blowing at thirty miles an hour, he might not be able to penetrate them. In that case, Larry and his glider would fall into the sea, and he would almost certainly drown. Finally he made his decision.

"Okay," Larry said, "I'll fly down. Anything to save the flight. But if I do this and you two make it to Europe, I want you to tell the world what I sacrificed."

The events of that day glimmer just out of reach of Larry's

memory. However, it was probably later in that day, after Max and Ben had suggested that he fly out of the gondola over the Shetlands, that he decided to clean up his hang-glider.

Gazing over the side, he saw that its wings were caked with sand, the bright orange sailcloth stained green by urine. Larry broke out a long aluminum pole that was designed to support the rain cover in case of a sea landing, and taped a square of cardboard to its end. Then, leaning over the edge of the gondola, he began laboriously to sweep the hang-glider with this makeshift broom. Each time he touched the glider, it rotated. He was tired and giddy. As he scraped the foul mud off the glider, his mind went back to his childhood. "It reminded me of those games," Larry recalls, "where they had the steam shovel and the bunch of little toys inside of a glass box full of sand, and you picked up these things and dumped them through a slot to try to get the prize out." He grew more and more impatient; each time he moved his head, the hose on his oxygen mask tugged at his head. His arms ached.

Some days before, Ben had thrown a sheet of rigid plastic over the side, and it had gone through the glider's sail, slashing it like a knife. Larry saw the cut as he poured several gallons of fresh water on the glider, to wash away the urine stains. Clean again, the glider was an object of affection. The cut in the wing wasn't serious; Larry trusted his glider, and he was going to fly it anyway.

In Bedford, new position reports came in from Nimbus. They showed that *Double Eagle II* had crossed the ridgeline, picked up new winds, and begun to turn to the east; it had left the storm behind. Bob Rice, stirred to poetic imagery, rumbled to Rich Schwoebel, "They have made a glorious turn to the east." From the pattern of the weather, it began to seem to Rice that *Double Eagle II* would, after all, fly the Atlantic from shore to shore — and that the far shore would be that of Ireland at the worst. If the winds freshened, and the speed of the balloon increased, it was entirely possible that Ben and Max and Larry would make England, or even France.

Rich Schwoebel agreed. That evening, Pat and Patty and Sandra, accompanied by Doc Wiley, Jim and Jo Mitchell, and Syd Parks, boarded a flight for London.

Over the Atlantic at 0100 Zulu, flying in bright moonlight, the captain of their TWA airliner raised *Double Eagle II* on the radio.

Pat Abruzzo and Patty Anderson rushed to the cockpit and talked to Ben and Max.

To Pat Abruzzo, Ben's voice sounded strong and confident, and hearing it, she was sure that *Double Eagle II* was going to make it to Europe. As for Ben, he had never had any doubts, once the balloon was in the air, and it was that confidence that communicated itself to Pat.

"How are you, honey?" Patty asked.

"Just fine," replied Max.

"We know you can do it . . . You don't sound very excited to talk to me."

"I don't? But I am. I can see you."

Patty was deliriously happy. Max could see her airplane! There was no sign of the balloon anywhere; it must be hidden by clouds, or perhaps it was flying beneath the belly of the plane. It seemed likely enough that Max could see the plane — after all, Dave Slade had seen the balloon from *his* plane. Not until later did Patty learn that Max had not been able to see her — he was using a figure of speech.

In the gondola, Larry sat in silence, wrapped in his sleeping bag, with a blanket drawn for extra warmth around his shoulders. Ben and Max chattered with their wives, Larry asked if he could speak to Sandra. Pat Abruzzo replied that Sandra was asleep and had asked not to be disturbed.

Ben and Max said goodbye to Pat and Patty, and Larry switched off the radios. Ben had the watch, and Larry huddled for warmth next to the feeble butane heater. A picture of Sandra, curled up asleep in the Boeing 747, formed in Larry's imagination. Another blank spot in our relationship, he thought; there are too many blank spots. She had not even talked to him. Loving her still, he had never in his life felt so lonely. Tears ran down his cheeks, and he hoped that his sobbing, inside the oxygen mask, would sound to Ben like normal breathing. He wiped the tears away, fearing that they might freeze on his face and give him away when morning came.

Larry had by now made friends with a number of hams. His best and truest friend was G4JY — A. H. ("Art") Davies, of Kinver, Stourbridge, West Midlands, England, the first voice Larry had heard

232

on the ham radio. Davies, who lived in a nursing home, kept what amounted to a twenty-four hour vigil on the frequencies used by *Double Eagle II*. Larry, delicately tuning the temperamental ham radio, could always bring in G4JY loud and clear. Davies, in turn, made contact with Howard H. Ferris in Concord, Massachusetts, only a few miles from Bedford. Ferris, a retired scientist, made the telephone patches to Schwoebel at the Bedford control center during the crucial final hours when the balloon was approaching the coast of Ireland. To Larry, Art Davies's voice, gentle and calm and English, was the voice of the good shepherd. He learned to believe that G4JY would always answer when he called. They set up a call schedule at four-hour intervals.

At 0150 Zulu on the morning of Wednesday, August 15, the fifth day, Schwoebel reached the balloon by telephone patch through Howard Ferris's radio in Concord and Art Davies's in England. Ben's strong voice, a bit tinny after passing through several thousand miles of atmosphere and a telephone line, told Rich that *Double Eagle II* was flying through clear skies at 15,000 feet. A thousand pounds of ballast remained — enough for one more night, in Ben's view. Rich asked if they had opened one of the small rip panels to limit ceiling and conserve ballast. Ben did not respond to the question. He and Max had discussed opening the duct; neither really wanted to take the chance.

"We'll give up all our ballast if we have to," Ben said.

Schwoebel replied: "I hope you can go through the whole day without ballasting."

Max made special note of that instruction. Ben's ballasting logs, so meticulous to begin with, had begun to deteriorate. Instead of recording each item as it went overboard, he had begun to group articles of ballast at intervals. Sometimes Larry and Max would disagree on how much ballast had been expended in a night watch while Ben was asleep. Then Ben would simply record the amount that seemed most likely to him.

Getting the ballast together for sunset each day was a laborious process. The entire gondola had to be unpacked. Items marked for use as ballast — dead batteries, useless equipment — would be piled in the center of the deck. Then everything else would be stowed away until the next day. The process took hours. The balloonists knew that some items were unaccounted for. The two fifty-pound sacks of Maine potatoes had vanished during the icing; nobody remembered throwing them overboard.

Max kept the navigational charts, laid their course, differentiated between the dozens of inaccurate navigational fixes they received from aircraft and the absolutely trustworthy Nimbus fixes provided by Rich Schwoebel. On the first flight, it had made Ben anxious, not to know precisely where he was, and this time he kept his own set of charts. Only that morning, Max had spent a long time trying to get a sextant sighting on the North Star; in the false dawn, Max had been able to see the star with his naked eye, but he had not managed to capture it in the sextant mirror. Ben said nothing.

If they stayed out of each other's territory, Ben and Max invaded Larry's with impunity. He resented more keenly every day the way in which they used his radios. Especially, he liked to talk to G4JY, and he did not like it when Ben and Max meddled in his relationship with the kindly, invisible Art Davies. Yet it was Ben who kept telling Larry that he talked too much.

"You say too much to me, and you say too much on the radio," Ben snapped. "Keep it down."

"You don't like my radio language?" Larry retorted. "Mine is better than yours. Mine is short and crisp. Yours is all full of bullshit."

Larry went on talking, asking questions to which he already knew the answers, just to keep conversation alive. He thought that if he fell silent, nobody in the gondola would speak for the rest of the journey. Afterward, grinning at the memory, Ben conceded that Larry had been right. They had been struck all but dumb by fatigue, altitude, and the weird suspension of the senses that takes place in an environment where there is nothing to hear, nothing to see except empty sky, and where a man is breathing oxygen instead of air. Maxie disciplined them to eat, heating drinks and making sandwiches, though they had no appetite. Larry forced them to talk. When Ben and Max did talk, they talked a great deal about the first flight. Larry listened with a pretense of interest to all their stories. He wanted their goodwill. "You can't be mad at a man," he said afterward, "when you are explaining something to him."

As a child, Larry spent many lonely hours in the croplands of the San Joaquin Valley, listening for the sound of his father's airplane returning for him. As a result, he recognizes the distinctive pitch of different aircraft engines in the way most people know popular tunes after hearing the first few notes.

At 0720 Zulu on the fifth morning, Larry heard the unmistakable drone of turboprops. The balloon's altimeter read 19,000 feet — a low altitude for a transatlantic passenger plane. Still, he knew the song of those engines. He tuned the VHF, and almost instantaneously, an American voice boomed over the loudspeaker. It was King Five Zero, a U.S. Air Force rescue plane out of Woodbridge, England. The HC-130 was flying a practice mission on *Double Eagle II*, and it gave the balloonists a precise navigational fix. They were at latitude 56.18 degrees north, longitude 23.29 degrees west, less than five hundred miles west-northwest of Ireland.

Aboard the Air Force plane was an ABC television crew. Bob Beattie asked the balloonists to describe their condition. The voices that came back to him were weary and fraught with anxiety.

Ben said that it was cold. He predicted a landing the next day. "If we make our destination, it should be okay," said Ben. "Otherwise we go into the sea."

Max, made impatient by the newsmen's frivolous questions, listened hard for any comment from the military personnel aboard. The aircraft commander, Captain Charles R. Stueve, mentioned that the HC-130 had been bucking eighteen-knot headwinds all the way from its base to the balloon.

On hearing this, Max's spirits plunged. Max thought that the plane had taken off from Prestwick, Scotland, many miles to the north of its actual base at Woodbridge, England. As Prestwick was almost due east of the balloon's position, a wind of only eighteen knots (about twenty-one miles an hour) would never get them to Ireland; they would fall into the sea a hundred miles off the coast, just as Cameron and Davey had done.

Max's despair was all the deeper because he had been con· vinced that *Double Eagle II* had picked up speed during the night. When he came on watch, relieving Ben at 0330, Ben had had news for him. Two hours before, the balloon had passed through some sort of seam in the atmosphere. The gondola moved out from under the envelope — a most peculiar thing for it to do. Looking up, Ben saw that the envelope appeared to be ten to fifteen degrees off the perpendicular.

"I think we went through some kind of high-altitude curl, or wind shear," Ben told Max. A wind shear is the place where two currents of air, moving in different directions, come together, causing an eddy that is similar to the one that occurs at the confluence of two streams of water.

"That's the best news I've heard on this flight," Max had said. "Maybe we've entered a high-speed wind system."

Ben agreed that this was possible; he had the feeling, too, that *Double Eagle II* had changed direction and was turning to the southeast, toward Ireland. It was only a feeling, but he went to sleep nearly convinced that his intuition was correct.

As Bob Rice was to tell the balloonists after the flight, the "wind shear" Ben had observed took place at the precise moment that *Double Eagle II* left the ridgeline and entered the windfield that would fling it over the coast of Europe.

King Five Zero told Max, who was asking for navigational fixes and winds aloft, that it would stay in the vicinity of the balloon for at least an hour. Max asked the navigator, Captain James W. Carlton, to give him another precise navigational fix at the end of that time.

When he did, it showed that *Double Eagle II* was moving at close to forty-five miles an hour, on a track of 120 degrees. They *had* made the turn, and they were on course for Ireland. Max laid in the course with a lighter heart. Ireland begins at longitude 10 degrees west, Scotland at 5 degrees; in those latitudes, that is a difference of some two hundred miles. They might make it after all, if speed and direction remained good — and if ballast held out. Max estimated that they would reach Ireland at midnight Zulu, and asked Captain Carlton to calculate landfall as well. Carlton's estimate was within thirty minutes of Max's own. "You will go into the Irish coast between Limerick and Shannon," said Carlton.

Boy, that's super, Max thought. He asked the Air Force plane to monitor their beacon, and to be prepared to fly back for a real rescue late that night.

"We're going to jettison our life raft at sunset tonight," Ben told King Five Zero, and the ABC cameraman on board caught a fine reaction shot of the pilot's horrified face as these reckless words came over his headset.

After King Five Zero flew away, *Double Eagle II* climbed

through 21,000 feet, and reached 23,000. The cold was intense, and the northern skies were pallid, with a solid cloud deck 15,000 feet below.

Max opened a discussion with Ben about ballast. They had already thrown over some of the radios and an armful of unexposed television film and film canisters. Ben and Max knew the hang-glider would have to go at sunset, along with the life raft and most of their food — even the greater part of their water. Max did not like to lose the water because he feared the effects of dehydration on their minds and bodies. As they would remain for at least another day at high altitudes, they needed the oxygen.

It was not the first time Max and Ben had openly discussed the ballast situation. The day before, woozy with fatigue, they had had a rambling talk about ballast, but had come to no firm conclusion. Ben had rummaged through the tool kit and flourished a hacksaw. "Just take and cut off the stern of the gondola," Ben had said. "That's a hundred and fifty pounds. We could do the same on the bow, and still keep the gondola floating."

Now both men were tense. Ben knew well enough that Max had doubts about his ballasting statistics, and Ben was prepared to defend them. He knew, down to the last ounce, how much ballast was aboard — knew it as a riverboat pilot knows a river with its sandbars and its rapids and its curves. The sequence of ballasting, all the way to landing, was laid out in Ben's mind.

Ben listed the things that would have to go: his potato-sack sea anchor, a wet battery, two oxygen bottles, the sextant, the life raft, ABC's $7,000 tape recorder, the sleeping box, the $8,000 Omega, all the radios and their antennas except the VHF.

Max listened. Ben was telling him things he already knew, but he understood the other man's need to dispel anxiety by dwelling on detail. Ben ticked off on his fingers the things they had left, and their approximate weight.

"You didn't mention the propane tank," Max said. "It's heavy, and I don't see that it's worth a hell of a lot."

"I don't agree."

Max was puzzled. Why didn't Ben agree? He honestly thought Ben had overlooked the propane tank.

"I want to throw it over," Max said. "The options are the propane tank or a bottle of oxygen."

"We've got enough oxygen to go around the world," Larry said.

Ben stared at Max in stubborn silence. Max was thinking, Ben must know we can't throw a heavy thing like a propane tank overboard while we're above land; it could fall on somebody and hurt them. To kill some poor Irish farmer with a damn propane tank would ruin the flight.

"I *won't* throw it over," Ben said.

"I don't see why not. We don't need it."

Ben exploded. "You didn't freeze your goddamn foot the last time, Max! I'm not going to lose my foot just because you want to throw away the propane, so get that through your head!"

Max, for the first time in their long friendship, was enraged with Ben. Larry, watching, feared that the two men might come to blows. Max had forgotten all about Ben's bad foot, and stung by his own sense of shame for having forgotten his friend's injury as well as by Ben's words, he struck back.

"No, I didn't freeze my foot and I don't want anything to happen to your foot this time," Max said. "But I don't care if you freeze your ass off!"

That, thought Max, was precisely what would happen if they were overtaken by the following storm and went into the sea. The gondola would almost surely broach. Even in survival suits, even in August, the Atlantic would kill them in hours.

As *Double Eagle II* wafted toward the shores of Ireland, with a solid cloud deck beneath it and the morning sun before it, Max watched the altimeter closely, tapping it nervously with a forefinger.

Each day, as the sun was directly overhead, the balloon had lost altitude. Why?

His mind returned to Cameron and Davey and their fall into the sea. Had they approached the French coast at a higher altitude, they would have made it.

Max thought: If you come into the coast at less than eighteen thousand feet, you don't go home. It's as simple as that.

Max was suspicious of the winds at 23,000 feet. Their speed would be some twenty miles an hour slower at that altitude than at 21,000 feet. He wanted to descend, somehow, into the swifter windfield.

At 0900 Zulu (nine hours into the fifth day), Larry contacted Art Davies in England, G4JY had already set up a telephone patch to Massachusetts with Rich Schwoebel through W1HZ, Howard Ferris.

Schwoebel, believing that the balloon had traveled more slowly through the night and morning than in fact it had done, told *Double Eagle II* that it could reach Ireland by noon the following day, assuming winds of twenty miles an hour.

Max seized the microphone. "We expect the Irish coast in about ten hours," he said. "We're at twenty-three thousand feet. We are traveling at forty to fifty knots."

"With forty knots [forty-six miles an hour]," Schwoebel replied, "we estimate it may be possible for you to reach the mainland if you can stay up one more night."

"We intend to stay up one more night. The option will depend upon the winds. We don't want to overfly and then get blown out at the end," said Max. "I have a technical question for Rich. If we go down to only eighteen to twenty thousand, will we be able to open the twenty-five-thousand-foot duct?"

"That's affirmative," Schwoebel replied.

Opening the duct would limit their ceiling, and conserve ballast.

Ben, taking over, told Rich that he planned to offload 700 to 750 pounds that night. Landing ballast was 400 pounds.* Schwoebel told him the nighttime ballast ought to be more on the order of 600 pounds.

"Do you feel that you might go to a much higher ceiling?" Schwoebel asked.

"Negative," Ben replied crisply. "No altitude control problem. No equilibrium problem. Question: in these circumstances, should we open the twenty-five-thousand-foot duct?"

Schwoebel, believing that they could control altitude through use of the valve, advised the balloonists not to open the duct.

"I think you guys are expert pilots," he said, "and I have a lot of faith in what you can do with the system."

Max came back on. "We expect to be in Ireland by ten o'clock tonight," he told Schwoebel. While Ben talked, Max had been plotting their track and velocity. He had listened with only half an ear to Ben's chatter about ballast figures — Max had his own estimates on that subject.

"We'll need to know landing winds," said Max. "We'll need to know what the velocity is. If they're high winds we'll go into the sea or a lake. If they're low, we can land."

Ben, listening, could not believe what Max was saying. Land in the sea? Land in a lake? At *night?*

Peter Leavitt of Weather Services came on, talking fast in his nasal eastern voice. "You're over the ridge and you're in the chute now. You couldn't pour on the coal at a better time."

"We're glad we made it," replied Max.

Ben bit his tongue. They had not made it yet, and if they landed in the sea, even if they could walk out of the gondola and wade ashore, *they would not have made it.* Wet landings did not count.

Max was playing "What-if?" again. In Ben's mind, Ireland was an option — it would count as a transatlantic crossing, but if they landed there, they would be Alcock and Brown, not Lindbergh. England was a better option. France was the real goal.

But Max, measuring and remeasuring with his calipers and punching out numbers on his calculator, believed that the winds, as they were now blowing, would put *Double Eagle II* above the English

* Final ballast that night, according to Ben's log, was 718 pounds.

Channel at noon the following day. On every day of this sunny flight, the balloon had lost altitude at midday. They'd be at zero ballast, or near to it, and if the balloon sank to a low altitude between England and France, the winds would die, and so would the flight. Better to be recognized as the men who landed in England, or even in Ireland, than the fools who tried to go too far, and took a bath in the Channel. We'll wait and see, he thought.

Just after 1100 Zulu, wispy cirrus formed above the balloon at very high altitudes. Max had lit the Coleman stove and was heating soup for lunch. He wore his oxygen mask. Normally, especially if the balloon was below 18,000 feet, he went without a mask and would sip oxygen from a tube, like a man smoking a waterpipe. That was dangerous around an open flame, even so feeble a flame as the one licking the charred bottom of their soup kettle.

At 1130 or so, the balloon began to vent as it reached its ceiling. Larry, watching the instruments, said, "We're going down."

"When it gets to four hundred feet per minute, let us know," said Max, intent on his cooking.

Ben and Max exchanged a few words about the descent. Perhaps the cirrus had something to do with it, or the usual mysterious midday descent. It did not worry them. They decided they would let *Double Eagle II* go down; superheat in the afternoon would bring it back up.

The sunset ballast was already prepared and lay in a heap on the deck. Larry had chopped up the sleeping box and the floorboards, and had thrown more of ABC's equipment — a recorder and some other items — on the pile.

Larry, gazing at the altimeter, called out the numbers. Now *Double Eagle II* was falling toward the cloud deck below, and the sea beneath it, at a rate of 400 feet per minute.

Ben ballasted off, carefully, and the rate of descent slowed to 200 feet per minute. Still, the balloon kept going down. The two American flags suspended from the envelope stood straight out. Gazing upward at the flags, Ben thought, We'll go down to twenty thousand, maybe a little lower, and bottom out.

Larry called out numbers: "Nineteen thousand, eighteen thousand, seventeen thousand." *Double Eagle II* plummeted through 15,000 feet and showed no sign of stopping.

"Ben," said Max, "I wonder what the hell is happening."

Ben got out his ballast tables, sat down, and began figuring with a pencil. In a few moments, after checking his figures again, he looked up.

"If we stop the descent any sooner than is absolutely necessary, we're going to lose the ballast we need to make the coast," he said.

"How far down do you want to go?"

"Right to the sea if we have to. I don't want to touch the water because the barograph would show that, and I don't know if they'd allow us the transatlantic record if we touched the water on the way across."

Max nodded. Their hot words of the morning forgotten, Max and Ben had an amiable discussion about the rules of the International Aeronautic Federation for transatlantic balloon flights.

"You know, Ben," Max said, "I always kind of wondered if it would have counted if Dewey had made it across, the way he was gonna go down and sit on the water all the time."

Larry could not believe that Ben and Max were as calm as they seemed to be. He wondered if they were playing their macho game again, as they had done in leaving their parachutes behind. Larry decided to be nonchalant, too. He threw a handful of papers over the side, and the three men watched them float away above them. All knew that this could happen only because the balloon was falling: the papers remained where Larry had laid them, on the palm of the wind.

It grew warmer as they descended, and they started to peel off clothes. There was no longer any need to breathe oxygen, so they removed their masks.

Ben gratefully scratched his stubble and said, "We ought to eat. We've got the masks off, and it's comfortable down here."

"God!" cried Larry. "How can you eat at a time like this?"

He looked over the side to check on their distance from the cloud deck; Ben kept saying that the reflective heat of the sun from the clouds would drive the balloon back up.

What Larry saw, thousands of feet below, was a huge blue hole in the clouds. The hole was perfectly circular. The balloon was falling right into it. Larry pointed down, tugging at Ben's sleeve. Ben and Max, sipping their soup, looked over the side.

"Max, it's just like what we had off Greenland," said Ben. "The big downs. It's like Greenland, all over again."

Larry flicked his eyes from one impassive face to the other. He had heard, to the point of ennui, about those downs between Greenland and Iceland. Now they were real to him.

"We can't go under those clouds, Ben, or we'll have a false sunset and we'll have to ballast to get back up," said Max. He pointed to the west. Towering cumulus, another storm, was coming up in their wake along the surface of the earth.

"We'll go back up," said Ben, unperturbed. "We'll just *ballast*."

With Larry still agape, Ben and Max discussed the alternatives. Ben did some more figuring in his ballast log.

"We've thrown over how much?"

"About one hundred and twenty-five pounds, I figure," said Max.

"Then we can't afford to give up any more. We'll go back up with the superheat to a much higher ceiling — maybe even twenty-nine five."

Ben and Max, frowning, considered the problem. It was not a total mystery to Larry, but he could not know what Ben and Max knew: if they did go as high as 29,000 or 30,000 feet, the flight was lost, unless they chopped off part of the gondola at sunset as crisis ballast.

"The answer," Ben said, "is to ballast off fastidiously, and wait it out to the very last minute. We buy ourselves two things: one, we give up the least amount of ballast, and two, we prolong whatever is happening, so that we hit the sunset on the way up. That way we won't go to maximum ceiling."

Max's face, as Larry watched it, twisted into an expression of sage agreement. They were at 8,000 feet, having lost 15,000 feet in fewer than sixty minutes. Larry looked over the side, into the great blue hole in the cloud deck below. *Double Eagle II* was falling straight into it still.

Larry turned around, and saw Ben fussing with the camp toilet. He was fumbling with a plastic bag, just as he fumbled with the radios, trying to fit it to the stool.

"What are you going to do?" cried Larry. He snatched the stool from Ben's hands, maddened by his ineptitude, and slid the plastic bag onto the rods.

Ben took the stool from Larry's hands, thanked him, dropped his trousers, and sat down.

"I am going to move my bowels." he said.

Later, Ben would tell Larry that he had chosen this act as a means of calming Larry's nerves. If that was his objective, he failed. Larry, watching him, felt exasperation churning around his heart, and he wanted to cry out, "Why aren't you flying the balloon?"

But he said nothing. Max cut loose several plastic bags of human waste that were hanging outside the gondola. "Fastidious ballasting," he said, and he and Ben laughed.

Even Ben wondered, as the balloon continued its inexplicable plunge toward the ocean, if it had developed a leak. Max had never dismissed this possibility; now it seemed to him more likely than ever. Perhaps the valve had failed; perhaps a rip had developed, as in the case of *Zanussi*. Ben and Max did not share these thoughts with Larry, and there was no need to share them with each other. Ben, after inspecting the exterior of the envelope, convinced himself that there was no leak, that the balloon was sound. They were in the grip of some atmospheric phenomenon, such as in the descent off Newfoundland early in the flight.

Double Eagle II was caught in an avalanche of air. No balloon had ever fallen so far, and lived.

Now Larry could hear the ocean through the circular hole in the clouds, as well as see it. The sea was calm; they were two hours ahead of the storm above weather ship *Lima*. But the roar of the waves was clearly audible. The balloon was at 4,000 feet. Max and Ben were finishing their lunch. They were through talking, and nothing had been said for several moments.

Larry took his eyes off the ocean. He had felt moisture on his skin; it reminded him of flying through clouds in a hang-glider. He looked out of the balloon, straight ahead of him, and saw haze billowing into the gondola.

"We're in the clouds!" he cried.

Max leaped to his feet and picked up a twenty-pound tape recorder. He hesitated a moment, then threw it over the side. The balloon stopped, then rose a few hundred feet, and stopped again.

Larry looked through the blue hole. "We're going to lose the flight," he said. "We've come all this way, and we're going to lose it."

"No, we're not," Ben said.

"We're in the clouds, for Christ's sake!"

"We're not in the clouds; we're in the hole," said Ben.

Larry did not see what difference it made. Being in the hole *was* being in the clouds. If the balloon fell through the hole, the winds would carry it under the clouds and Larry feared that *Double Eagle II* would never have the ballast to break through the overcast, back into the uplifting heat of the sun.

The balloon hung motionless at 4,500 feet. It was very warm. The air is warmer than the balloon, Max thought, and it has been all the way down. That would account for it.

They waited fifteen minutes. Though the sun was strong, *Double Eagle II* did not start back toward its ceiling. Max opened their last bottle of Perrier water and passed it around; they threw the bottle over. Larry, thinking he must do something to relieve the tension, urinated over the side and the others followed suit. They poured some water overside.

Nothing happened. *Double Eagle II* hung in the milky afternoon sky like a punctuation mark upon a blank page.

In Concord, Rich Schwoebel picked up the telephone at 1420 Zulu, expecting to hear voices, even jubilant voices, from *Double Eagle II*; the balloonists had been scheduled to transmit a report through G4JY and Howard Ferris at 1400 hours. They were a bit late, but Schwoebel wasn't worried — as a veteran ham he knew that it sometimes took time to make contact on the amateur band. Larry's skill in tuning the equipment despite handicaps of inexperience and stress and fatigue had filled him with admiration.

Instead of the crackle of a long-range ham transmission, Schwoebel heard a chipper English voice. A British Airways flight had sighted the balloon an hour and twenty minutes earlier, about three hundred miles west of the Irish coast. *Double Eagle II*, at that time, was at 16,500 feet and descending.

Descending? Schwoebel's heart fell. He did not permit himself to speculate on the reason for the balloon's descent, or even to believe without reservation the report from the airliner. Quietly, he mentioned the problem to Bob Rice. The two scientists reviewed the weather data: the balloon had passed over the high-pressure ridge and was now part of a new weather system that was moving fast toward the European land mass. It was flying in good weather, with the sun aglow. In theory, *Double Eagle II* could not undergo a loss of altitude in such circumstances. Schwoebel and Rice waited tensely for a transmission from the balloon. Howard Ferris told Schwoebel on the telephone that he and Art Davies, G4JY, had been trying, along with an army of hams from the Mediterranean to the Great Lakes, to raise the balloon, but nobody had made contact with Larry.

At 1500 Zulu, with the gondola touched by tendrils of cloud swirling out of the great hole beneath it, Larry turned on the ham radio. He tuned it with his quick fingers to the proper frequency, and in a matter of seconds he found the fatherly voice of G4JY, quivering and tinny at the very edge of audibility. Turning the vernier knob, Larry finally brought Art Davies's voice up to full volume.

"We've run into a bit of a problem," Larry told G4JY. "We were at twenty-two thousand feet [sic]. We're now at forty-five hundred."

An atmospheric disturbance, described by Art Davies as "an equatorial whistle that's giving me a heck of a job," prevented Schwoebel from talking directly to the balloonists. Davies, however, could hear both Schwoebel and *Double Eagle II*, and he passed the words they spoke from the gondola to Bedford and back.

"Ask what is the nature of the problem," Rich said. His voice was calm, but tight with strain.

Ben replied, in a strong, unruffled tone: "Excessive superheat loss."

RICH Understand. Ask him his ballast situation.

BEN This is Ben. Ballast adequate for night. Balloon extremely slack. Does not seem to respond to afternoon superheat.

RICH Do they feel they are stable at forty-five hundred now?

BEN Affirmative.

RICH Stand by for winds at five thousand. Would it be advisable to have rescue in the area?

BEN Negative. Tomorrow would be soonest rescue mission necessary. If we go in, we will give Mayday at that time. Ask Rich if extreme altitude loss today normal in his opinion.

RICH In my opinion, it is not normal, but they may be in an unusual situation. I would advise them to use whatever ballast they have to hold balloon at this altitude and take advantage of west winds into Ireland.

BEN   That's a Roger. Ask Rich his opinion if [higher] altitude possible without ballast.

RICH   Very difficult to say. Just have to see what occurs. I'm sorry I can't answer that.

BEN   This is *Double Eagle*. Thank you very much for your help. I'll give the mike back to Larry, here.

Larry took the microphone from Ben's steady hand. The older man lolled back in his deck chair, with Max beside him in another chair, and tapped the glass of the altimeter. The needle remained steady at 4,500 feet.

Larry thought that Ben had left a lot out of his conversation. How did he know they would not need rescue tonight? Larry spoke eagerly to his friend G4JY.

"Is there any chance you could have some other people in England monitor this frequency in case of the eventuality of a water landing, a water landing?" he asked. "We'd find it necessary prior to ditching to give you a call. If anything happens it'll happen this evening, because this is our last night out."

Art Davies's voice, reassuring and sympathetic, came back immediately: "Several of us are on the frequency and I feel sure we'll be monitoring all night. Good sailing to you, Larry."

Larry switched off the set. He felt better for having talked to another human being, especially G4JY, and as his spirits rose, the balloon rose, too. It went up rapidly to 6,500 feet — and then sank again to 4,500.

"Well, fellows, that's it," said Larry. "We're not going back up."

"Larry," said Ben. "Get that idea out of your head. We're going back up."

"I'll bet you," Larry said. "I'll bet you a hundred dollars we won't go back up to twelve five."

It was to Ben that he offered the bet. Larry does not gamble — "I won't bet that fat makes grease," he says of himself — but he had watched Ben at the gaming tables in Las Vegas, putting down thousand-dollar wagers.

"I don't want to take your money," Ben said. "We are going *up*. We're going up to twenty-six five."

Larry pulled out his wallet. It was stuffed with money — he had brought along eight hundred dollars or more, figuring that he might land in a place where nobody knew him, and might need airplane fare back to the States. Neither Max nor Ben had more than three dollars with them. Max, too, refused the bet, but Larry insisted.

"All right, I'll bet you ten dollars," Max said at last.

"Ten dollars! Make it a hundred."

Max nodded, and Larry thought, contemptuously, Big bet for Maxie — ten dollars.

The sun kept shining. The envelope heated, the helium expanded, and *Double Eagle II* began to climb. Larry watched the altimeter. Finally the needle touched 12,000 feet, then 12,500. Larry took a hundred-dollar bill out of his wallet and, grinning, flung it at Max.

Max handed it back to him. "I don't want it," he said.

"Keep it — a bet's a bet!" said Larry with a joyous guffaw.

It was very important to him that Max keep the hundred dollars. Larry half-believed that the balloon would fall again if he refused the money. In making the bet, he had been wagering on a superstition, though he calls it playing the odds.

If you bet, he had thought, the odds are against your winning. I'll bet we won't go back up. Maybe the odds will work, and I'll lose. Then we'll go back up. That will be the best bet I ever lost.

Double Eagle II, gathering speed as it gained buoyancy in the thinning air, rose to 25,000 feet. There, the effects of the afternoon cooling — the sun was now beginning to color the western sky — halted its ascent.

The balloon vented helium through the duct as it climbed. This action gave Larry a bad moment; he feared they would have to give up more ballast than they could afford. The disputes on this subject between Ben and Max had left their mark on him, though in his loyalty he was absolutely convinced that Ben was right.

They were back on oxygen, of course, and as the balloon climbed into the frigid upper atmosphere Ben and Larry had put on successive layers of clothes. Max seemed comfortable enough in his Norwegian sweater and an unzipped jacket. To Larry, this indifference to cold seemed hardly human.

Max, during the upward journey, had reworked his calculations, and he was now certain that the balloon would cross the coast at about

248

ten o'clock that evening. Passing airliners gave them tracks and wind speeds. They were heading straight for Limerick at fifty miles an hour. Even during the great down, *Double Eagle II* had continued to fly toward Ireland.

Laboriously, snuffling in their oxygen masks, the three men prepared for the night ballasting again. The heap of stuff they had assembled that morning had, of course, been somewhat reduced as a result of the great down. Frugal as they had been, they had used some three hundred pounds to keep *Double Eagle II* above the clouds. Larry clambered all over the gondola, dismantling its nonessential parts, clipping antennas, disconnecting radios. With a pang, he cut the heavy antenna of the amateur band. They would need it no more because they were in touch with Shannon control and with passing aircraft by VHF. Everything belonging to ABC except the exposed film and the camera lenses went on the pile.

They assembled all the food and most of the water — it would go. They had another discussion about the life raft. Max thought it useless; he would save water before the life raft because if they went down in the gondola and survived, they could not live without fresh water. Ben was thinking still of chopping up the gondola itself to reduce weight. If they did that, then the gondola wouldn't be seaworthy, and the raft would be needed. It was a big, six-man raft with a radar-reflective top and its own store of emergency gear, including a device to turn sea water into drinking water.

"Nobody," said Max, "has ever turned sea water into drinking water." They decided to ballast the raft, after taking a vote.

The hang-glider could not be released over land unless Larry was flying it. The craft could fly thirty miles by itself, and perhaps decapitate someone as it came whistling in to land. There was no vote on this question: Max and Ben let Larry decide.

"We can take it," Ben said, "but these are the alternatives — we can throw over a wet battery, reducing our power supply for the radio. We can throw over oxygen bottles and maybe not have them when we go back to high altitude in the morning."

"Let it be the hang-glider," Larry said.

Max added Larry's parachute to the pile.

"You can keep this if you want to," Ben said. "We'll throw you out over Ireland."

249

Ben and Max joshed him about the chute, and how, from the earliest days in Albuquerque until their arrival in Maine, he had urged them to bring their own parachutes.

"I'll tell you what's really on my mind," Larry had told Ben before takeoff. "If I have to jump, you bastards will try to beat me up and take my parachute away from me."

When all the ballast was collected, Ben surveyed it. The entire port side of the gondola was strewn with the stuff, and in the failing light it looked to Ben like the world's largest mouse's nest — bits of wiring, fittings, Styrofoam, splintered boards pried from the floor and the interior bulkheads, tape recorders, the sextant. Larry ran a total in his head: $14,000 for photographic equipment, $2,000 apiece for their film magazines, $20,000 worth of radios. It boggled the mind. Ben worked out another set of figures.

"Seven hundred and eighteen pounds," he said.

Max looked at the pile and stirred it with his toe. "Where?" he asked. "Where is the seven hundred eighteen pounds?"

"I can't tell you where every single piece is, Max. It's all over the place, hidden. But it's there. It's all there."

"I don't believe it."

They were flying very high. The sun was fading. Ben felt a slight numbness in his foot, as he always did in the chill of the night at extreme altitudes.

"You don't *have* to believe it," he said, and turned away.

"We need four hundred pounds for tomorrow."

"We've got it. There is no question about making it, Max. None. All we have to do is survive tonight's ballast, and we've got the ballast for tonight."

Max sat down. There was no point in going through the inventory again. Ben was doing just that — he had been doing it all the way across the ocean. In his mental inventory, he included everything — their clothes, Larry's wallet, even the trail ropes. Nobody, so far as he knew, had ever landed a helium balloon without trail ropes. But he was as buoyantly confident now as he had been on the first day, breathing oxygen or not breathing oxygen, fatigue or no fatigue, that he could do it.

Ben thought: We could go in without ballast, we could ballast off the trail ropes to stay aloft; we could go in by valving very, very carefully, just ever so delicately; if it's during the sunlight hours, I say it's no problem, no problem at all — I learned years ago how to handle an airplane, you handle her as you would a very fine lady: you fly the balloon the same way.

Ben kept these thoughts strictly to himself.

At sunset, their Lear came out to meet them, beautifully flown by Don Sellers and John Calcott, who had piloted it across the Atlantic. The ABC crew was aboard, and Larry decided that this was a good moment to drop his hang-glider. If it were on film he would, in a way, always have it. He had dreamed for months of his descent, circling the balloon — and dreamed, too, of the photographs of himself in flight with *Double Eagle II* in the background. "They would," said Larry afterward, still in the grip of regret, "have been the most thrilling photographs in the history of hang-gliding and ballooning."

As the Lear circled *Double Eagle II*, Larry and Ben unhooked the two D rings that held the hang-glider to the load ring, and at a signal from the cameraman aboard the Lear, Larry released it. The glider dropped its nose, then flew back up and trembled, motionless, before Larry's face. He thought it was going to fly into the gondola. Then it slid backward, nosed over, and did three loops, its form as graceful as a girl's against the sunset. It circled down, a long slow descent, with Larry watching it all the way. He felt as though a million-dollar bill had blown out of his hand.

Double Eagle II had already begun its sunset descent. The balloonists ballasted off, and it seemed to Ben that the craft would never come to equilibrium. He knew that it would take every item he had laid out on the deck in order to stop the balloon, but he kept wishing that he were wrong, that something had changed. He didn't want to give all those things up.

They threw over the high-frequency radios that had never worked, and some ABC equipment. Max, in a hypnotized moment, placed his navigational calculator on the ballast pile; it weighed only three ounces and had cost $700. Larry thought, Why doesn't he just throw over three ounces of money? It would have been cheaper. Ben quietly rescued the calculator and tucked it away. Syd Parks's homing beacon, which had saved Ben and Max in the first flight and guided airplanes to them all through the second flight, went overboard; it weighed less than two pounds. Even the sextant went.

At last, Larry could throw the maddening Omega navigational

device over the side. He did so with a grunt of satisfaction and watched it fall; as it plunged toward the clouds, it spun at an ever faster rate. Parts of it began to fly off. Larry watched, fascinated, and cheered as the machine fell and fell, destroying itself as it went, and finally disappeared.

Ben picked up the bundle containing the life raft and staggered to the gunwale with it. As he dropped it, its inflation cord tangled with his oxygen regulator and nearly pulled him overboard. Another example of Ben's dexterity, thought Larry with a fond grin. The raft inflated with a whistle of gas and a popping of rubber and spun into the clouds, sailing on the air currents, as Larry thought, like a giant Frisbee. Larry pulled the rip cord on his parachute, and watched it deploy and float for what seemed hours. Looking over the side, he kept glimpsing the hang-glider, soaring and glinting far below. Ben had brought along a .44 magnum pistol; he had intended to use it in case of attack by polar bears should the balloon be forced down on the ice pack. He ballasted it. Larry wanted to shoot it first.

"No!" cried Ben. "You shoot that thing off at night and it's like having a blowtorch in your hand. You might burn a hole in the balloon."

Larry wanted to say, "Helium doesn't burn, remember?" But he held his tongue.

As darkness fell, *Double Eagle II* descended to 13,000 feet. They threw over their oxygen masks, and the balloon came to equilibrium. They had thrown away perhaps $30,000 worth of equipment. A jar of Skippy peanut butter weighing one and a half pounds remained in the gondola, and they would land with it the next day in Miserey.

The air all around them was filled with the chatter of hams. G4JY was trying desperately to raise Larry. In their last, tense conversation with Schwoebel, after the big down, they had agreed to come back on the air at 1700 Zulu. But Larry had disconnected the radio. *Double Eagle II* was flying with nothing but its VHF radio and transponder. Larry, in another miracle of cleverness, had jury-rigged the remaining radios to a twelve-volt marine battery that Syd Parks had put aboard at the last minute. The alkaline cells that had given them so much trouble all the way across the ocean were all gone, over the side.

Larry talked on the VHF with Shannon approach. Radar told them they were twenty miles off the coast, then fifteen miles.

"Ben, Ben!" Larry shouted. "I see lights."

Ben and Max stood up — the empty gondola rocked like a rowboat now with every step they took — and saw, far away, lamplight in the windows of scores of cottages. Below them were solid clouds, but it was clear over the land.

Shannon approach called. *"Double Eagle*, you have just crossed the coast of Ireland," said the laconic voice of the controller.

Larry looked down and saw nothing but clouds. He had imagined that the lights they saw were those along the shore.

"Shannon approach, this is *Double Eagle*," Larry responded. "Are you sure?"

"Sir, my radar is never wrong."

"Roger," said Larry Newman. "Thank you very much."

He and Max Anderson and Ben Abruzzo, the first men to cross the Atlantic Ocean in a balloon, said nothing at all to one another. It was 10:02 P.M., 2202 Zulu, on Wednesday, August 16, 1978 — 117 hours and 59 minutes after liftoff.

Later, the Lear came back, and Bob Beattie asked them to give a cheer to reenact their crossing of the coast. They lifted false, hoarse voices for the microphones, and then floated on, beyond the clouds and over green fields and crooked limestone walls, clearly visible in the moonlight.

The dogs in Ireland began to bark, and it took the men in the balloon a breath or two to recognize the sound: they had grown so accustomed to the hush of the ocean sky.

The night was so clear and the full moon so bright, when at last *Double Eagle* II flew beyond the cloud deck over Ireland, that Larry, awake and flying the balloon, could see the color of the grass two miles below.

Max had gone to sleep soon after they started inland. Ben remained on watch for some three hours, with Larry at his side. The balloon was not stable; it kept losing altitude. Through a hole in the clouds, they ballasted off the three rubber survival suits, and as these fell, they filled with wind so that they looked like portly headless men flying down to pay their respects to the banshees and the leprechauns. The sight, and the thought, tickled Ben and Larry, and they laughed uproariously together for the first time in days. Ben used some of their precious lead shot, ballast of the last resort, letting it trickle through his fingers all across Ireland.

They heard cars on the roads below, and the dogs barking, and (a puzzlement to them all) the brisk rattle of gunfire. The shooting lasted for a long time. A Piper Aztec rendezvoused with *Double Eagle II* when it was two hours inside Ireland, and some London newspapermen aboard the plane chatted with Ben and Larry on the radio.

After Ben went to sleep, Larry called Shannon control every twenty minutes, asking for vectors and ground speed. He plotted their course and saw that it was perfect: if they maintained this track they would pass just south of London at midmorning.

Larry put his hand into his pocket and fumbled for coins. He couldn't find any, and he felt a stab of anxiety. Here we are, he thought; we're over Ireland. It looks like a mighty big country, and France is probably twice — three times, ten times! — as big; I don't know because I've never been to France. What are we going to do if we land in a field and our support crew doesn't get there? How are we going to let them know where we are? God, we'll probably have to hike to a pay phone and I don't have any French coins, and I don't even know if they have pay phones out in the countryside in France. What if we land in some farmer's field in France? What if he gets mad and shoots us with a shotgun? Nobody knows this balloon is coming, and if we land and destroy their crops they're really going to be mad and they certainly won't let us use their telephone. Maybe we can bundle up the balloon and hide it, and then go find our people.

Larry worried for another hour, until *Double Eagle II* reached the eastern coast of Ireland. The harbor lights along St. George's Channel had long been in sight, and when they were directly below, Larry woke Max. He showed Max, on a sectional aircraft map, precisely where they were. Then he lay down and fell fast asleep.

When Larry woke, two hours later, with the rising sun in his eyes, he looked over the side. *Double Eagle II* was approaching the jagged coast of Wales. Inland, overlying the whole countryside, was dense ground fog.

"Boy, it's going to be tough if we have to land in England," said Larry, "because you can't even see the ground."

Max gazed in silence for several minutes at the shrouded ground below. He had always liked Britain and the British. He thought of Alcock and Brown; one of them, he had read, had climbed out on the wing of their plane over the Atlantic and knocked ice off the engine with a hammer. That was a guts game. He thought, It isn't over yet. In a little while Max lay down and went to sleep again.

The balloon superheated slowly, but finally it began to climb. Larry was taking dozens of photographs, as he had done all the way across the Atlantic. He had learned to enjoy using the camera; he had even made a mount for it, to attach to his hang-glider, so that he could photograph *Double Eagle II* as he flew around it. A wave of sadness and disappointment washed over him as he remembered the glider in its long pilotless flight.

"Ben, let's pull the two [altitude-limiting] rips Rich put in, just for the hell of it," Larry said.

255

"Okay," Ben said. "You do it."

Larry thought that this was a tremendously generous act on Ben's part, to let him pull the riplines. He was pleased by Ben's confidence in him. He tugged both lines at once, and dozens of yards of nylon tape cascaded down upon him, and Ben gave a yelp of laughter. Larry pulled the tape off his own head and shoulders and dumped it on Ben's, and took a picture of him. Max slept through the hilarity.

With the two rip panels out, the balloon could not rise above 20,000 feet, owing to the automatic venting action created by opening the triangular holes inside the duct.

Double Eagle II climbed rapidly to 13,500 feet and started across the Bristol Channel, which separates Wales from the English county of Devon. Now it was full morning, and airplanes and helicopters were swarming round the balloon. Larry was astonished at the amount of traffic. One little plane had come out to meet them over Ireland, and he had expected that there might be another over England. Larry, seeing all the different kinds of airplanes, began to realize that he and Ben and Max had done something that interested the world.

Larry was enjoying himself, working the valve. To keep the balloon at a reasonable altitude, Ben had been releasing helium in two- and three-second bursts. Larry overvalved by a second or two and *Double Eagle II* began a steady, shallow descent at a rate of fifty feet per minute. There was no spare ballast with which to correct this, as every ounce would be needed at landing, but Ben was not concerned. He felt certain that superheat would take the balloon up again. He lay down to rest.

After Ben had closed his eyes, *Double Eagle II* went all the way down to 8,500 feet and came to a virtual halt above the oily calm waters of the Bristol Channel. Watching the ships below and gauging their speed against that of the balloon, Larry believed that *Double Eagle II*'s speed was no more than ten miles an hour. Besides, as ground radar confirmed, their track was not taking them toward Devon and France by the most direct route.

Max thought it wise to discuss the option of a landing in England. The sunset before, talking to Bob Beattie before crossing the coast of Ireland, Max had said, "We'll try for England or France if these high winds hold — but it will probably be England." Obviously, the high winds were not holding. They had had serious problems every time they crossed a body of water that lay near land: the Gulf of St. Lawrence, the Denmark Strait, the waters around Newfoundland, the approach to Ireland. Now they had a problem over the Bristol Channel. Fifty miles away lay the English Channel.

"Paris is the pearl of great price," Max said after the flight, "and you'd better weigh it well on the scales of realism each time you make a decision to go for it."

Ben was up now, surveying the situation. There was no doubt in his mind that the sun, hotter than any they had felt for days, would heat the balloon and lift it into a windfield that would sweep *Double Eagle II* across England and into France.

"You know, Ben," Max said, "maybe we ought to consider the option of landing in England."

"England? Why?"

Max, jesting, said, "They speak English in England."

Ben did not see the joke, nor did Larry. Both men were half-blinded by fatigue. "I don't want to land in England," Ben said. "England is not the place to land. France is the place to land because it is the Continent. England is an island and it's the second-best choice."

If Ben did not grasp Max's humor, Max did not perceive Ben's irritation. He revived the game of "What-if?" and spoke about their shortage of ballast, about the problem of midday cooling and the perils of a descent over the English Channel.

"It's a possibility, Ben, that we'll go down in the Channel, given all the factors. If that happens, we'd have done no better than Cameron and Davies. If we make France, we've done it all. If we opt for England, we will have done well. If the wind dies . . ."

"But we're not going to land in the Channel," said Ben, hotter by the minute; Max was questioning his ballast figures again. "We're going to make it across. We have enough ballast. I accept these odds."

"Well," said Max, "the English are famous for their pomp and ceremony, and we'd get a grand welcome here — and in France, there is that language barrier." It bothered Max that he did not speak or understand French. When he had heard it spoken on his trips to France, he had thought it a lovely language — the language of love and diplomacy.

Max's sally did not lighten Ben's mood. Larry started to speak to Ben, and told him that he, personally, favored going on. But Ben cut him short.

"We're mad, we're all unhappy," he said.

Max, if he noticed Ben's anger then, did not remember it afterward. He had raised the questions he believed needed to be resolved, and a decision had to be made. He still feared treachery from the English Channel, but he put his mind, now, to the problem of getting across. The decision would be made at the coast.

Ben, of course, had already made *his* decision — *France*, Lindbergh's France, and nothing less.

They dropped an oxygen bottle into the water, and, as Ben had anticipated, *Double Eagle II* climbed out of the calm above the Bristol Channel and entered a windfield that took it at good speed across Devon and Somerset. Ben and Max and Larry did not know precisely where they were, and would not know until they landed later in the day, because they had no charts of England and France, just a large-scale map of Europe. It showed only large cities, major rivers — it was of no more use as a navigational aid than a page torn from a geography book. The detailed charts of Europe had either been left behind or ballasted.

It was about ten-thirty in the morning of Thursday, August 17, as they crossed the land, and below them, as far as they could see, they saw light flashing from thousands of mirrors. In all the villages and cities of southern England, the people had come out to signal them welcome in the brilliant morning sunshine, and *Double Eagle II*, winking back with its own small mirror, flew across this mellow countryside on a pathway of light.

Airplanes carrying reporters and well-wishers swarmed around the balloon, and Larry talked to them with zest. "Of course, for all purposes, the crossing of the Atlantic Ocean has been completed," he told British Southern Television. "England was a delightful sight, and now maybe we'd like to sample some French wines."

At the first opportunity, he gave credit where credit was due: "The man who is coordinating the balloon is Richard Schwoebel. He designed the flight profile, and with the help of Bob Rice of Weather Services in Bedford, the flight went almost exactly as they predicted."

As *Double Eagle II*, flying at 14,000 feet, came in sight of Poole, an unmistakable voice broke through the babble on the VHF like a stone through a window.

It said, "LARRY! THIS IS YOUR FATHER! I'M SO PROUD OF YOU, SON, I'M READY TO CRY."

Herb Newman had taken Laker Airways from New York to London at a cost of $135, spent $10 for a bed at the Fielding Hotel, near Covent Garden in London, and in the morning had taken a train to Christchurch and a taxi to Bournemouth airport. There he had rented a single-engine Cessna 172. He was in the little plane now, 2,000 feet below the balloon. Larry could see the Cessna, its nose in the air, chewing weakly at its ceiling.

"I can't get up to you, Larry. I'm going to get a better airplane," Herb Newman cried. "I'll be there when you land."

With the Isle of Wight in view, more familiar voices came over the air. Pat Abruzzo and Patty Anderson and Sandra Newman flew by with a camera crew in a chartered De Havilland jet. Larry spoke to Sandra at last: "It's going really fine. I miss you. I love you." Sandra told Larry that she missed him and would see him in France. The sound of Sandra's voice transported Larry from joy to depression. "Pavlov would have loved my reaction," he says.

Ben was overjoyed to hear Pat's slow, calm tones again. But then she, of all people, said something to him that raised his hackles. "Ben, I know you," said Pat Abruzzo. "Don't push it too far." That's a hell of a thing for Pat to say to me, Ben thought. Max and Larry heard Pat's words, and Ben did not like that — his own wife was confirming over the radio that it was his nature to push things to the limit, to push too far.

London approach passed them a message from the Smithsonian Institution. Would Ben and Max and Larry give *Double Eagle II* to the Smithsonian, to be displayed beside *The Spirit of St. Louis* and other legendary American aircraft? They answered that they would be honored to do so.

Double Eagle II left England behind just before midday, and as Max had predicted and Ben had known all along, the balloon would be above the English Channel at high noon, the most dangerous time of the day. At the coast, the balloon was at 14,800 feet and climbing, traveling at about thirty miles an hour. Ben and Larry began to suck oxygen through the rubber tubes attached to the regulators, having ballasted the masks the night before. The undiffused pure oxygen made their throats raw. Once again, Max did not use oxygen, and once again, Larry wondered what sort of heredity had produced such a strange metabolism.

To conserve batteries, Larry had been using the VHF to transmit as little as possible. *Double Eagle II* rose to 15,500 feet, and behind them, the sky above England was filled with puffy cumulus.

The Cherbourg Peninsula came into sight, and London approach handed the balloon over to the Cherbourg tower. The coast of France was clear, but as far inland as the eye could see, the earth was hidden by a solid cover of clouds. Don Sellers, calling from the Lear, told them that the tops of the clouds were at 7,000 feet and the bottoms at about 3,000; he would fly ahead to Paris and give them a report on the skies along the route.

They were crossing the Channel on a diagonal, heading southeast from England, so that the crossing would be as long as 120 miles; the straight-line distance is about forty miles. Max, working with the big, clumsy map, wondered if they would have the speed and duration to make it. The same thought entered Larry's mind when he saw a warship below them, and on the same course as *Double Eagle II*. The ship was passing them. Cherbourg approach told them that their ground speed was forty miles an hour, but it did not seem to Larry, who had been plotting their course from radar sightings transmitted to him from ground stations, that they could be moving that fast if a ship could pass them.

Max watched the smoke from another ship's stack, *blowing toward England*. Was *Double Eagle II* moving in the wrong direction? A rogue wind could still fling her back out to sea. In fact, the balloon had turned away from Cherbourg, and was now heading on a more northeasterly track, toward Le Havre. Neither Ben nor Max could judge the angle of approach, but Larry could clearly see Le Havre with the naked eye — its industrial smoke and its great harbor and jetty. With binoculars, he could see a huge supertanker tied up at the port.

Through binoculars, Ben saw that *Double Eagle II* appeared to be paralleling the coast. Perhaps they would not, after all, make France. Pat's words rang in his memory: maybe she was right, maybe he had pushed it too far. Was she going to prove her point with the whole world looking up at Ben in *Double Eagle II?* But then Ben saw that the balloon had turned, and was, after all, heading straight for Le Havre. Radar confirmed the change of course.

The ubiquitous Dave Slade, flying above the Channel in a Piper Navajo, called on the radio and talked to Ben.

"We're planning to go into Le Havre," Ben told him. "That apparently is going to be our destination, and we're going to have to land before sunset because of minimal ballast."

"Say again your intended landing," said Slade.

"Le Havre, we think it'll be Le Havre," Ben replied.

Hearing this, Max once again began silently to juggle options. If they were going to land on the coast, then it made sense to land in the water. He and Ben and Larry could make a completely controlled landing in the harbor; it would be far safer than attempting to put *Double Eagle II* down inland. There, they would have to contend with power lines, trees, buildings. In his mind's eye France was a thicket of houses; he had never been in Normandy, but he had always pictured it, and all of Europe, as built-up, oversettled, crowded.

Double Eagle II was about thirty miles from land. Max could see his breath; he exhaled twice and watched the little cloud of moisture form. Were they passing through a layer of cold air? Would the balloon go into another big down, like the one off Ireland that Ben called the Cold Sink? *Double Eagle II* should have been climbing, but it was not doing so. At its present ground speed, the balloon should pass over Le Havre in about an hour. Max thought the moment had come to suggest a harbor landing: if they were going to do it, they would need the time remaining to prepare for it.

"You know, Ben," he said, "we could put her down in the harbor."

Once again, Max was posing an alternative, a sensible one, in his mind. Ben didn't see anything sensible about it. He took the oxygen hose out of his mouth and said, "Max, we are not landing in the water."

Max told him why he thought they should consider a harbor landing: "Ben, landing her in the water is definitely the safest way to land. We can take her right in to the shore, control the approach by valving, use the ropes."

"If we land in the water," Ben said, "we may drown. Plus, we'll lose the balloon. We've come three thousand miles and we're going to go the last thirty and land on land."

Max thought that was a reasonable enough view of the matter.

Ben knew as well as he did what the hazards inland were. If he wanted to take the risk of doing what no one had ever done before — bringing a free manned balloon down on land after a three-thousand-mile journey, well — that was Ben's way.

Just as Max was putting it out of his thoughts, Larry perceived the discussion between Max and Ben as a bitter quarrel. He leaped into it.

"In case you guys don't know it," Larry said, "there's a third man in this gondola — me. And I have a vote, too."

"Vote," said Ben.

"I want to land on land. I don't want to land in the water."

Max shrugged; even while they were over England, Larry had discussed landing on the coast, as he recalled it. He had been under the impression that both Ben and Larry wanted to put *Double Eagle II* down on the coast. Over England, while talking to Doc Wiley on the radio, Larry had said, "Maxie and I, we figure we're going to land . . . either in Cherbourg or Le Havre. If it's not that, it's in the drink." What was "in the drink" if it wasn't a landing in the water?

Moments later, an interviewer from French radio came on the air, and Max, struggling to penetrate the man's heavy accent without offending him, finally understood his question: "What reason for you, this travel?"

"Well, sir, as balloonists, we were anxious to find if the Atlantic could be crossed in a balloon," said Max in his most gallant tone. "Also, we should like to duplicate the flight that Lindbergh made to Paris and we feel it is an accomplishment and an honor . . . to reach the coast of France. If we can go under the clouds to Paris, we may try and do it."

They received a final message from Bedford: "Over the next two hours, descend carefully, fifteen thousand to ten thousand, taking you within five miles southwest of Le Havre, continue slow descent over subsequent two hours to five thousand feet. Bob and Rich."

"Tell them," Ben radioed, "that those are our intentions, and they are reading our minds from three thousand miles away."

Ashore in France, Pat and Patty and Sandra watched *Double Eagle II*, pulsing like a star with the afternoon sun glittering on its silvered sphere. They were on the ground with Doc Wiley at Deau-ville, a few miles south of Le Havre on the sandy coast; not far away were Omaha and Utah beaches, and Max did not realize until long afterward that he had flown by these hallowed places.

Max, speaking to Doc in the grounded De Havilland, suggested that Pat and Patty rent a car and chase the balloon to its landing. "We'll put it down near a highway so they won't break their high heels," he said. "Tell Dave Slade to have cold beer at the landing — cold beer," Ben added. Larry, still worried about transportation from the landing site, asked Dave to fly to Paris, rent some cars, and drive out to meet them.

Double Eagle II crossed the French coast at 1430 Zulu, (4:30 P.M. European daylight time), passing over the mouth of the Seine and across the city of Le Havre, where thousands stood, unnoticed by the balloonists, in the streets.

Once inside France, flying at 13,700 feet and descending through gentle valving, they maneuvered into a windfield that carried them toward Paris. The radio exploded with congratulations in French and English and a mixture of the two, and Paris approach control gave them this message: "We are closing Le Bourget airport for you." If *Double Eagle II* stayed on its present track, and if the sun lasted long enough, Ben and Max and Larry could land on the very airfield where Lindbergh had touched down fifty-one years before. Ben thought that would be a fitting end to the flight, and Le Bourget — not just France, not just Paris, but the grail itself — became his chosen destination.

Ten or fifteen miles ahead of them, the balloonists saw a solid cloud deck covering the French countryside.

"We can penetrate those damn clouds, Ben," Max said, "if we've got the ballast."

"If we get decent separation, and hit it just right, yes."

Larry did not wholly understand what Ben and Max were talking about: he had never landed in a balloon.

"You got to get a little velocity going, Larry," Ben explained. "Hit the top of the clouds at maybe two hundred and fifty feet per minute — slower than that and the heat reflected off the clouds will send you back up." He gave a devilish smile. "Trouble is, when you come out of the bottom of the clouds, you're really hauling the freight.

Now you've got to ballast off, maybe all the ballast you have, and if you don't do it right, you hit the ground like a damn rock, and you don't walk away from it."

It was clear to Larry that Ben would *enjoy* diving the balloon through the cloud deck. "How do you know whether you've done it right?" he asked.

"There's no formula," Ben replied. "It depends on feeling. Experience. We'll take her down just like we did off Iceland."

Larry, looking anxiously ahead, saw that the clouds, many miles ahead of the balloon, were beginning to break up, and as they flew on, the clouds parted before them. "Look at that, it's like the Red Sea," said Ben. "We've got Moses with us, old Larry."

Ben, checking with aircraft and with Paris control, was convinced that the balloon was tracking straight for Le Bourget. Max, working with the chart, began to think that their course would take them south and west of the city. They figured that they had an hour and a half to sunset, perhaps a little more. They would fly on. The clouds kept parting before them, as if a hand were sweeping them away.

Max, in preparation for landing, rummaged in his ditty bag and got out the several chains he wears round his neck on formal occasions. He put them on, and brushed off his flight suit, and lay down to take a short nap. Over the Channel, he had opened a can of turkey, and he still had the taste of it in his mouth. He thought, I wonder why we saved that turkey till the last minute? It was delicious.

Ben, too, went to sleep. Larry, drinking in the verdant beauties of Normandy, talked again to his father on the radio. Herb Newman, now in a twin-engine Piper Apache, was scouting ahead for landing sites. He told Larry that the track of *Double Eagle II* would carry the balloon south of Paris.

"I sure am proud of you, Larry baby, you sure are something to see and hear on the radio," cried Herb. "I just hope I can be there when you land to give you the shirts I had made up for you in New York — that's how much confidence I had in you."

"We know about the shirts," Larry replied. "But now, Dad, you can cool it on the shirts. I'm proud of you and I'm so glad you're here. We'll talk about it tonight over dinner, okay?"

Herb Newman, before leaving New York, had gone to Queens

Boulevard and had three T-shirts made, lettered with the name of the balloon and those of the pilots — Larry's name on top. For himself, he had one made that said GROUND CREW. He figured that this would be useful in getting by any French security that might be guarding the balloon.

When Max woke, he consulted the chart. It confirmed his belief that even if they kept flying they were going to miss Paris. Besides, he thought, there isn't enough time to get there. The sun was setting behind them, and late afternoon cooling had already begun. He studied the ground; farmers were working the fields, and the dust from their tractors was blowing briskly from west to east. That meant that *Double Eagle II* would be landing with a reasonable ground wind, and could therefore land in a relatively small field. They passed over a forest, and Max saw more woods in the distance.

"Ben," he said, "maybe we ought to start thinking about putting her down."

But Ben was thinking about Le Bourget. "I just don't understand you," he said. "What's the great anxiety about getting on the ground? We still have daylight."

"The balloon is flying heavy. We don't have enough ballast to stop a down — we've already used half our ballast. We don't want to land in one of those damn forests, Ben."

"There's plenty of open country. We're closing on Paris." Ben knew precisely what the ballast situation was — knew better than Max, or anyone. They had all the ballast they needed.

"Ben, we're not closing on Paris. We're paralleling Paris," said Max.

"Like hell we are!" Ben said.

The two friends fell into a tight-lipped silence.

"Well, what the hell," said Ben finally. "Let's take her down and go sightseeing."

He valved a bit — it required thirty pounds of pull on the line to open the valve at the top of the balloon and his arms were beginning to ache — and finessed *Double Eagle II* down to about 5,000 feet.

In the distance they could see a considerable town among the lush green fields, and the spires of an ancient cathedral reached above its rooftops. The balloonists, because they had no proper map, did not know its name. It was Evreux, capital of the department of

Eure, sixty-seven miles northwest of Paris, seat of the counts of Evreux. Standing on the slopes of the valley of the Iton, it had been a flourishing town at least since Gallo-Roman times.

At Le Bourget, Patty Anderson and Pat Abruzzo were distraught. The ABC television crew had taken off in two helicopters, leaving the wives stranded at the airfield. Doc Wiley had been unable to get hold of another helicopter. He had been talking to Paris control, and it appeared that *Double Eagle II* was going to land short of Paris, somewhere in the vicinity of Evreux. There was a military airfield there, and Doc was attempting to get permission to land there with the De Havilland or the Lear.

Patty had heated words with the ABC producer. She felt betrayed, abandoned. She thought of leaping into a car and joining the stream of traffic that was pouring out of Paris in the direction of the landing site. French radio was a babble of description of the approaching balloon and its pilots: The New Lindberghs. A British newsman tried to help, but his helicopter had left. Every helicopter in France and England had been chartered by the press; there were none to be had.

Doc Wiley finally got permission to land at the military airfield at Evreux, but the De Havilland, having just taken on a full load of fuel, was too heavy to land there. Doc hired another plane, but the pilot refused to land without written permission from the military authorities. At last he found a pilot who was willing to fly Pat and Patty and Sandra to Evreux, but at that moment he learned that the balloon had already landed. Wiley, his ingenuity for once defeated, loaded the wives into cars and took them to the American Embassy; Ben and Max and Larry would come there as guests of the ambassador straight from the landing.

For Pat and Patty, being part of a triumphal welcome at the embassy was not enough. On the breakneck ride into Paris, they fought for self-control.

"Max was landing in France — his dream, and I wasn't there," Patty says. "The greatest moment of his life and I wasn't there to share it with him. I'll never get over it."

With the sun weakening, and with only 375 pounds of usable ballast aboard, Ben still hoped for Le Bourget, or at least the outskirts of Paris, but he realized that he was cutting it close. Pat's words came back to him again; her warnings were usually worth listening to.

While over the Channel, Larry and Max had vented the oxygen from their remaining bottle, and the gas from the propane tank, so that they would not explode when dropped from the balloon. A few miles short of Evreux, Ben valved *Double Eagle II* down to about 300 feet. He cut loose the heavy metal tanks above a tilled field, and heard them strike the ground, sending up a noise like the thuds of three quick punches. Larry watched the tanks bury themselves in the soil; they simply vanished into the ground like animals darting into their burrows.

A farmer was harrowing in an adjoining field, and Max saw, again, that the wind was blowing the dust away from Evreux. Ben and Larry were waving and shouting to some people on the ground; these French peasants, though they looked upward at *Double Eagle II*, made no response.

This field looked to Max like a good place to land, and he said so to Ben. Ben had just ballasted a heavy wet battery, and the balloon was beginning to climb.

"Land?" said Ben. "We don't land while we're in an up. We'll bust our ass."

"We've landed hard before," Max retorted.

"Not," said Ben through clenched teeth, "with the whole world watching us."

The balloon climbed very fast to about 2,000 feet, and overflew Evreux. With its cathedral standing on an eminence and its twisting medieval streets and its queer old rooftops, it looked enormous to Ben.

Just beyond the town, Max saw a triangular field, suitable per- haps for a landing. Ben rejected it. He rejected two or three more — the balloon was too high, the field was too small. Ben wanted to go as far as *Double Eagle II* would go. He wanted to fly her into the sunset. By now he knew that Le Bourget was beyond his reach, but he did not want the flight to end before he had taken it into its final second.

Max was annoyed that they had not landed short of Evreux, where they ballasted the tanks and the battery. The field had been ideal. There had been no crowd to molest the balloon, and it would have been a lovely picture to remember, coming to rest with that beautiful town as a backdrop. Ben wished with all his heart that Max would stop pointing out landing fields. He wanted to land everywhere! Ben's exhaustion was like a soldier's pack upon his back, and he felt a good deal of irritation with Max.

When only thirty-five minutes of daylight remained, Ben spotted another field ahead, beyond a little village. There were power lines at both ends of the field, but it was near a highway, and it is a point of ballooning pride and etiquette to land near a road.

Ben said, "All right, we'll put her down."

He picked up the microphone and made the last transmission of the flight: "All aircraft in the area, *Double Eagle* is landing."

The words came hard, and as he uttered them, Ben realized that the flight was over. He was overcome by sadness. But he and Max and Larry still had work to do — the most difficult job of all, and the one for which he believed this crew better fitted than any on earth. This was the job, never done before, of landing a transatlantic balloon on the soil of France, with all hands safe and primary communications equipment intact.

"Larry," he said crisply, "cut the wires and stow the radio."

Ben and Larry had moved the trail ropes to the port side of the gondola in preparation for landing. They planned to come in broadside, with Ben valving, Max ballasting, and Larry dropping the ropes.

To Larry, Ben said, "Have you got your knife?"

"It's too dull to cut anything. I've been stabbing sandbags with it all the way from Maine."

Ben handed him an extra knife from his own belt. "When I tell you to drop the ropes, cut 'em loose and shake 'em out," Ben told Larry. "Don't just throw the ropes, or they'll get tangled into a rattail and we won't get the proper use out of them."

Double Eagle II, descending at 200 feet per minute, just the rate and angle that Ben wanted, came sweeping over the village of Miserey, toward a barley field golden and ripe for the harvest. For the first time they saw that the highway was choked with cars. Max, looking down, saw hundreds of people leaping from their cars and running toward the field. The sky was filled with circling aircraft; there were helicopters all around, and immediately behind the balloon, though Ben and Max and Larry did not see it, was a press

268

helicopter. The wash from its blades blew *Double Eagle II* over the ground, filling the slack envelope as wind fills a spinnaker.

Max said, "Larry, drop a rope."

Ben said, "Don't you dare touch those ropes until I tell you!" They were approaching a power line. Larry had seen the power line; he did not need Ben's warning.

Now the balloon was descending over a cornfield at the edge of the barley field, and it seemed to Larry that it was moving at tremendous speed. Ben was valving, delicately. The gondola passed over the power lines.

Larry shook out two trail ropes, and Ben cut loose a third. Larry dropped the fourth, moving through this whole sequence with such speed and skill that Max was filled with admiration. Max's admiration for Larry's physical skills, his quick mind and steady nerves, had grown throughout the flight. He thought, Larry's done his job and done it well. I've been pretty glum, and without Larry I might have been worse. He's cheered us up the whole way.

By the time the ropes dropped, *Double Eagle II* was so close to the ground that they touched the corn. Dragging through the cornfield, the ropes slowed the balloon — though not enough because the helicopter was still whirling behind it. As the ropes took up weight, the gondola rushed toward impact, and Max saw that they were going to land in the cornfield. He did not want to ruin the farmer's crop, so he threw over a bag of sand, and *Double Eagle II* leaped upward like a horse pricked with the spur. At that instant, Ben pulled the rip line, and *Double Eagle II* came back down and touched the soil of France.

Max and Ben, horrified, saw two men running directly at the gondola as it descended toward them. If they hit these people, they would kill them. "Get out of the way!" they shouted in English, but the Frenchmen, laughing and waving, kept running at the gondola. They swerved out of harm's way, laughing and crying out words in French.

As the gondola struck and dragged, Max cried, "Rip!" He turned to see Ben with the rip line already spilled all over him. Max laughed aloud: Ben looked like he had taken a spaghetti bath. With the main rip panel open, helium gushed from the long split in the envelope. Ed Yost had told them that the envelope, once ripped, would empty in twenty seconds.

The envelope was still vertical, and the gondola was still dragging over the ground, driven by the wind from the helicopter. The gondola was tipping over. Larry ran to its high side, shouting and signing frantically to people on the ground to seize the trail ropes. A man in a white coat seized one rope, and soon others joined him. Larry reached down and grasped the outstretched hand of a man running behind the gondola, and pulled him aboard as living ballast. He pulled another body into the gondola, and another. The people were laughing and striking him on the back. It was painful, and he felt a flash of anger. At last he had hauled enough people into the gondola so that their weight stopped its skidding progress.

Double Eagle II was motionless. The envelope gave up the last of its helium, and fluttered to the ground. More and more people clambered into the gondola.

Ben leaped out. He had a single thought: take care of the balloon. Men and women and an army of children swarmed over the inert envelope; they clawed at it, seeking to take a piece of it as a souvenir. Some fell to their knees and tried to rip the tough nylon with their teeth.

Ben's pent-up emotions overflowed. Larry was standing in the gondola, grinning into a television camera. Max was nowhere to be seen. The balloon was being attacked by a mob. He stood where he was, with the laughing, exalted people, thousands of them, tumbling around him into the tall grain. Their feet trampled the barley into perfume. Nobody recognized Ben as one of the pilots. He felt two things — sadness that it was over, and something nearly like regret that the Atlantic had at last been conquered by men in a balloon. What was left? Ben remained where he was; he wanted desperately to be alone, and he realized that he could be no more alone than he was now.

Max was still in the gondola, seconds after touchdown, when a young man wearing a white coat, perhaps the same one who had grasped the first trail rope, seized his arm. Wearing a look of professional solemnity, he wrapped a blood pressure cuff around Max's bicep, inflated it, and listened with a stethoscope to the pulse in his elbow. Max thought, I wonder if the French are crazy? The young man nodded, gave Max a reassuring pat on the shoulder, and turned away.

Max looked into the crowd, and to his astonishment saw the corpulent figure of Herb Newman. Herb had his arms around Larry, and he was crying; his cheeks shone with tears. Larry put his head against his father's chest and said, "Dad! We did it, Dad!" Herb pulled the special T-shirt over Larry's unresisting head; Larry held up his arms like a child being helped with his pajamas. Herb Newman, using his old expertise from San Joaquin Valley days, had landed the Apache in a nearby field, flashed his Bernalillo County, New Mexico, honorary sheriff's badge at an ambulance driver, and got to the scene of the landing sooner, even, than the ABC crew.

Max clambered out of the gondola, which was now filled to overflowing with dancing French people, all of them pummeling Larry. Max wandered through the crowd, looking for Ben and thinking to help him with the balloon. He could not find his friend, and he saw that the crowd, although it was already being charged by squads of police, could not be controlled.

Max returned to the gondola. A bottle of champagne had been opened, and Larry's hair was wet with it. Max stood back, watching the scene with bemusement, and when Bob Beattie got him in front of a camera, Max said what was uppermost in his mind: "I think I'm going to owe the farmer some money for his crop." The destruction of the barley bothered him; all the way across France, he had worried about destroying some farmer's crop, and now they had done just that.

Ben emerged from the crowd and started fussing with the gondola. He wanted to save their logs, the barographs, the film. He could not get near any of these things, and some were taken away by souvenir hunters.

The police were growing increasingly nervous, and they urged the balloonists to leave. Ben, infected by the joy of the crowd, felt that he owed it to them to stay a little longer. Larry and Max were escorted to a helicopter, and even inside the flying wedge of burly policemen, they were touched and slapped by their hysterical welcomers. Max worried about the people; the police were being awfully rough with them. When Max and Larry, at last, were inside the helicopter that would fly them to Le Bourget, the crowd clawed at the skin of the machine and pounded on the windows. The pilot simply started the motors, and people fell to the ground in terror as the blades whirled above their heads. Larry's horrified eyes were fixed on a man who stood beneath the flashing rotor blades with a child on his shoulders. They got out of the way just in time.

Ben left in the last helicopter and joined Max and Larry at the airport. Shiny limousines awaited them, and after more television interviews (someone took a beer out of Ben's hand and replaced it with a glass of wine when the cameras rolled), they were driven to the American Embassy.

The Faubourg Saint-Honoré was jammed with a cheering throng, including the entire half-naked chorus line from the Lido, in costume. Ben and Max and Larry fought their way through the crowd and found their wives and kissed them.

As they passed through the line of security men and started up the steps of the embassy residence, a tiny woman emerged from the crowd and touched Ben's hand. Max paused, to see what she wanted, and Larry joined in.

"I am Jacqueline Citroën," she said in English, "and I was the little girl who gave Charles Lindbergh his first bouquet when he landed at Le Bourget. I so wanted to be the first to greet you."

Madame Citroën showed them a photograph of herself as a child, standing between Lindbergh and a man she identified as her father. She asked Ben and Max and Larry and their wives to come with her to the house of her son, André de Saint-Sauveur, president of the French Ballooning Federation. She and her son wished to give them a *champagne* to celebrate their triumph.

They went as they were, unbathed and unshaven, Ben and Max in their flight suits and Larry in the T-shirt his father had given him. All Paris, from people of fashion to screaming journalists, seemed to be in the room with them at the Saint-Sauveurs'.

Maxie Anderson, seated on a sofa with Ben and Larry and all their wives, was overcome by the certain knowledge that he had been here, in this place, at just this moment, in some other time and in some other life. Never before had he had such a feeling. He felt Patty squeezing his hand, but everything swam away, and for an instant the noisy salon, filled with the excited rattle of French and the explosion of flashbulbs, seemed as silent as the sky. Maxie smiled and smiled, and even the cameras could not make him stop.

Afterword

The single bed, carved and enameled in the French style, in which Charles Lindbergh slept on the night of May 21, 1927, had been returned to the American Embassy residence in Paris by Anne Morrow Lindbergh. Samuel Gamon, the chargé d'affaires, told the balloonists that one of them would have the honor of sleeping in this bed.

Ben and Maxie and Larry tossed a coin, and Larry won. The first of hundreds of telegrams arrived: an invitation from President Carter to call on him and Mrs. Carter at the White House.

After leaving the reception at the house of André de Saint-Sauveur, Larry and Sandra went to dinner at Maxim's as the guests of Madame Citroën. Herb Newman, who accompanied them, became the first person to be admitted to Maxim's while wearing a T-shirt and a baseball cap. Ben and Max, and Pat and Patty, returned to the embassy residence. Both men fell immediately into a deep sleep. Larry, returning in the small hours of the morning, found the Lindbergh bed uncomfortable after five nights on the deck of the gondola, and spent the night on the floor of the Lindbergh suite.

The balloonists and their wives flew to London, and treated Don Cameron and Christopher Davey and the support crew of *Double Eagle II* to a dinner of smoked salmon and saddle of lamb at the Savoy. On returning to France, they were received by the mayor of Paris and by ministers of the French government. In a ceremony at Evreux, which had recently celebrated the anniversary of its liberation by American troops in World War II, Ben and Max and Larry received the first of the many decorations that would be bestowed upon them. They paid Roger and Rachel Coquerel, owners of the barley field in which *Double Eagle II* had landed, a thousand dollars for the damage done to their crop by the excited crowd. Ben slept that night in Lindbergh's bed, and Max did so on a subsequent trip to Paris; neither was troubled by insomnia.

On their return to Albuquerque, they were greeted by a cheering throng of tens of thousands of their fellow citizens, who contrived to have a ticker-tape parade in a city where few buildings are more than four stories high. Sixty hot-air balloons lined the triumphal route from the airport to the new Civic Center, and six more balloons hovered overhead, gas burners whooshing, while the governor of New Mexico, the mayors of Albuquerque and Santa Fe, the entire New Mexico congressional delegation, and most of the other political figures of the state joined in welcoming the heroes home. The U.S. Congress voted to strike a special gold medal for the balloonists, an honor that had previously been bestowed on very few (Lindbergh and Neil Armstrong among them).

The tendency of *Double Eagle II* to lose altitude at noon was explained after the flight. Too great an area of the balloon's sphere had been covered with silver reflective paint. The sun, when directly overhead, shone upon the silvered area, and too little heat was absorbed to keep the helium inside at full expansion. The gas cooled and contracted, and the balloon descended at the precise hour when theory dictated that it should rise. No other manned balloon had ever reported this effect. Richard Schwoebel coined a phrase to describe the phenomenon: midday cooling.

The great down off the coast of Ireland was never definitively explained, but Robert Rice and Schwoebel believe (to simplify greatly) that *Double Eagle II*, having left the high-pressure ridge and flown into another weather system, entered a descending column of warm air. Because the envelope, chilled by high-altitude temperatures, was colder than the air surrounding it, it fell 19,500 feet before regaining equilibrium. The warm-air column probably caused the "blue hole" into which *Double Eagle II* seemed to be falling; in effect, the warm air punched a circular hole in the cloud deck. The way in which the pilots reacted to this situation was, according to Schwoebel, absolutely correct. Ben's decision not to ballast on the way down probably saved the flight.

Ben and Max returned to their families and their businesses, and both men have been mentioned as candidates for the governorship

274

of New Mexico. Larry and Sandra Newman separated soon after their return to Albuquerque, and subsequently were divorced.

All three men have been affected by their celebrity. Ben Abruzzo, always a zestful public speaker and an enthusiastic worker in patriotic and civic causes, undertook a schedule of appearances that left him almost as fatigued as his flight across the Atlantic. "I very much prefer the flight and the before to the after," says Pat Abruzzo, commenting on the pressures of fame. "It's very difficult for Ben at times, having all these people all over him. We've never done it before. I have had to learn how to handle it. In public, your personal relationship must be set aside. And there'll be no gazing at each other, there'll be no pats on the arm or shoulder, no arm around the waist. It doesn't fit in."

Larry Newman met more people in the six months following the landing in Miserey than he had known in all his earlier life. He has been delighted to learn how naturally he belongs in the company of celebrated men and beautiful women. He has lost none of his impulsive candor. Muhammad Ali chartered the partnership's Lear jet for a lecture tour, and took a great liking to the airplane and to Larry, who flew the plane himself. At a small college in Kentucky, the champion called Larry to the stage from the audience, introducing him as "Randy Newman," one of the *Double Eagle II* balloonists. Back aboard the Lear, seated in the copilot's chair, Muhammad Ali asked Larry if he had appreciated his gesture. "It was great," Larry replied, "but if you ever call me 'Randy' again, Ali, you can take the bus." Though Larry received hundreds of letters from new admirers and old acquaintances after his adventure, he had no word from Baxter Richardson, the friend of his childhood.

Of the three balloonists, Maxie Anderson has remained closest to home. He has spoken mostly to small groups within New Mexico. Like Ben Abruzzo, he believes that the flight had great symbolic meaning for Americans, and particularly for youth. Max has spent a good deal of time addressing young people, and he has been especially attentive to requests from the cadets of Missouri Military Academy. In 1978 he was named Copper Man of the Year by his colleagues in the metal industry, and earlier this year, William Woods College in Fulton, Missouri, awarded him an honorary doctorate.

In April 1979, Ben and Maxie and Larry were presented with the National Geographic Society's John Oliver LaGorce Medal.

275

"The really important thing about the flight," Ben said in his acceptance speech, "was that we brought happiness, we brought pride, to the entire world. Or at least that was what the world said to us."

Max, after thanking Rich Schwoebel, Bob Rice, Doc Wiley, and the rest of the ground crew for having guided him and his companions across the Atlantic, spoke of the view from *Double Eagle II*: "The world . . . has beauty that is indescribable. The world is passing below you. You find humility, which is very hard for men like Larry, Ben, and me. But it is good to have found it."

Larry devoted the whole of his brief speech to a message of thanks to Herb Newman. "I had my hero, Charles Lindbergh," he said of his youth, "and I had my father, his support and his love. I want to thank you very much, Dad." He gave his gold medal to his father. Herb Newman wept, and he was by no means alone.

On May 27, 1979, Ben and Max flew together once again, launching from Long Beach, California, in the twenty-seventh James Gordon Bennett Balloon Race, an event revived after a lapse of forty-one years. Piloting *Double Eagle III*, a 34,500-cubic-foot polyethylene balloon filled with helium, they flew a point-to-point distance of 560 miles, landing in a remote area of Utah thirteen miles north of Dove Creek, Colorado, after forty-seven hours and seven minutes aloft. They won the race, in which sixteen other balloons from ten nations competed, and brought the James Gordon Bennett Cup back to the United States. It had last been won by an American in 1932. Throughout their flight across California, Nevada, Arizona, and Utah, Ben and Max flew an American flag eighteen feet long.

Of all the sights they saw on all their flights, the one that lives most brightly in their memories is the flag: fluttering its warning when the balloon rose and fell, rippling at last above the hedgerows of Normandy, where so many Americans had gone before them.

Acknowledgments

Ben Abruzzo, Maxie Anderson and Larry Newman wish to acknowledge the help and support of these friends:

Marian Adle
Leonard Aiken of Oak
  Creek Films
Irv Alward
Carl and Marie Anderson
Dr. and Mrs. Gary Anderson
Nancy Baker
Lucien Bicheron
Jay Blackwood
Marla Kay Blount
George Boyden
Peter Briggs
Chantal Burns
Ernest Butterfield
John Calcott
Denise Cardinet
Sister Celestia
Jacqueline Citroën
Mr. and Mrs. Roger Cocherel
Dana Connor
Bill Cutter
Sid Cutter
Mr. and Mrs. Jack Daniels
Mr. and Mrs. Dennis Doherty

Pete Dominici
Malcolm Forbes
Gene and Mary Garriott
Glen Giere of ABC
Dr. and Mrs. Sam Ginestra
Pierre Giraudet
Garth Gobeli
Ed Gorin of CBS
Bill and Mary Grady
Jack and Shirley Hammack
Mike Hand
Ambassador and Mrs.
  Arthur Hartman
Natalie Houq
John Irick
Willie Jackson
Glenda Jenson
Dick Kent
Brad Knott
John Koller
Bertrand Larcher
Joel Le Theule
Ralph Levenson
Dr. Luft

Manuel Lujan
Mr. and Mrs. Doug March
Lois Martin
Ross and Nancy McAllister
Tracy McGill
Camilla McGuire
William Morgan
Dr. and Mrs. Ed Murphy
Mrs. Don Myrland
Keith Naylor
Ray Nelson
Herb and Irene Newman
Perini Group
Jack Pfieffer
Tom Price
Buddy Rice
Bill Rose

Harold Runnells
Our many friends at St.
    Timothy's Church
Count André de Saint-
    Sauveur
Dee Schelling
Jack Schmidt
Bill Snyder of Oak Creek Films
Jean-Pierre Soisson
Mr. and Mrs. Merle Sprague
Ralph Stedman
Karen Wike
John Wilcos of ABC
Jack Wilderman
Paul Wood
Chris Yates
Ruth Zubizarreta

and the people of Albuquerque, New Mexico; Marshfield, Massachusetts; Presque Isle, Maine; and Rockford, Illinois.

Our thanks also go to the following organizations:

Air France
Albuquerque *Journal*
Albuquerque *Tribune*
BBC
Gamma
Imperial Manufacturing
    Company
KGGM

KOAT
KOB
Nordhaus, Moses & Dunn
Sandia Peak Ski Company
Sandia Peak Tram Company
Trans World Airlines
Union Carbide—Eveready Batteries
World Balloons

Flight Paths of
Double Eagle – – – – – – – – – – – –
Marshfield to Iceland, Sept. 9–12, 1977
and Double Eagle II ——————
Presque Isle to Miserey, Aug. 11–17, 1978
⊕   24 hour position